MORE
THAN
DANCING

MORE THAN DANCING

Essays on Afro-American Music and Musicians

EDITED BY
IRENE V. JACKSON

Prepared under the auspices of the Center for Ethnic Music, Howard University

Contributions in Afro-American and African Studies, Number 83

Greenwood Press
Westport, Connecticut • London, England

Library of Congress Cataloging in Publication Data

Main entry under title:

More than dancing.

(Contributions in Afro-American and African studies,
ISSN 0069-9624 ; no. 83)
Includes index.
1. Afro-Americans—Music—Addresses, essays, lectures.
2. Music—United States—Addresses, essays, lectures.
I. Jackson, Irene V.   II. Series.
ML3556.M68   1985   781.7'296073   84-8990
ISBN 0-313-24554-1 (lib. bdg.)

Library of Congress Catalog Card Number: 84-8990
ISBN: 0-313-24554-1
ISSN: 0069-9624

First published in 1985

Greenwood Press
A division of Congressional Information Service, Inc.
88 Post Road West, Westport, Connecticut 06881

Printed in the United States of America

10 9 8 7 6 5 4 3 2 1

In Memory of
Lula Vere Childers (?-1946)
Founder of the School of Music, Howard University
Warner Lawson (1903-1971)
Dean, College of Fine Arts, Howard University, 1961-1971
Mark Fax (1911-1974)
Professor of Music, Howard University, 1947-1972

Contents

Illustrations

Preface

This volume, a project of the Center for Ethnic Music at Howard University, is an outgrowth of a symposium on African and Afro-American Music, sponsored by the Center in the fall of 1978. The symposium, conceptualized by W. Komla Amoaku (formerly on the staff of the Center) brought together eight scholars, four of whom have essays in this volume. The agenda included Fela Sowande, "Traditional African Music"; Pearl Williams-Jones, "Black American Gospel Music in Continuity and Change"; Irene V. Jackson-Brown, "Musical Practices of Blacks in Mainline Denominations: Some Preliminary Explorations"; Portia K. Maultsby, "African Musical Concepts Retained in United States Black Music"; Olly Wilson, "The Association of Movement and Music as a Reflection of a Black Conceptual Process of Music Making"; Mantle Hood, "A New Hybrid? Black-American Vis-a-Vis Afro-American Music"; Bruno Nettl, "The Role of Preservation in Ethnomusicological Theory"; and Doris Evans McGinty, "The Role of Ethnic Music in General Music Education." Four essays from the symposium have been revised for publicaton here.

When I assumed the directorship of the Center for Ethnic Music in 1979, there had not yet been established a mechanism for disseminating the papers from this important symposium. It was clear to me—through my participation in the symposium and from numerous requests for copies of the papers—that the proceedings had to be published. I envisioned a publication that would include

the work of the original participants, all of whom are music special-
ists—ethnomusicologists and musicologists—as well as scholars
from other disciplines who had in various ways "interpreted" African and Afro-American music. And so, I set about identifying these
scholars and asking them if they would be interested in participating in this project. During this same period, I approached James
Sabin, of Greenwood Press, with the idea for such a project, and he
encouraged me to write a prospectus.

The original prospectus included thirteen essays. But by the time
the project reached completion, there were twenty-one essays, il-
lustrating the range of research currently being conducted.

This project has had, it seems, a long history. The first draft of
the manuscript was completed in 1981; several revisions followed.
In 1983, the manuscript was accepted by Greenwood. Upon review
of the manuscript, James Sabin decided that the manuscript should
be published as two volumes. The first would focus on Africa,
South America and the Caribbean, and the second volume would
center on the United States.

Thus, this volume is one part of a work originally conceived as
one study. The two volumes can stand alone, yet together provide
the larger picture.

The directorship of the Center for Ethnic Music became vacant in
the fall of 1981. As of this writing, a new director has not been
named. The Center continues as a reference and resource place.

Royalties from this work will go to Howard University to promote research and study of Black musics and musicians.

My appreciation extends to all the contributors, who answered
countless queries, returned numerous calls, and willingly reviewed
many drafts of their essays, and a special colleague who, after the
fifth telephone call from me on the same day, answered my question and commented, "You *are* thorough," giving me the push I
needed that day.

Many individuals have contributed to this project in both tangi-
ble and intangible ways. The former dean of the College of Fine Arts
at Howard University, Thomas J. Flagg, provided the necessary
funds for the book's publication. Lonye Rasch and Janet Johnson
gave technical assistance and were my right and left hands in the
preparation of this manuscript.

I wish also to thank Carrie Hackney, former librarian of the College of Fine Arts, for her help, as well as two former graduate students at Howard, Felicia Coleman and Velma Lewis, for their assistance. I hope they profited from being a part of this project. I wish also to acknowledge the support of James Sabin and Margaret Brezicki of Greenwood Press.

To my family, both nuclear and extended, who provided me with the emotional support to take on such a task, who somehow endured as a good portion of my emotional energy was consumed seeing this book to fruition, I say I could not have done this without you.

I wish also to thank the editors and authors who gave permission for articles to be published here.

Again, I must extend my deepest appreciation to the contributors, my colleagues, who have patiently awaited the publication of this book. Their unfaltering cooperation over these past four years will never be forgotten.

MORE
THAN
DANCING

IRENE V. JACKSON
Introduction

This volume of essays is about music as cultural expression, or music as an *aspect* of culture. The notion of music as cultural expression was formalized into a scholarly discipline in the 1950s after Jaap Kunst used the term—with a hyphen—as the title for his 1957 book.

Ethnomusicology has its antecedents in comparative musicology and anthropology. Several scholars—George Herzog, Mieczyslaw Kolinski and Klaus P. Wachsman—who formed the Berlin School worked in an area of musicology called "comparative musicology." These scholars laid much of the foundation for ethnomusicology in the United States. In 1955 with the founding of the Society for Ethnomusicology, ethnomusicology as a scholarly discipline was firmly established in this country. The anthropological component of ethnomusicology owes a great deal to the work of anthropologist Alan P. Merriam who defined the field of ethnomusicology as the "study of music in culture" in his book, *The Anthropology of Music* (1964).

While there is no *one* definition of the field and no *one* scholarly approach, as a group, ethnomusicologists are usually interested in understanding music from the standpoint of its socio-cultural context—why a music is used as it is, what a culture expresses about itself through its music, and what the music expresses about a culture.

The essays here have evolved largely from what I call "foundation studies." A major early work by an American was Alan P.
Merriam's "Characteristics of African Music," which was published
in the *Journal of the International Folk Music Council* in 1959. This
article must be singled out since it had a far-reaching effect on African and Afro-American music research. In 1952, another American
scholar, Richard A. Waterman, published "African Influence on
Music of the Americas," as part of the proceedings of the twenty-
ninth International Congress of Americanists. Waterman's article
examined the dispersion of African music to the New World, providing a foundation for the study of African music in New World
contexts. His interest in New World Black music stemmed from his
1943 dissertation, "African Patterns in Trinidad Negro Music."
Merriam like Waterman was concerned with African survival in
the New World writing a dissertation in 1951 called, "Songs of the
Afro-Bahian Cults: An Ethnomusicological Analysis."

This collection of essays linked by a thread connecting Black
communities in Africa, South America, and the Caribbean with
Black communities in the United States has been inspired by several
important works that analyze the musical meaning of Africa and
Africa in the New World. These works have appeared in several
disciplines.

In religion, for example, there is C. Eric Lincoln's *The Black
Experience in Religion* (1974); in anthropology, *Afro-American
Anthropology* (1970), edited by Whitten and Szwed; and in folk-
lore, *Mother Wit from the Laughing Barrel* (1973), edited by Alan
Dundes.

Several books—collections of essays—on African and Afro-
American music have emerged within the last twenty years and
have prompted this collection. Works that readily come to mind
include *Reflections on Afro-American Music* (1973) by Dominique-
René de Lerma, Eileen Southern's *Readings in Black American
Music* (1971), and *The Social Implications of Early Negro Music in
the United States* (1969) by Bernard Katz as well as Klaus P. Wachs-
mann's collection, *Essays on Music and History in Africa* (1971)
and *African Music in Perspective* (1982) by Alan P. Merriam.

In the field of ethnomusicology, several collections have inspired
this work: David McAllester's *Readings in Ethnomusicology* (1971)
—directly prompted this work—and books of essays on various

world musics such as *Eight Urban Musical Cultures* (1978), edited by Bruno Nettl, *Contemporary Music and Music Cultures* (1979) by Charles Hamm, et al., and Elizabeth May's 1980 collection, *Musics of Many Cultures: An Introduction* and *Discourse in Ethnomusicology and A Tribute to Alan P. Merriam* (1981) edited by Carol Card, et al.

The scholarly community has not yet been offered a collection of essays that tackles music and musicians of Africa and the African diaspora from an ethnomusicological standpoint. In spite of increase in publications on African and Afro-American music and in the field of ethnomusicology, at the time of this writing there has not yet been a book largely ethnomusicological in perspective, that examines African-derived music of the United States. Thus, in this regard, this volume and its companion work on African music and Afro-Latin music collection are singular.

An ethnomusicological perspective allows for the participation of scholars in other disciplines. As McAllester (1971: xii), in his introduction to *Readings in Ethnomusicology* notes, there is ". . . a heterogeneity of the backgrounds of the scholars who are making contributions to the field [ethnomusicology]. The presence . . . of linguists, archivists, dance ethnographers, ethnologists, sociologists, psychologists, and others serves abundant notice that this is not a field for the music specialist alone. . . . [There are] almost as many approaches . . . as there are scholars."

This collection brings together scholars in sociology, English literature, anthropology, and Afro-American studies, in addition to scholars in various music disciplines. By extending the following comments to the whole of Black culture, without regard to geographical boundaries the raison d'être for a multidisciplinary approach to research in Black culture is expressed well: "Given the complex, multilayered, and polyphonic nature of Caribbean culture, any analysis . . . requires *ab initio* both an interdisciplinary and multidisciplinary approach" (Crahan and Knight 1979: vi).

The approach here is interdisciplinary and the research current. The majority of scholars whose essays appear here have been trained within the last decade; therefore, much of the fieldwork which provides the data for these essays has been carried out within the last ten years. By the same token, the volume also has the perspective of many years of research through the work of senior scholars Stephen E. Henderson and Doris E. McGinty, the first American woman to receive a degree in musicology from Oxford University, who demonstrated her interest in Black music over twenty years ago in a 1960 article, "African Tribal Music: A Study of Transition," which appeared in the *Journal of Human Relations*.

The essays in this collection are wide ranging—from the function and use of music to historical and sociocultural examinations to the music of a specific locus. Areas for further scholarly inquiry are identified—music among Blacks in Washington, D.C., for example. Overall the collection identifies new topics for future research.

The first essay by Olly Wilson provides a pivotal essay to the first volume on African and Afro-Latin music. He analyzes what he calls a "Black conceptual approach to music-making," delving into the relationship betwen African and Afro-American music as based on a shared conceptual approach to music-making.

In chapter 2, Portia K. Maultsby identifies those musical genres and performance practices in Black music of the United States that are strongly grounded in a West African tradition, examining the sociocultural context that gave rise to these genres and practices.

Scholars of Afro-American music are increasingly focusing on musical traditions and musical activity within a certain locus. Chapters 3 and 4 by George L. Starks, Jr., and Doris Evans McGinty, respectively, are examples of this.

George L. Starks, Jr., describes musical activity on several islands off the coast of South Carolina, collectively called the "Sea Islands." The basis for his discussion are songs that he collected during fieldwork undertaken during the 1970s.

Doris Evans McGinty reveals that during the nineteenth and early twentieth century Washington, D.C., was a center of Black musical activity. She explores the extent of this activity, disclosing for the first time the significance of Washington, D.C., as a mecca of Black musical talent and activity.

The religious music tradition of Blacks in the United States has received a great deal of attention in scholarly circles. The next three chapters, 5, 6, and 7 point to the *new* direction that research on the religious music of Afro-Americans in the United States is taking.

I examine the musical activities of Blacks in the Episcopal church in chapter 5. This is a new research direction, since scholarly attention has not been given to the religious musical activities of Blacks in what are called "mainline denominations." It has been largely assumed that these activities were and are not distinctively "Black." The larger issue addressed in my essay is the religious musical tradition of Afro-Americans, and the activities of Black Episcopalians are a part of this tradition.

Studies of Afro-American gospel music have appeared at an increasing rate in the last five years. A pioneer in gospel music research is Horace Clarence Boyer who, in chapter 6, displays rare technical competence in his theoretical analysis of what he calls "traditional" and "contemporary" gospel.

Mellonee V. Burnim's essay, chapter 7, outlines those concepts which regulate and shape gospel music as a vehicle for expression among a majority of Black Americans. She uses data collected in several Black churches (designated as "Apostolic") as a basis for her discussion.

The next three chapters look at secular genres. In what he calls an "exploratory investigation," in chapter 8, James B. Stewart looks at how rhythm and blues *function* in Afro-American culture and analyzes Black male-female relationships as they are reflected in the texts of rhythm and blues.

Chapters 9 and 10 analyze blues texts; here blues are regarded as both music and poetry. Stephen E. Henderson, in chapter 9, skillfully calls attention to the blues poetry of Sterling Brown, poet and professor emeritus of Howard University. Henderson assesses Brown's work in relation to what he calls "the stylistics of Afro-American culture in which it [Brown's poetry] is saturated." In chapter 10, Loretta S. Burns looks at imagery and theme in blues lyrics, with attention to the structure of these lyrics.

The final essay, chapter 11, by Lorraine M. Faxio examines an important source for the documentation of music in Afro-American culture, thus calling the attention of scholars and researchers to a most important research collection.

These essays are meant to be provocative—offering new insights for further research and study.

REFERENCES

Crahan, Margaret, and Franklin Knight. 1979. *Africa and the Caribbean: The Legacies of a Link*. Baltimore: Johns Hopkins University Press.
McAllester, David. 1971. *Readings in Ethnomusicology*. Middletown, Conn.: Wesleyan University Press.

The Association of Movement and Music as a Manifestation of a Black Conceptual Approach to Music-Making

The relationship between African and Afro-American music has been an intriguing question for almost as long as individuals have been aware of the existence of strong Black musical cultures on both sides of the Atlantic. The full nature of that relationship has never been adequately examined, however. Most studies tend to make comparisons on the basis of the presence or absence of specific musical characteristics.[1] Hence, the common occurrence of such well-known African musical characteristics in Afro-American music as antiphony (call-and-response patterns), pentatonic scales, cross rhythms, and "offbeat phrasing of melodic accents" is usually cited as evidence of the interrelationship of the musics. While this approach is certainly necessary and valuable as far as it goes, it is inadequate in expressing the full nature of the relationship, because this approach deals with foreground aspects of the music and not the guiding background factors which, in fact, determine the presence of these foreground features.

The artistic output of any culture reflects the collective cultural attitudes and values of that culture. Western art, for example, reflects attitudes toward time and space that are the result of particular developments in Western society. A composer writes a piece of music that has a beginning, a middle, and an end, and he assumes the piece will be listened to as a process that occurs within the dimensions of linear time.[2] Because these aspects of the musical events seem to be so basic, the Westerner assumes that they are uni-

versal and takes them for granted. It is precisely these assumed
aspects of the musical experience that form the Westerner's basic
conceptual approach to either making or experiencing music. Therefore, not only will an analysis of foreground aspects of music be
enhanced by an understanding of background factors but the total
musical experience cannot be adequately probed without taking
them into consideration.[3]

As a result of their collective cultural experiences, the sub-
Saharan African peoples share a conceptual approach to music-
making. One element in this multidimensional perspective is a
belief in the affective power of music, a view of music as a force
that is capable of making something happen. Another is the attitude that the musical experience should be a functional, multimedia
activity in which many kinds of collective human output are inextricably linked. Hence, a typical traditional ceremony will include
music, dance, the plastic arts (elaborate masks and/or costumes),
and, perhaps, ritualistic drama or poetry. There are many other
aspects, some of which still lie undiscovered to this point.[4]

The relationship between African and Afro-American music is
based upon the continuity of an African conceptual approach to
music-making within the Afro-American context. The retentions of
this approach and the values they reflect provide us with a viable
framework with which to analyze relationships between African
and Afro-American music, as well as between various types of
African music. The commonly retained core is a set of attitudes
which are revealed in the manifestations of specific foreground
musical characteristics.[5] In this study, I would like to concentrate
on one aspect of this conceptual approach: the relationship
between music and body movement.

In traditional sub-Saharan musical cultures body movement
must be seen as an integral part of the music-making process. Although it is true that physical motion, especially as dance, frequently
accompanies music in many cultures, in most instances that physical activity is extrinsic to the act of making music. That is, it is seen
as something which accompanies the musical experience, something
which is not absolutely necessary in order for the music to exist. In
sub-Saharan cultures, conceptually, the two activities are viewed
as interrelated components of the same process.[6] The Western conceptual assumption of a division between consciously organized
sound (music) and movement associated with that sound (dance)

usually does not exist here. That is why in many traditional music-making situations the dancers and the musicians frequently are one and the same. An example of a common performance practice which reflects this conceptual view is the elaborate physical body movement characteristically associated with playing musical instruments. The Yoruban dundun[7] player moves his arms, head, shoulders, feet, and legs as he performs a praise song for an elder of the community during a festive occasion. It is important to note that those movements are not capricious gestures of ecstasy but actions necessary to produce a particularly desired effect from the musical performance. The movement is part of the music-making process and therefore intrinsic to the music.

Scholars of African music, while not formulating the concept in these terms, have long been aware of the special relationship between physical body motion and music in African cultures.

John Blacking (1973: 27), speaking of Venda music, says:

Venda music is founded not on melody, but on a rhythmical stirring of the whole body of which singing is but one extension. Therefore, when we seem to hear a rest between two drum-beats, we must realize that for the player it is not a rest: each drum-beat is the part of a total body movement in which the hand or a stick strikes the drum skin.

Kwabena Nketia (1974) treats the same topic in a chapter entitled "Interrelations of Music and Dance." Among the points he makes is the following:

Although purely contemplative music, which is not designed for dance or drama, is practiced in African societies in restricted context, the cultivation of music that is integrated with dance, or music that stimulates affective motor response, is much more prevalent. For the African, the musical experience is by and large an emotional one: sounds, however beautiful, are meaningless if they do not offer this experience or contribute to the expressive quality of a performance. (Nketia 1974: 206)

Later on, in discussing response to music, Nketia (1974: 207) emphasizes the importance of physical body motion:

Affective response to music may be shown outwardly in verbal or physical behavior. The values of African societies do not inhibit this: on the contrary, it is encouraged, for through it, individuals relate to musical events or performing groups, and interact socially with others in a musical situation. Moreover, motor response intensifies one's enjoyment of music through the feelings of increased involvement and the propulsion that articulating the beat by physical movement generates.

Finally, Rose Brandel (1961: 33), in discussing work songs of Central Africa, states:

The paddler who flexes his arms and bends his body in a symmetrical, purposeful rhythm begins to identify himself with the sound and feel of paddling. The paddle cuts the water; the water swishes; his hands grip the handle of the paddle sending it forward, around, and back in some time relationship to the cutting and swishing; his muscles stretch and his bones may creak; the boat has a myriad of motions and countermotions: all in some interrelated complex of rhythm which causes him to hear and sing something that seems to flow with the rhythm. The paddler's song comes into being.

Another common example of this phenomenon is in the usage of various sound producers on the body of dancers in traditional societies. These sound makers, usually on the arm, ankle, or waist, have a characteristic "buzzy" sound and are important components of the normal musical ensemble. The sound that they produce is determined by the nature of the dancers' movements. Therefore, the movements of the dancers have two dimensions: actual dance and a means to produce an important component of the music. Obviously, these functions are inextricably linked. The dance is the music and the music is the dance.

There are, of course, other examples of this phenomenon, but those cited (found throughout sub-Saharan Africa) should suffice to support my thesis that in traditional African cultures motion and music are viewed as interreacting aspects of the same act.

This attitude is an important part of the approach to making music which the "African exiles" brought with them as subliminal cultural baggage when they came to the Western Hemisphere. It thus provides us with a potential tool for understanding the rationale behind certain choices that were made as Afro-American music developed. In the course of this essay I will focus on three developments in early Afro-American music: (1) the association of movement and music in religious Afro-American music; (2) the association of movement and music in the work song; and (3) the involvement of Blacks in marching bands from the colonial period through the present.

RELIGIOUS AFRO-AMERICAN MUSIC

The first development in Afro-American music history that reflects the presence of this motion and music concept is the adoption of Christianity by large numbers of Blacks. Prior to 1740, the number of Blacks who had adopted Christianity was relatively small; however, by 1830, the number of Blacks who professed belief in Christianity became a significant percentage of the total Black population in the United States (Raboteau 1978: 93-150). In the interim, not only were large numbers of Blacks converted to the Methodist and Baptist Protestant denominations, but the earliest independent Black churches were established.

There are a number of interrelated factors which explain this phenomenal development, but one which is frequently overlooked is the fact that several aspects of the common form of worship used by the Protestant revivalist movement in the United States at that time were consonant with several traditional West African practices. From about 1740 through 1830, America was caught up in the first great evangelical movement,[8] a revivalist trend that grew out of the evolvement of Methodism in Europe. The emphasis of this Movement on Christ as a personal savior and on outward individual expressions of spiritual intensity struck a responsive chord in the Black masses that were initially on the periphery of rural camp meetings which came into prominence in the early nineteenth century.[9] The religious fervor was so appealing to Blacks because they had a deeply internalized positive attitude toward outward physical expressions of spiritual zeal. Moreover, because the revivalist movement supported individual expressions of religious fervor, these revivalists were more tolerant of physical motion as part of the religious experience than the older non-revivalist religious denominations of the eighteenth century.

As a result, the Blacks who subsequently formed a large part of the great camp meetings began to adopt Christianity in large numbers. Within this milieu, they could pursue with impunity their predilection for combining physical body motion with music in the form of rhythmical hand clapping, foot patting, head bobbing, rocking back and forth, and even dancing. At least philosophically —if not always in practice—this body movement was encouraged, particularly by the Methodists and nonhierarchical Baptists. Thus, Herskovits' conditions for "cultural syncretism"[10] appear to be met here. Hence, the probability of the "reinterpreted" African practice being retained was increased.

Chronicles of early Afro-American music are filled with accounts of the association of physical body movement and music. Before the mass conversions of slaves, Rev. Morgan Godwin, who arrived in York County, Virginia, in 1665, complained about the religious dance of the non-Christian slaves:

Nothing is more barbarous and contrary to Christianity, than their . . . idolatrous dances and revels; in which they usually spend the Sunday. . . . And here, that I may not be thought too rashly to impute Idolatry to their Dances, my conjecture is raised upon this ground . . . for that they use their Dances as a means to procure Rain; Some of them having been Known to beg this liberty upon the Week Days, in order there unto.[11]

In 1779, Alexander Hewatt commented that the majority of the Negroes in South Carolina were "great strangers to Christianity, and as much under the influence of Pagan darkness, idolatry, and superstition, as they were at their first arrival from Africa. . . ." Hewatt was particularly disturbed that Sundays and "holidays are days of idleness . . . in which the slaves assemble together in alarming crowds for the purposes of dancing, feasting and merriment."[12]

Perhaps the most thorough contemporaneous discussion of the use of physical body motion in early Afro-American religious music is by the frequently quoted Methodist evangelist, John Watson (1819: 28-31), who complains about musical practices of Blacks at the Philadelphia Conference:

In the blacks' quarter, the coloured people get together, and sing for hours together, shout scrapes of disjointed affirmations, pledges, or prayers, lengthened out with long repetitious choruses. These are all sung in the merry chorus-manner of the southern harvest field, or husking-frolic method, of the slave blacks; and also very greatly like the Indian dances. With every word so sung, they have a sinking of one or the other leg of the body alternately; producing an audible sound of the feet at every step, and as manifest as the steps of actual negro dancing in Virginia & Co. If some, in the meantime sit, they strike the sounds alternately on each thigh. . . . The evil is only occasionally condemned and the example has already visibly affected the religious manners of some whites.[13]

In one paragraph, Watson provides evidence of the distinctiveness of early Black religious musical practices, the use of a myriad of physical body motions associated with music (from body percussion to a shuffling dance), and the fact that these "indulgences" in bodily exercises were beginning to influence white Methodists—all clear testimony to the continuity of African behavioral patterns within the context of Protestant revivalism.

Scholarship in the area of Afro-American Christianity contains frequent references to the association of movement and music in the form of religious dancing in general, and the "ring shout" or "runnin sperichil" in particular.[14] Raboteau (1978) devotes a large segment of his book to eighteenth- and nineteenth-century accounts of religious dancing, which he demonstrates was very widespread. Particularly noteworthy is a quote from Morgan F. Davenport (1917: 92-93), who compares ecstatic religious behavior in Northern Ireland with that witnessed in Kentucky:

I wish in closing to call attention to the difference in type of the automations of Kentucky and Ulster. In Kentucky the motor automations, the voluntary muscles moving in violent action, were the prevailing type, although there were many of the sensory. On the other hand, in Ulster the sensory automations, trance, vision, the physical disability and the sinking of muscular energy were the prevailing types, although there were many of the motor.[15]

The distinction in kinds of ecstatic behavior led Herskovits (1958: 231) to state that "it is just in the forms of motor behavior remarked on as characteristics of the "automations" of the [white] Kentucky revivals that aboriginal modes of African worship are to be marked off from those of Europe." Finally, John and Alan Lomax (1947: 334) concluded the following after observing ring shouts that persisted into the twentieth century:

We have seen shouts in Louisiana, in Texas, in Georgia and the Bahamas; we have seen voodoo dancing in Haiti; we have read accounts of similar rites in the works upon Negro life in other parts of the Western Hemisphere. All share basic similarities: (1) the song is "danced" with the whole body, with hands, feet, belly, and hips; (2) the worship is, basically, a dancing and singing phenomenon; (3) the dancers always move counter-clockwise around the ring; (4) the song has the leader-chorus form, with much repetition, with a focus on rhythm rather than on melody, that is, with a form that invites and ultimately enforces cooperative group activity; (5) the song continues to be repeated for sometimes more than an hour, steadily increasing in intensity and gradually accelerating until a sort of mass hypnosis ensues. . . . This shout pattern is demonstrably West African in origin.

Although the Lomaxes were discussing ring shouts performed in the twentieth century, the characteristics of these dances appear applicable to eighteenth- and nineteenth-century religious dances as well.

The point to be made here is that the basic conceptual approach to music-making that Blacks brought with them from Africa found a responsive environment in evangelical worship. Because of this, it spawned a tradition of important music in America. The Black spiritual developed because it fulfilled the basic goal: to integrate body movement and music. While my analysis suggests that Blacks were motivated to adopt Christianity because the form of worship possible in that religion at that historical moment was consonant with traditional West African practice, I am not suggesting that this factor was the only one. Obviously, there were a number of inter-related factors that contributed to this development. Patterned behavior within the context of musical performance, however, is an important one that is frequently overlooked. In a comparative analysis of African and Afro-American "spirit possession" (another distinct form of behavior that is commonplace within the context of a religious musical experience), several scholars[16] point out two factors that must be taken into account: "the faith-context" or theo-logical interpretation and meaning; and "the patterned style of outward response by which the ecstatic experience is manifest" (cf. Raboteau 1978: 63-73). After discussing the considerable differ-ences between the African and the Afro-American faith-contexts,

Raboteau (1978: 64-65) makes the following statement regarding behavior patterns:

It is in the context of action, the patterns of motor behavior preceding and following the ecstatic experience that there may be continuity between African and American forms of spirit possession. While the rhythms of the drums, so important in African and Latin American cults, were by and large legally prohibited and hence forbidden to the slave in the United States, handclapping, foot patting, rhythmic preaching, hyperventilation, antiphonal (call-and-response) singing, and dancing are styles of behavior associated with possession both in Africa and in this country.

Although Raboteau was specifically discussing spirit possession, his comments regarding general behavioral patterns could also be applied to the continuity between African and Afro-American religious music; that is, although the specific theological context as well as the specific music differs, the general musical behavioral patterns are very similar. Put another way, the two musical practices share the same general behavioral patterns in the process of music-making, though the specific manifestations of that shared conceptual approach vary in detail.

The approach to music-making in which body movement is seen as an integral part of the musical process is also illustrated in other forms of Afro-American music. The work song is a vivid example.

THE AFRO-AMERICAN WORK SONG

In the work song, the physical activity of work is incorporated as a means of producing the song; conversely, the song is part of the work. This relationship differs from the "whistle or sing while you work" ethic one finds in many cultures. In the latter case, the song of the whistler accompanies the work activity and may indirectly assist the worker in his work by drawing attention away from the laborious task. In the American and the Afro-American contexts, however, the physical activity is a part of the music-making process. Janheinz Jahn (1961: 224), in discussing the African work song within his exposition of the Bantu philosophical system, gives perhaps the most provocative analysis of the relationship between work and song:

Song and dance do not have the purpose of lightening the work, but in song and dance Nommo is doing the real work, and conjuring up the latent forces of nature, while the work itself is only an addition. The meaning of the work lies in the song and dance; they are not a purposive means for the end of lightening the work, even though their influence has that effect. The song is not an aid to the work, but the work an aid to the song.

Independent of whether or not one agrees completely with Jahn's analysis, it is instructive to note that his assertion is based on an assumption of music's inextricable association with movement. Consider, for example, Leadbelly's performance of the popular worksong, "Take This Hammer." The sound of the hammer is part of the song, it is absolutely essential. That is why folk singers find it necessary to simulate the sound of the hammer when the song is sung outside of its original functional context. The first line of the song is not "Take this hammer . . . ," but "Take this hammer—*pow!*" Thus, the music-making activity is also a work activity. Work is an integral part of the music.

THE MARCHING BANDS

Another development in Afro-American history that reflects the concept of physical body motion as an integral part of the music-making process is the long association Americans of African descent have had with marching bands. From as early as the Revolutionary War to the present, Black people in the United States have been associated with the marching traditions. Chroniclers of the Revolutionary War cite many examples of the involvement of slaves and free Blacks with martial music. Eileen Southern (1971a: 74) cites a Virginian Act of 1776 which specifically mandates that Blacks "shall be employed as drummers, fifers, or pioneers." With respect to the War of 1812, she states:

[Although there is] little on record in regard to black army musicians in the War of 1812 . . . more black musicians must have been active during the war because of the number of all-black brass bands that began to appear soon after the war—especially in New Orleans, Philadelphia, New York and sections of New England. After the war, for example, the Third Company of Washington Guards (Philadelphia) organized a Negro band under the leadership of Frank Johnson that was destined to become internationally famous. Johnson, a Negro, earned for himself a reputation as one of the best performers on the bugle and French horn in the United States. The black musicians who composed the military bands of the early nineteenth century undoubtedly acquired their training—as well as their instruments—during the War of 1812. (Southern 1971a: 77)

The activities of Black military bands during the Civil War have been well documented. James Monroe Trotter, a member of a Black regimental band during the War, and the author of the first biographical history of Black American music, *Music and Some Highly Musical People* (1878), included the following in an article entitled, "The Schoolmaster in the Army":

In quite a number of the colored regiments, military bands were formed, and under the instruction of sometimes a band teacher from the north, and at others under one of their own proficient fellow-soldiers, these bands learned to discourse most entertaining music in camp, and often by their inspiring strains did much to relieve the fatigue.[17]

Trotter (1878), Colonel Thomas Wentword Higginson (1870), and Eileen Southern (1977), as well as others, provide copious documentation of the excellence and widespread involvement of Black military bands during the Civil War.

From the end of the Civil War through World War I, Black brass bands enjoyed a high point. Perhaps as a result of the influence of the French military tradition, throughout the entire former Louisiana Territory brass bands were highly involved in the popular American pastime of playing marching music. Indeed, the important appearance during this time of musical genres such as ragtime and early traditional jazz was profoundly influenced by the involvement of Blacks in brass marching bands.[18] On the east coast during World War I, there were a number of outstanding Black infantry bands with James Reese Europe's world-famous 369th Infantry Band setting the standard.

Finally, during more recent times, Black military bands, drum and bugle corps, and college and university marching bands continue to be in the forefront of the American marching band tradition. Of particular note in the last fifteen years is the role played by Black college and university marching bands in revolutionizing the spectacle of football half-time shows.[19] Clearly then, from the time of the Black fifers and drummers of the Revolutionary War, through that of the internationally acclaimed bands of Frank Johnson[20] and James Reese Europe, up to the contemporary "Marching One Hundred" of Florida A. & M. University, the Black presence in the American marching band tradition has been significant.

I suggest that the long tradition of Black marching bands is a reflection of an African and Afro-American conceptual approach to music-making. The very nature of the marching band fulfills the ideal of treating music and motion as complementary facets of one process. In most marching music, the process of marching becomes a component of the music. The synchronized steps of a massed group of marchers and the resultant regular tactics this physical act produces provide a basic periodic pulsation, in the framework of which the band plays music. This regular pulsation, the basis of the music's rhythmic foundation, is thus literally produced by the act of marching. Hence, motion is an inextricable aspect of the music. Given their particular cultural bias toward merging motion and music, Americans of African descent would be particularly attracted to this mode of music-making. The historical evidence seems to corroborate this view.

We can see that African and Afro-American music reflects underlying conceptual approaches to the process of music-making. One of these conceptual approaches, the peculiar association of motion and music, provides us with a framework within which to analyze the historical development of the music and its "foreground features." It is this conceptual background which functions as the constant, the core of "African roots of music in the Americas." Although the outer features of the music may change, this core is retained. For example, Afro-American work songs may differ from African work songs, but the nature of the role of work in both songs stays the same. What has been retained by them is a basic approach to the role of work and music.

Although I have concentrated here primarily on developments in early Afro-American music, there is evidence that this conceptual approach is equally operative in contemporary Afro-American music. Several writers on contemporary Afro-American music, while not dealing with the subject in the terms put forth in this paper, address the question of physical motion and music. For example, A. B. Spellman (1966) discusses the role of movement in the performance of a specific jazz artist, and Charles Keil (1966) notes that motion is a part of the ritualized performance of the popular blues singer. Moreover, although there has been no systematic analysis of the role of movement in contemporary music, the well-known body movement of contemporary jazz, soul, blues, and gospel performers suggests that this principle is still very much intact.

NOTES

1. Among these studies are Courlander (1963); Merriam, et al. (1956); Roberts (1972); Schuller (1968); and Waterman (1952). A summary of these studies and the outline of a different approach to the problem may be found in Wilson (1974). In addition to the above, there are other comparative studies between specific genres of Afro-American music and African music, such as Oliver (1970).

2. There are, of course, exceptions to this basic assumption, particularly since twentieth century developments in Western music.

3. For further discussion of the role of culture in framing aesthetic values, see Meyer (1967) and Merriam (1964).

4. See Armstrong (1971) and Jahn (1961) for a more complete discussion of African aesthetics.

5. Cf. Herskovits (1958) for a thorough study of African retentions in the Western Hemisphere. Significant to my discussion is Herskovits' "theory of reinterpretation" in which he asserts that "African exiles" reinterpreted traditional African cultural patterns to conform to their new social situation, while retaining a core of essentially African values.

6. See Nketia (1974: 206-217).

7. The dundun is an hour-glass shaped drum.

8. See Chase (1955) for further discussion of music in the "Great Awakening."

9. See Southern (1971a: 93-99; 1971b: 62-64); Chase (1966: 237-243) and Maultsby (1974) for a discussion of involvement by Blacks in the revivalist movement of the nineteenth century.

10. See Herskovits (1958) for further discussion.

11. Cited in Epstein (1973: 79-80).

12. Cited in Epstein (1973: 81) and Raboteau (1978: 94).

13. Cited in Southern (1971b: 62-64).

14. See Southern (1971a: 160-62).

15. Cited in Herskovits (1958: 230-231) and Raboteau (1978: 86).

16. For further discussion of spirit possession in African and Afro-American contexts see Bourguignon (1970) and Walker (1972).

17. Published in Wilson (1887: 505-507) and cited in Stevenson (1973: 383-404).

18. See Schuller (1968: 63-88); Blesh (1971: 63-88) and Russ Russell (1971).

19. During the 1950s, Black university marching bands, led by the Florida A. & M. University "Marching One Hundred," began to march a very fast cadence (= ca. 240-360), and to use popular rhythm and blues songs as part of their repertoire. Following the first appearances of these bands on national television during the half-time shows of the National Football League Championship and All-Star Games, this marching style became part of the standard practice of university marching bands all over the United States.

20. See Eileen Southern (1977: 3-29) for a thorough discussion of Frank Johnson's widely acclaimed concerts in London and Philadelphia. Robert Stevenson (1973: 383-404) also discusses Frank Johnson's illustrious career.

REFERENCES

Armstrong, Robert Plant. 1971. *The Affecting Presence*. Urbana: University of Illinois Press.

Blacking, John. 1973. *How Musical Is Man*. Seattle: University of Washington Press.

Blesh, Rudi. 1971. *They All Play Ragtime*. New York: A. A. Knopf.

Bourguignon, Erika. 1970. *Ritual Dissociation and Possession Belief in Caribbean Negro Religion*. Afro-American Anthropology. New York: Free Press.

Brandel, Rose. 1961. *The Music of Central Africa*. Hague: Martinus Nigjoff.

Chase, Gilbert. 1955. *America's Music*. New York: McGraw-Hill.

Courlander, Harold. 1963. *Negro Folk Music U.S.A.* New York: Columbia University Press.

Davenport, Morgan F. 1917. *Primitive Traits in Religious Revivals*. New York: Macmillan Company.

Epstein, Dena J. 1973. "African Music in British and French America." *Musical Quarterly*, 59, No. 1.

Herskovits, Melville. 1958. *Myth of the Negro Past*. Boston: Beacon Press.

Higginson, Thomas Wentworth. 1870. *Army Life in a Black Regiment* (n.p.).

Jahn, Janheinz. 1961. *Muntu*. New York: Grove Press.

Keil, Charles. 1966. *Urban Blues*. Chicago: University of Chicago Press.

Lomax, John A., and Lomax, Alan. 1947. *Folksong U.S.A.* New York: Duell, Sloan & Pearce.

Maultsby, Portia. 1974. "Afro-American Religious Music: 1618-1861." Ph.D. dissertation, University of Wisconsin.

Merriam, Alan et al. 1956. "Songs of a Rada Community in Trinidad." *Anthropos*, 51: 157-174.

Merriam, Alan P. 1964. *The Anthropology of Music*. Evanston: Northwestern University Press.

Meyer, Leonard B. 1967. *Music, The Arts and Ideas*. Chicago: University of Chicago Press.

Nketia, J. H. Kwabena. 1974. *The Music of Africa*. New York: W. W. Norton and Company.

Oliver, Paul. 1970. *Savannah Syncopators*. London: November Books Limited.

Raboteau, Albert. 1978. *Slave Religion: "The Invisible Institution" in the Ante-Bellum South*. New York: Oxford University Press.

Roberts, John. 1972. *Black Music of Two Worlds*. New York: Praeger Publishers.

Russell, Russ. 1971. *Jazz Style in Kansas City and the Southwest*. Berkeley: University of California Press.

Schuller, Gunther. 1968. *Early Jazz*. New York: Oxford University Press.

Southern, Eileen. 1977. "Frank Johnson of Philadelphia and His Promenade Concerts." *Black Perspective in Music*, Spring.

_____. 1971a. *Music of Black Americans*. New York: W. W. Norton and Company.

_____. 1971b. *Readings in Black American Music*. New York: W. W. Norton and Company.

Spellman, A. B. 1966. *Black Music: Four Lives in Jazz*. New York: Shocken Books.

Stevenson, Robert. 1973. "America's First Black Music Historian." *Journal of the American Musicological Society*, 26, no. 3, Fall: 383-404.

Trotter, James Monroe. 1878. *Music and Some Highly Musical People*. New York: Johnson Reprint Corporation.

Walker, Sheila S. 1972. *Ceremonial Spirit Possession in Africa and Afro-America*. Leiden: E. J. Brill.

Waterman, Richard, 1952. "African Influence on the Music of the Americas." In *Acculturation in the Americas*, ed. by Sol Tax. Chicago: n.p.

Watson, John. 1819. *Methodist Error*. Trenton: n.p.

Wilson, Joseph T. 1887. *The Black Phalanx: A History of Negro Soldiers of the United States*. Hartford: The American Publishing Company.

Wilson, Olly. 1974. "The Significance of the Relationship between Afro-American Music and West African Music." *Black Perspective in Music*, Spring.

West African Influences and Retentions in U.S. Black Music: A Sociocultural Study

During the late 1960s scholars began to reexamine Black history[1] and culture[2] in the context of an African past. Many pioneer writers interpreted aspects of Black American culture to be adaptations and imitations of white American culture.[3] Thus, significant African influences in Black dance, folk tales, speech patterns, religious beliefs, and musical practices were rarely acknowledged or were misinterpreted.

Current evidence reveals that West Africans did not sever all attachments to their native country after being exported to the New World. Ties with Africa persisted at conscious levels and in their memories (Epstein 1977: 127). Customs, beliefs, and cultural practices were orally transmitted from generation to generation. Thus, the African world view and frame of reference "continued to exist not as mere vestiges but as dynamic, living, creative parts of group life in the United States" (Levine 1977: 5).

Simpson, in summarizing Herskovits' conception of culture, defines it as the "summation of the behavior and the habitual modes of thought of the persons who constitute a particular society at a given time. While these persons conform to the ways of the group,

The research for this study was funded in part by a grant from the Afro-American Arts Institute, Indiana University. This chapter has been revised and reprinted by permission of the author and THE WESTERN JOURNAL OF BLACK STUDIES, Black Studies Program/Washington State University Press, Pullman, Washington, Vol. 3, No. 3 (Fall 1979), pp. 197-215.

they vary somewhat in their reactions to the situations in which
they find themselves." (Simpson 1973: 97)
    According to Levine culture is a process, rather than a fixed con-
dition. More specifically, it is

the product of interaction between the past and present. Its toughness and
resiliency are determined not by a culture's ability to withstand change,
which indeed may be a sign of stagnation not life, but by its ability to react
creatively and responsively to the realities of a new situation. (Levine
1977: 5)

For three and one half centuries, Blacks have reacted creatively as
they have adapted to a multitude of new environments in the United
States. The culture they created drew from new environmental factors as well as West African traditions.
    The various genres that constitute the Black musical tradition
serve as a repository for historical events that have defined and
governed Black existence since importation from West Africa. The
songs of this tradition communicate and document the philosophies, values, attitudes, aspirations, feelings, hardships, relationships, work experiences, social status, community life, mode of behavior, aesthetic priorities—in other words, the world view which
has been a part of Black culture throughout each stage of its evolution. These songs also illustrate cultural continuity, as well as the
levels of change that West African concepts have undergone in
Black culture.
    The retention, reinterpretation, revival or disappearance of West
African concepts in U.S. Black music existed in relationship to the
social structures and life-styles that defined the boundaries of Black
experience in the New World. The varying social structure of the
southern plantations and the segregated nature of rural and urban
communities enabled Blacks to resist imprisonment by standards
that the larger society sought to impose. In this essay, I will explore
the circumstances that contributed to the preservation of West
African concepts in three centuries of U.S. Black music. Within this
context, I will identify musical genres and corresponding stylistic
features, which reveal that a West African heritage is the source for
the musical norms and practices that govern Black musical
performance.

THE SOCIAL ENVIRONMENT OF BLACKS
PRIOR TO 1865

The first Blacks to live in the United States were given the status of indentured servants. They lived in Virginia and constituted a very small percentage of the total population. Information about their social environments and life-styles is limited, but evidence indicates that, beginning in the 1640s, their status was reduced to that of a slave. In the 1660s, slavery was given legal sanction and began to evolve as an institution in the southern and northern colonies.[4] The specific system of slavery varied from colony to colony, governed by the size of the slave population, which increased or decreased with the demand for free labor. Social environments and life-styles of slaves were defined by the particular system of slavery that encompassed their existence.[5]

In the northern colonies, slavery existed on a very small scale and legislation attempted to limit the number of slaves imported. During the eighteenth century in New England, for example, the Black population did not constitute more than three percent of the total population.[6] The slaves generally lived in the homes of their masters and worked beside them on farms, in stores, and in houses. They were regarded as children in need of constant guidance and care. Many of their daily activities were dictated by the master and his family, since they attempted to define the slaves' cultural frame of reference. The exposure of slaves to white culture was immense and, when in the presence of the master or other whites, they adopted or at least adhered to the larger society's customs.[7] When apart from whites, however, they engaged in familiar African activities.

In the southern colonies, the social structure of farms and plantations governed the slaves' social environment. The majority of slaves lived on large farms or plantations that were located some distance from the master's house. Because they had limited contact with the slaveholder and other whites, they defined their own values, behavioral patterns, modes of thought, and norms of existence which, in turn, provided the foundation for the evolution of an Afro-American culture.[8]

The only bondsmen who came into constant contact with whites were house servants, skilled slaves, and those who lived on small

farms. Their quarters were either attached to or situated very near
the house of the slaveholder and the master closely supervised their
daily routines. Frequently exposed to white cultural values and customs, these slaves adopted those which coincided with the expectations of their masters.[9] Herskovits believed that this exposure,
however, proved insufficient cause for them to abandon their African modes of thought and behavior. He emphasizes that they were
constant victims of "severe punishment that followed even unwit-
ting conduct that displeased the ever-present masters" (Herskovits
1958: 115, 134). Thus, they relied on traditional cultural values as a
means of self-preservation and identity.

MUSICAL TRADITIONS OF BLACKS PRIOR TO 1865

For more than one hundred and fifty years, slave traders—and
later slaveholders—unknowingly helped to preserve African concepts in the Black American musical tradition. During the long
voyage from West Africa to the Americas, slaves were forced to
engage in physical exercises to preserve their health. They jumped,
sang, and danced in a manner that was unquestionably African. Instruments of African and European origin provided the accompaniment during such activities. Crew members played European instruments, such as bagpipes, harps, and fiddles while slaves played
African instruments that the captain or one of his crew brought on
board. Africans, upon arriving in the New World, brought their
songs, dances and instruments as well as other cultural components
of their native country.[10] Thus, the slaves were exposed to two
distinct musical traditions.

The slaves' exposure to aspects of Euro-American culture and
their continued involvement in activities of West African origin encouraged their participation in two distinct musical traditions. One
was associated with Euro-Americans and the other, which later
evolved into an Afro-American tradition, represented the various
West African cultures.

Blacks were introduced to Euro-American musical traditions as
they were instructed in the concepts of Christianity and trained for
the military. Legislation encouraged masters to instruct their children and servants alike in the principles of Christianity. Rudiments
of psalm singing were included in this religious education since for

more than half the Colonial Era, psalms were sung during all religious activities and at many ceremonial, educational, and informal gatherings. The legalization of slavery as an institution in the northern colonies did not interfere with the religious status of slaves. They attended Sunday and other religious services with their masters and, from their segregated seating area, participated in the singing of psalms. Similarly, when slaves conducted their own religious activities, they opened and concluded them by singing psalms (Southern 1971: 33-42).

Northern slaves also participated in the holiday celebrations and informal secular activities of whites. In these settings, they sang European ballads and played European instruments (drums, trumpet, and fife), which they learned to play during military training. Slaves often provided entertainment for the informal dances and other social activities of whites. Here they played the fiddle, flute, and other instruments, which were either purchased by their masters or made by bondsmen from local materials. Many taught themselves to play these instruments, while others received instruction from their masters (Southern 1971: 48).

In spite of constant exposure to and participation in cultural activities of whites, northern slaves organized their own social activities and celebrated their own holidays in an African fashion. Perhaps the most spectacular and festive occasions were " 'Lection Day" and "Pinkster Celebrations." On 'Lection Day, celebrated from about 1759 to 1850 in the New England colonies, the slaves elected Black governors or kings and staged an elaborate parade that involved over one hundred slaves. The festive activities culminated with wrestling, jumping games, and singing and dancing to the fiddle, tambourine, banjo, and drum. Reports indicate that all of these instruments were of African origin except the fiddle. The texts of songs combined African languages with "broken and ludicrous English" (Southern 1971: 49-50).

Pinkster Day[11] was a three- to seven-day holiday celebration organized by slaves in the northern and southern colonies. Documentation reveals that thousands of slaves and free Blacks gathered together and participated in traditionally African activities. Wild animals were exhibited and individuals engaged in rope dancing and bareback riding. Following the appearance of the elaborately dressed king, there was dancing and singing. A banjo and a drum made from a wooden ell-pot and covered with sheepskin provided the musical accompaniment.[12]

The unique character of this event prompted the novelist James Cooper to record his impressions:

It is true, there are not now [1845], nor were there then [1757], many blacks among us of African birth; but the traditions and usages of their original country were so far preserved as to produce a marked difference between the festival, and one of European origin. . . . (Quoted in Epstein 1977: 67)

During the seventeenth and eighteenth centuries, slaves living in the North and South participated in other activities that were believed to be distinctly African in origin. Missionaries often described these activities in writings of the day while they accelerated their efforts to stop the slaves' African practices which were often described as "heathenish and savage manners."

As early as 1665 and as late as 1899, missionaries, travelers, slaveholders, and slaves themselves commented about the African origin of dances, instruments, and songs associated with slaves.[13] A slave born in 1849 reported that at Christmas celebrations, African-born slaves would sing some of their songs or tell stories about African customs (Epstein 1977: 129).

An army general, upon returning to his plantation about 1782, discovered his slaves engaged in a party. They were astonished at his appearance "and every now and then some one or other would come out with a 'Ky!' and the old Africans joined in a war-song in their own language of 'Welcome the war home' " (Epstein 1977: 41).

Instruments such as the banjo, musical bow, quill or panpipes, flutes, balafo or xylophone, triangle, tambourine, and a variety of drums made from barrels, kettles, gourds, and tree trunks and covered with goat or sheep skin, were constructed and played by slaves and were so prevalent that whites became suspicious of their use and function. Slaveholders eventually realized that slaves were using some of these instruments to communicate messages about illegal gatherings to plan insurrections. Legislation not only prohibited slaves from assembling without the supervision of whites, but also banned the making and playing of drums, horns, and other loud instruments. Enforcement of such legislation varied from colony to colony, at most curtailing rather than preventing the slaves' use of these African-derived instruments.[14]

Throughout the seventeenth and eighteenth centuries, southern slaves continued to participate in African and African-related social activities. Slaveholders generally did not object to them as long as they did not interfere with the slaves' daily work routine. While performing various types of work, ranging from field labor to domestic chores through industrial labor, slaves were encouraged by their master to sing. The songs imparted a rhythm to group labor and simultaneously relieved boredom and passed the time (Epstein 1977: 63-76).

In the nineteenth century, missionaries intensified their earlier efforts to prevent slaves from engaging in African-derived activities by converting them to Christianity. Prior to this time, southern slaveholders generally were not receptive to converting slaves, since they feared it would alter their established status. But slowly, they were convinced that Christian teaching would improve their slaves' behavior and general obedience and thus consented to religious instruction (Epstein 1977: 100-111). Many slaveholders assisted the missionaries with the conversions. They allowed Blacks to attend outdoor camp meetings associated with the Revival Movement. Some slaveholders built "praise-houses"[15] on their farms and plantations.[16]

In spite of such efforts, the slaves' understanding and acceptance of Christianity was superficial. They interpreted Christian concepts and practices in an African context, adding an emotional component and unconventional musical expression to their practice of Christianity. These modifications were criticized by missionaries throughout the nineteenth century. In an attempt to discourage Black congregations from spontaneity and emotional responses to Christianity, Charles Colcock Jones made the following comments:

. . . the public worship of God should be conducted *with reverence and stillness on the part of the congregation*; nor should the minister—whatever may have been the previous habits and training of the people—encourage demonstrations of approbation or disapprobation, or exclamations, or response, or noises, or outcries of any kind during the progress of divine worship; nor boisterous singing immediately at its close. These practices prevail over large portions of the southern country, and are not confined to one denomination, but appear to some extent in all. . . . I cannot think them beneficial. (Jones, 1842. 39-40, my italics)

Jones also advocated teaching Blacks the proper way to sing psalms and hymns. He believed that if more emphasis were placed on psalm and hymn singing,[17] slaves would be encouraged to

. . . lay aside the extravagant and nonsensical chants, and catches and hallelujah songs of their own composing; and when they sing, which is very often while about their business or of an evening in their houses, they will have something profitable to sing. (Jones 1842: 265-266)

Although missionaries made every conceivable attempt to modify the slaves' musical practices, their efforts were unsuccessful.

Many slaves were allowed to conduct their own religious services during the latter half of the eighteenth and throughout the nineteenth centuries. When unsupervised by whites, they defied all rules, standards, and structures established by the various denominations and sects. They encouraged spontaneous verbal, nonverbal, from twenty minutes to several hours. As late as 1859 and 1863, misclapping, foot-stamping, shouting, groaning, outcries, musical interjections, an intense level of involvement, dancing and other forms of bodily movements, and antiphonal singing that lasted from twenty minutes to several hours. As late as 1859 and 1863, missionaries and other whites reported their "shocked reactions" to Blacks' services. By this time, however, Blacks had established a distinct theology, a structure for their services, and a religious musical tradition that represented the reinterpretation of white Christian concepts to conform to the principles and practices of West African rituals. In this way, they freely worshipped their chosen God in a manner that was familiar to them.[18]

In the absence of whites, Blacks freely reinterpreted songs taught to them by missionaries and made them conform to their own musical aesthetics. Henry Russell, an English musician who toured the United States from 1833 to 1841, had this to say about the reinterpretation of a psalm tune he heard while visiting a Black church service at Vicksburg, Virginia:

When the minister gave out his own version of the Psalm, the choir commenced singing so rapidly that the original tune absolutely ceased to exist—in fact, the fine old psalm tune became thoroughly transformed into a kind of negro melody; and so sudden was the transformation, by accelerating the time, that, for a moment, I fancied that not only the choir but the little congregation intended to get up a dance as part of the service. (Russell 1895: 84-85)

Other descriptions reveal that slaves occasionally borrowed melodic ideas and textual themes from Protestant musical traditions. They reinterpreted the songs by changing melodies and rhythms, replacing original texts with new ones that combined English words and phrases with those of African origin. They added refrain lines and choruses and wove shouts, moans, groans, and cries into the melody. They substituted faster tempos for the original ones and incorporated complex foot-stamping, hand-clapping, and bodily movements.[19]

Thus, much of the religious music the slaves created was sung according to principles that govern group singing in West African traditions. The style was antiphonal, with song lengths undetermined. Although a few of the songs reportedly were sung in harmony, singing in a heterophony appears to have been the common practice. Repetitive texts were spontaneously improvised, with phrases taken from sermons, the Bible, Protestant songs, and the slaves' sacred and secular experiences. Although many of the religious songs (later known as spirituals) were communally conceived, individuals also sang them as a form of personal expression.[20]

The secular musical tradition of Blacks incorporates many traits from the religious tradition. It includes work songs, songs of in-group and out-group satire, nostalgic songs, nonsense songs, children's songs, and play songs, as well as lullabies, field cries, and calls, created by individuals as a means of personal expression and communication.[21]

The abolition of slavery in many northern colonies around 1800 only served to make Blacks subject to discriminatory legislation, which again placed restrictions on their mobility. Limited involvement in everyday affairs of the society at large forced them to establish communities and institutions where they could define their own mode of existence and cultural frame of reference (Litwack 1961: 14, 64). There were also a number of free Blacks in the south whose position was a precarious one in that their "color suggested servitude, but [their] status secured a portion of freedom" (Wade 1964: 249). Only a "portion of freedom" was theirs because legislation, expressing the everpresent and unyielding hostile attitudes of whites toward Blacks, barred free Blacks from participating in the society at large. Thus, many Blacks took refuge in African churches and Black fraternal societies. Only a few sought to penetrate existing institutions.

As African churches sprang up in the North and South, the fears and hostility of whites were heightened. It was common knowledge that these churches served many functions in the Black community: not only were they religious centers, social centers for adults and children, care centers for the poor, and school houses, but also meeting centers for the political activists and hideouts for slaves. The expansive functions of these churches hampered the control the whites sought to maintain over the Black community.[22]

It should be noted that there were two classes of free Blacks—the elite middle class of the northern colonies and the middle-poor class of the southern and some northern colonies, each with a culturally distinct musical tradition. The elite middle class, representing a very small percentage of all free Blacks, shared the social and cultural values of whites. In spite of being resented by the larger society, many of these Blacks divorced themselves from other free Blacks and attempted to socialize with the white community. Generally, they attended the white Episcopal or Presbyterian churches when permitted or they became members of affiliate churches comprising Blacks of the same social and economic status.[23] When they conducted their own services, they strictly followed the established liturgy and sang from the official hymnal. In the nineteenth century in the Episcopal church, for example,

they were accustomed to use *no other worship* than the regular course prescribed in the Book of Common Prayer, for the day. Hymns, or Psalms out of the same book were sung, and a printed sermon read. . . . No extemporary address, exhortation, or prayer was permitted, or used. . . . (Quoted in Epstein 1977: 196)

When Blacks initially attended these churches, white ministers insisted that they follow the established order of worship and only sing the songs that were included in the official book of denomination. The elite middle class of free Blacks continued to strictly adhere to the policies of both the Episcopal and Presbyterian churches (Maultsby 1975: 409; Epstein 1977: 23).

The middle-poor classes of free Blacks sought refuge from the legal restrictions and hostility of the white world by establishing their own churches. In these Methodist and Baptist institutions, they freely expressed themselves, structuring their services to meet the needs of the congregation. The theology, structure of service, mode of operation, and musical tradition were the same as those found in the "praise houses" under slave leadership. Thus, the musical tradition and practices associated with free Blacks of the middle-poor classes represented the continuity of the cultural tradition from slave to free Black.[24]

THE SOCIAL STATUS AND ENVIRONMENT OF BLACKS AFTER 1865

When slavery as an American institution was abolished at the end of the Civil War in 1865, emancipated Blacks found themselves rootless and confused. This situation temporarily disrupted their communal solidarity. Individually and in small groups, Blacks attempted to establish new lives within the larger society. Many migrated from rural areas to cities and from South to North in search of socially, politically and economically suitable areas for settlement. Others sought to take advantage of educational opportunities and emulate white values and modes of behavior. Their strides toward "self-improvement," however, were resented by the larger society, which responded by heightening its legal and illegal efforts to hamper and control the freedmen's mobility.[25]

While the fourteenth amendment to the U.S. Constitution, passed in 1866, guaranteed equal rights to all Blacks and the Civil Rights Act of 1875 ensured them use of public facilities, Blacks were forced to remain totally dependent on the larger society for their survival.[26] Job opportunities were limited and, as a last resort, many of the freedmen worked as sharecroppers on the land they

had farmed as slaves. The nature of the sharecropping system pre-
vented them from becoming economically independent of the land-
owner. Those who did not work as sharecroppers could find jobs
only as domestic servants, janitors, truck drivers, chauffeurs, and
delivery boys.[27]

In an attempt to create a meaningful existence, Blacks re-established
their communities and institutions. They reshaped old values and
adopted new ones when necessary. They relied on past cultural
norms for cohesive social interactions, self-identification and group
stability. As they were consistently barred from participating in the
mainstream of American life and subjected to discriminatory legislation and an inferior status, Blacks responded with new forms of
musical expression.

Their post-Civil War music reflected their precarious status. In
blues, gospel music, rhythm and blues, rock 'n' roll, soul, and funk
we can observe the range of life-styles that were practiced within
diverse structures of segregated rural and urban environments.
These musical genres express the sentiments, experiences, and contemporary world view of Blacks during each stage of community
development. The musical style of these genres illustrates a continuity of concepts and practices from the eras of slavery which, in
turn, drew from West African musical concepts for their
foundation.

THE MUSICAL TRADITIONS OF BLACKS AFTER 1865

For many decades following the Civil War and even after the
evolution of new forms of folk expression, Blacks continued to sing
songs of the past. White northerners, who migrated South to teach
the freedmen, constantly complained about this. Black school children, for example, preferred to sing their own songs as opposed to
those the teachers were teaching. At the end of a school day,
teachers reluctantly granted permission for the children to "shout"
and sing their own songs. A visitor observing this activity at a
Beaufort, South Carolina, school in 1866 commented:

The words of their hymns are simple and touching. The verses consist of
two lines, the first being repeated twice. . . . As I looked upon the faces of
these little barbarians and watched them circling round in this fetish dance,

doubtless the relic of some African rite, I felt discouraged. . . . However, the recollection of the mental arithmetic seemed a more cheerful view of the matter. (Quoted in Epstein 1977: 281-282)

Other descriptions reveal that the freedmen continued singing spirituals and adapting revival hymns and other songs to their criteria of performance (Epstein 1977: 274-281).

Secular music remained in the repertoire of the freedmen and became increasingly important in their postbellum culture. The work and social conditions of freed Blacks differed only slightly, if at all, from the conditions they had known as slaves. Unhampered by missionaries, who had formally discouraged the singing of secular songs, this music became commonplace in contemporary Black society. New songs served new needs. Many new songs combined the musical structures and poetic forms of old secular and religious songs with new musical and textual ideas. Others were based entirely on new material, but performed according to standards that defined the Black musical tradition (Levine 1977: 190-270).

THE BLUES

By the twentieth century, the blues had become a major form of Black expression. James Cone contends that the blues is a secular substitution for the spiritual, since it depicts the "secular" dimension of the Black experience (Cone 1972: 112). The role of the blues performer overlaps with that of the preacher; they both function as spokesmen and historians for the Black community. Through their texts, the bluesman and preacher console and comfort, while they comment on the social realities that affect the lives of Blacks. As Ferris (1978: 79-80) expresses it, "Though sacred and secular language separate their song traditions, the preacher and blues singer deal with familiar themes of suffering and loneliness. While one finds his solution in God, the other turns to his love."

Many blues performers received their musical training in the Black church. This, coupled with their religious beliefs, motivated many to include religious songs in their repertoire. Generally, these songs were not performed in public, but were recorded and sold in the Black community. Thus, the religious message of the bluesmen was heard by all—whether churchgoer or not (Levine 1977: 179).

In their secular songs, bluesmen often called to the Lord as they expressed grief of a secular nature. Sometimes, they shifted between blues and hymns (Ferris 1977: 79). In view of this overlap, it is possible to conclude that principle, rather than practice, has separated and continues to separate the secular from the sacred musical traditions. After all, secular concerns provided the textual content for the Black preacher, who emphasized that spiritual guidance will deliver one from "secular" hardships and help one resist the temptations of the "secular" world. These themes are reflected in the text of Black religious music as well.

Besides its religious impact, blues were the main type of songs used for entertainment. The blues performer provided the music for dancing in clubs, at barbecues, house parties, and other social gatherings. His music also helped Blacks to pass the time.

Some of these performers also played for white audiences. Those who performed regularly for whites developed "a musical repertoire which [was] markedly different in both style and content from blues played in the Black community" (Ferris 1978: 91). In catering to audiences outside the Black community, the blues performer drew songs from the Euro-American musical tradition and modified his performance to conform to the non-Black environment. He adapted his text to represent the white, rather than the Black perspectives on a given subject and tailored his vocal and instrumental styles to adhere as closely as possible to the musical standards and aesthetics the white community understood (Ferris 1978: 92-97; Levine 1977: 270-297).

A closer look at blues musical structure illustrates that it is derived from both secular and religious musical traditions. Its improvisatory nature emphasizes melodic and textual repetition, making use of call-response structures in the context of verses. The blues incorporates West African vocal devices such as slides, slurs, bends, dips, grunts, moans, song-speech utterances, and interjections and makes them an integral part of the melody.[28] Accompanying instruments, played in melodic and percussive styles, often include the guitar, fiddle, piano, harmonica or, sometimes, jugs, a wire nailed to the side of a house, and other ad hoc instruments.[29] For over eighty years, the essence of the blues tradition has remained the same. Amplified instruments in the 1940s, a rhythm section in the 1950s, and horns in the 1960s are perhaps the only significant, yet superficial, additions that this tradition has experienced. The melodic and percussive instrumental styles developed by blues performers provided the basis for the emergence of a twentieth century religious music that was characterized by a rocking beat.

GOSPEL

Gospel music is a by-product of the late nineteenth and early twentieth century Black "folk church." This church, associated with the Holiness or Pentecostal sects, was a contemporary version of the plantation "praise house." Its character "reflects the traditional cultural values of Black folk life as it has evolved since slave days, and is a cumulative expression of the Black experience" (Williams-Jones 1977: 21).

The Black "folk church" can be distinguished from other twentieth century Black churches denominations by the structure and nature of its service, religious and philosophical concepts, and the socioeconomic background of its members. The official doctrine of the Black church encourages freedom of expression that unveils itself in spontaneous testimonies, prayers, and praises from individuals. Unlike independent Black churches, the Black "folk church" did not evolve from white Protestant denominations. Its musical repertoire, therefore, is distinctly different from that of Protestant churches,[30] representing a continuation of age-old musical traditions and practices, adapted to reflect twentieth-century attitudes, values, and life-styles of the poor and uneducated.

Spontaneously improvised songs, folk spirituals, and revival hymns, altered to conform to the aesthetic priorities and social needs of Blacks, constituted the religious music of the first postbellum Black folk churches. These songs, known as "church songs," were manifestations of sermons chanted and sung by Black preachers, whose emotional and repetitive styles motivated spontaneous responses, often in song. Hand-clapping, foot-stamping, and later drums, tambourine, piano, organ, guitar, and various types of horns and ad hoc instruments not only provided accompaniment but also heightened the intensity of the service.[31] The use of these instruments as an essential part of religious rituals in the Black folk church appears to have contributed to the emergence of gospel as a distinct and original body of twentieth-century Black religious music.

Today, although free-style improvisations continue to give birth to gospel music, the large body of standard gospel songs are composed by individuals. Performers use the musical score as a framework from which to interpret and improvise, using stylistic and vocal devices emerging from a West African derived Black aesthetic (Williams-Jones 1975: 379).

Ironically, the gospel prototype and later gospel music first reached Black masses as a composed piece of music from ministers and members of the Methodist and Baptist churches, who recently had moved from the South to northern cities. In offering an explanation for this occurrence, Boyer (1978: 37) states that "while the gospel song was born in the Holiness church, its members were not the first to receive recognition as gospel singers. Until the forties, Holiness churches did not allow their members to sing their songs before non-Holiness persons." It appears that the pioneer was the Methodist minister, Charles Albert Tindley, who wrote his first songs between 1900 and 1906. Some were hymn-like verses set to melodies and rhythms of folk church songs (associated with the folk church), while others were adaptations of spiritual and revival songs. It was not until 1921 when Thomas Dorsey composed his first religious song in an attempt to capture the spirit of urban life-styles that the foundation and style for an original twentieth-century form of Black religious music was established. Dorsey's ragtime, boogie-woogie piano style, his blues-based vocal melodies and harmonies, and the spirit with which he expressed his belief in the teaching and powers of Jesus Christ gave rise to the Black gospel idiom.[32]

For more than seventy years, gospel music has served as a major source of inspiration for urban Black communities. During this time, its musical content and directon have been altered to capture the essence of contemporary social problems, values, attitudes, and life-styles of Blacks who are reacting to social structures and political climates imposed by the larger society. These alterations, however, do not change fundamental concepts, aesthetics, and practices. Rather, they expand upon them. Since the 1920s, standard church instruments, such as the piano and organ, as well as a variety of horns and percussive and modern electric instruments have been added to the traditional accompaniment of handclapping and foot-stamping. These instruments are played in contemporary idiomatic styles, associated with secular musical traditions of the time. They provide a driving, percussive, and polyrhythmic accompaniment for the electrifying and intense vocal style characteristic of gospel performers (Williams-Jones 1970: 211).[33]

The gospel performer's improvisatory style highlights antiphonal structures within a chorus-verse format. Much emphasis is placed on melodic and textual repetition and variation. West African vocal devices including moans, grunts, wails, shouts, cries, gliding pitches, song-speech utterances and verbal interjections work together to create motifs which, in turn, form the vocal melodies. To increase the intensity of their performances, gospel singers often use other devices such as sudden juxtaposition of extreme vocal registers (movement from the high to low vocal range) sudden dynamics changes, breathing either between syllables of words or between words within phrases and the production of airy tones. Williams-Jones (1975: 337, 382), in emphasizing the importance of these airy tones states that "the audible breath intake and expulsion of air acts as a rhythmic factor and is an essential part of Black timing and rhythmic pacing."

The large body of gospel music embraces many traditions and styles that extend from spirituals, hymns, and blues to contemporary jazz, pop, soul, disco and funk. In addition to creating completely original compositions, composers and arrangers of gospel consciously and unconsciously derive melodic and textual content from these other genres. The form of gospel ranges from a strict call-response structure to a three-line blues format to complex four- and five-part structures. Most gospel songs, however, are based on call-response and two-part forms (chorus-verse or verse-chorus) and their structure may vary from performance to performance.

The improvisatory nature of gospel and its lack of a predetermined song length allows performers to expand and contract established forms at will. A standard chorus-verse structure, for example, may be expanded into a chorus-verse-chorus-verse-chorus-extended chorus structure (Boyer 1978: 42).

Perhaps the greatest secular influence on gospel has been various instrumental styles. Former blues and jazz musicians were among the first to become instrumentalists for gospel singers. Orally transmitted from generation to generation, the style and musical vocabulary, first introduced by Dorsey, was combined with contemporary secular genres to create a new form for gospel style. Thus, the secular-orientated direction of present-day gospel is highlighted by the "beat" and modern gospel uses the musical vocabulary and instrumental styles characteristic of jazz, soul, disco, and funk (Boyer 1977: 46-49; Williams-Jones 1970: 211).

Gospel music has captured the essence of twentieth century Black existence and has become one of the most meaningful forms of expression for the Black community. Beginning in the Holiness and Pentecostal churches and the store-front Baptist and Methodist churches, it has now found a home in many of the large middle-and upper-middle class Baptist and Methodist churches. The impact of gospel has been so great that its colorful kaleidoscope of oratory, poetry, drama, and dance, coupled with its musical style provides a reservoir of musical resources that form the foundation of Black forms of popular music.

Prior to 1920, ninety percent of all Blacks lived in the South, eighty percent of these in rural areas. During and after World Wars I (1914-18) and II (1939-1945), masses of southern rural Blacks migrated to urban cities throughout the United States in hopes of escaping social, economic, and political discrimination. Life in these urban centers did not meet their expectations. Discrimination forced these Blacks—who by 1930 constituted twenty percent of the total Black population—to live in ghettos. Once again, their music reflects their struggles to survive in this new environment.

SOUL

The evolution of "soul music," a by-product of the 1960s Black Power movement, contributed to the general acceptance of Black pride and self-awareness. Performers of soul music encouraged Blacks to return to their African heritage for ideals, values, and inspiration. In their songs, they discussed existing conditions and offered solutions for change. Before the Black Power movement emerged, Black music disclosed the Blacks' inferior socioeconomic status and inability to improve their situation. The music created during and after the years of this movement announced the determination of Blacks to stimulate change through their own active efforts.

The renewed focus on an African past intensified the revival of West African musical concepts that had either been lost or been preserved only in residual form. The intense emotional nature of soul songs reflected the new spirit and convictions of Blacks that would soon alter the social, political, and economic structure of American society.[34]

Soul music may best be described as the secular counterpart of gospel. Many of its performers either are now or were once gospel singers; consequently, they use every vocal device idiomatic to gospel singing and preaching as they continue to find new ways of expressing traditional values, attitudes, and philosophies.

It appears that the larger society's various attempts to stamp out all vestiges of an African heritage in the culture of Black Americans have brought little, if any, significant results. The retention of many aspects of West African musical traditions through the seventeenth and eighteenth centuries illuminates the strength of the slaves' communal solidarity. The emergence in the nineteenth century of an identifiable Black musical tradition based on African concepts demonstrates clearly that the slaves refused to accept the essence of their white masters' culture. The continued evolution of a distinctly Black musical tradition in the twentieth century highlights the ability of Black communities to maintain and revive traditional values as a means of preserving their heritage in spite of external opposition.

THE PRESERVATION OF WEST AFRICAN
MUSICAL CONCEPTS

It is really West African concepts, more so than elements, that have been retained in U.S. Black music. Many African elements, as well as genres, have disappeared due to external pressures, social upheavals, and environmental changes; in their place, are fundamental substitutes. These new genres, however, adhere to many basic West African musical principles. As J. H. Kwabena Nketia (1977: 5) notes:

When musical types or the items of a given repertoire are lost through social upheavals or loss of interest, new ones are created in the style of the tradition, using its vocabulary and idiom, or in an alternative style which combines African and non-African resources that have become an integral part of the musical experience of peoples of African descent and those who share in their tradition.

The lack of African resources forced alterations in traditional concepts. The tempered tuning of western instruments, in addition to the nature of the English language, forced Blacks to deviate from certain principles of melodic structure, organization, and function. However, this situation challenged Blacks to explore new means of melodic expression, which, unconsciously, were founded on the original African concept. With "blue notes," "bends," and other techniques, they produced pitches unavailable on Western instruments and uncommon to Western scale structures, thereby exhibiting new ways to employ old concepts.

In spite of common conceptual roots, modern twentieth century Black music sounds less African than eighteenth and nineteenth century Black music. The superficial sound differences are a product of changes in the social climate, increased bicultural experiences, elemental substitutions, and the use of electronic instruments, which range from guitars, organs, and pianos to clavinets, synthesizers, and an assortment of external sound attachments. Nketia (1977: 16) in viewing this reality from a conceptual framework, believes that "African roots in the Americas must be viewed in terms of creative processes which allow for continuity and change."

Current research efforts, in addition to the accessibility of authentic sound recordings, enable us to pinpoint West African roots in twentieth-century Black music. We can identify African influences and retentions in seven conceptual categories: (1) social functions, (2) community function of musicians, (3) principles of music-making, (4) textual content, organization, and structure, (5) melodic traits, (6) vocal stylistic features, and (7) musical instruments.

SOCIAL FUNCTION

As West African music, U.S. Black music serves a variety of social functions. Music is the heartbeat of Black communities, woven into the daily routines of its members. Twentieth century technological advancements make it possible for Blacks to enjoy recorded music as an extension of live participatory performances. As they listen to Black-oriented radio stations and hear recordings of their favorite artists, Black Americans are entertained and comforted. The music, a part of their domestic, occupational, and political worlds, serves a functional purpose. Blacks respond to and become involved in recorded religious and secular music by singing familiar refrain lines and choruses, snapping their fingers, clapping their hands, and moving to the beat. They also express their approval by interjecting comments such as "Sing it baby," "Tell the truth," "Play your horn," "Tickle them keys," and "Get down and jam."

Live performances of secular Black music are organized social events. Though performances are billed as concerts, Blacks interpret them to be a time for "letting loose" and "jamming with the artist." Promotional materials frequently advertise concerts with such phrases as "Come and be moved by," "Come and jam," or "Come and party" with so and so. Live performances of religious and secular music are, in reality, social occasions which, through community involvement, promote group cohesion and mass communication. Traditionally, Blacks have been involved in the process of music making; this involvement is fundamental and governs Black music today. Despite the commercialization of most forms of recorded music, twentieth century live performances are of the same character as those that took place in the slave quarters and "praise houses" of the seventeenth century.

The improvisational nature of the music encourages spontaneous group involvement, manifested through hand-clapping, foot-stamping, fingerpopping, bodily movement, dance, and verbal and nonverbal interjections. Individual performers frequently alter their songs to accommodate a kind of—"we are here to jam"— philosophy of the audience. Ad lib or "rapping" (secular)/ "sermonette" (religious) encourage verbal and physical responses from the audience. The audience is free to participate in any way, sometimes even joining performers on stage. Audience participation increases the emotional intensity of the musical event, and often the success of the live performance is determined by the degree of audience involvement. The nature of individual and group performances of Black music reveals four attitudes that are fundamental to Black culture: (1) a common set of values regulates the behavior of the community; (2) the freedom of expression is tolerated and highly regarded; (3) group participation represents audience approval and serves as a source of encouragement for performers; and (4) musical events stimulate group cohesion and mass communication.

COMMUNITY FUNCTION OF MUSICIANS

Black musicians serve as spokesmen, counselors, politicans, historians, entertainers, and role models for the Black community. Through their songs, they address concerns, problems and social issues that pervade the Black community. Through their philosophical comments and words of wisdom, they provide counsel, comfort, and encouragement. With their songs of praise or criticisms, they influence community opinion and in this way exert social control.

As historians, documenting the history of Blacks, Black musicians are a valuable reservoir of information. As entertainers, they heighten spirits, relieve boredom, provide dance music, and help unify the community as they are the source of that initial emotional spark which energizes members who gather to "rap," "joke" and socialize for hours. Successful performers are role models for young Blacks who attempt to imitate their life-styles. In general, Black musicians along with Black preachers are the backbone and source of inspiration for the Black community.[35]

PRINCIPLES OF MUSIC-MAKING

The process of music-making, both in West Africa and Black America, extends beyond mere sound production. Bodily movements and their dance manifestations constitute an integral part of the process. In all genres of Black music, various forms of motion, including head movement, shoulder jerking, foot-tapping, hand-clapping, arm extension, body swaying, and other types of physical movement accompany the production of sound. These motions are executed in rhythm with the music and display an emotional response to it.

Physical movement also functions as a nonverbal means of communication. It expresses ideas that cannot be captured in sound, exaggerates subtleties in the sound, and articulates and dramatizes the feelings and philosophies of the performer. In the Black musical tradition, motion and music are conceptualized as one process; they do not constitute the fusion of two separate entities (Nketia 1974: 206-230; Epstein 1977; Levine 1977: 16, 200-201; Courlander 1963: 34).

Colorful and flamboyant costumes add another dimension to the music-making process. While an extrinsic factor, the wearing of costumes is synonymous with Black musicians. In recent years, Black artists have added stage props and other visuals to enhance their performances, providing another vehicle for expression that is a traditional African concept.

TEXTUAL CONTENT, ORGANIZATION AND STRUCTURE

As we have seen for over three centuries, Blacks in America have used music as an avenue for unrestricted verbal expression. The textual themes of their songs, derived from individual and group experiences, express hardships, aspirations, relationships, protests, praise, criticism, reactions to contemporary social issues, and belief in the powers of Jesus Christ. Some performers improvise verses on the spot; others compose new ones and combine them with lines and verses. Often, sacred and secular content are interchanged as imagery and metaphor facilitate in-group communication.[36]

Many of the lyrics repeat ideas over and over again in original and elaborated forms. Narrative prose constitutes only a small part of the repertoire; perhaps because—since the performer and audience share common experiences—general details are understood by all and, therefore, can be omitted. It also may be that the presentation of several thoughts would require more concentration and, as a result, interfere with the listeners' active participation. The general economy of words accommodates freedom of expression and flexibility, which Blacks value highly (cf. Keil 1966; Garland 1969).

Since most genres in the Black tradition are designed for solo singers and a group, the basic form assumes a call-response structure—A-B-A-B, A-B-C-B, A-B-A-C, or A-B-C-D. In post-Civil War genres, these structures have been incorporated into strophic, binary, ternary, and larger sectional forms. The use of call-response in this context is a stylistic rather than a structural trait, thus representing the reinterpretation of an African concept. Songs have stanzaic structures with extensive textual repetition and variations generally assume one of the following structures: A-A-B, A-A-A-B, A-B-C-B, or A-B-A-C.[37]

MELODIC TRAITS

Analysis of melodic traits is an area of Black music that has possibly been grossly neglected. Due to the limited amount of analytical data available, I can make only an initial attempt to summarize inconclusive findings. Vocal music uses one of six types, consisting of three, four, five, six, seven or eight pitches (excluding octaves) of various intervallic structures. The latter three scales appear to be common to the tradition. In the pentatonic scale, three structures dominate: M2-M2-m3-M2, M2-M2-m2-M2, and m3-M2-M2-m3. The most common hexatonic scale structure is M2-M2-m2-M2-M2-m2, while the major scale and mixolydian mode are common to the heptatonic scale structure.[38]

Pitches do not always correspond exactly to instrumental tunings since vocalists and instrumentalists use various techniques to alter tone. Melodic structures are based on intervallic sequences, which emphasizes the unison (repeated pitches). Important pitches resulting from stress and repetition appear to be the first, third, and fourth or fifth scale degrees. Melodic contour frequently moves in a downward direction. Ranges of individual phrases extend from a unison to a perfect octave plus a major second, while total song range extends from a perfect fourth to a perfect octave plus a perfect fourth. The syllabic nature of melodies associated with the antebellum Black music and related forms distinguishes them from gospel and popular melodies with their melismatic nature.

The most obvious melodic feature all Black music genres share is the extensive use of repeated pitches, which frequently are accompanied by one of the following rhythmic motifs: (1) series four pitches of equal durational value, (2) triplets, (3) dotted rhythms, and (4) pitches of short durational value followed by those of longer value.[39]

VOCAL STYLISTIC FEATURES

The most striking stylistic characteristics of Black music are the improvisation techniques and other vocal devices performers employ. Throughout Black existence in America, various writers, foreign travelers, and casual observers have attempted to describe this distinguishing feature. The vocal style, encompassing characteristics of West African traditions, is an extension of the Black preachers' style of developing sermons. Creating a cross between speech and song, the performer dramatizes his delivering with rhythmic moans, grunts, wails, shouts, glides, bends, dips, cries, hollers, vocables (words composed of various, possibly meaningless sounds), falsetto, and melodic repetition. Interjections and irregular phrasing rhythmically punctuate the song. Airy tones, sudden and drastic changes in dynamic levies, and singing in very high or very low registers enable the performer to achieve musical contrast.

MUSICAL INSTRUMENTS

All genres of Black music use a variety of manufactured, self-constructed, and ad hoc instruments. Musicians of most folk idioms make greater use of self-constructed and ad hoc instruments than do musicians of urban traditions. As folk musicians construct instruments from local materials and turn everyday objects into instruments, they are continuing an African practice. Many of the self-constructed instruments, such as the banjo, washtub bass, diddley bow, kazoo, and blowing jugs are reinterpretations of African stringed and wind instruments. Pots, pans, spoons, sticks, jawbones, blades, spring teeth from harrows, wagon clevises, washboards, frying pans, lard cans, and glasses serve as substitutes for African drums, beaters, bells, scrapers, and flutes. Blacks have adapted European instruments to African function. For example, the triangle has replaced the African bell and tambourines substitute for the calabash rattle.

In the seventeenth and eighteenth centuries, slaves used some instruments that were indigenous to Africa. The "marimba Brett" or *sansa*, the mouth-bow, panpipes, gourd rattle, calabash rattle with external strikers, "belt of bells," wooden horns, hand gong, balafo or xylophone, conch shell trumpet, and various drums are examples of African instruments that have been retained in the musical tradition of blacks.[40]

The playing techniques Blacks have developed while performing on Western and African-derived instruments illustrate another re-interpretation of African concepts. In learning to play a variety of Western instruments, Black musicians have applied traditional techniques that had been passed aurally from generation to genera-tion. In adapting to natural limitations and tempered tunings of these instruments, musicians have extended the ranges by altering established fingerings, using unconventional embouchures, and assuming unique playing positions. They have explored alternative methods for producing tone and sound effects. Muting and sound distortion through physical manipulations and use of external devices have become commonplace among Black performers.[41]

West African principles dictate which instruments performers choose. Since much of Black music emerges from an emotional and polyrhythmic foundation, instrument selection is based on range, timbre, and potential ability to be played in a percussive manner. In up-tempo gospel and soul music, for example, the bass and rhythm guitars, piano, and organ assume two functions: the bass provides a melodic and rhythmic foundation from which other instruments derive melodic, harmonic, and/or rhythmic patterns. The melodic line assigned to the bass generally is a phrase-length motif, which is repeated throughout a section, if not the entire piece. This pattern may be equated with the time-line concept associated with West African music. The rhythm guitar plays a series of short, repetitive, harmonic, and rhythmic patterns, which often are interchanged with short repetitive melodic motifs. The piano, organ, and the rhythm guitar complement each other by al-ternating between melodic and harmonic patterns of different rhythmic orientations. When horns are added to the rhythm section, they generally play a variety of two-, three-, and four-note motifs in a highly percussive manner. The drummer's role includes keeping of the time and accenting of certain beats, among other things. When percussive instruments are added, they double-time the beat of the drum, accent part of the rhythmic patterns assigned to other instruments, or play entirely different patterns.[42]

The combination of the various rhythmic patterns results in syncopated and polyrhythmic structures. The overall sound that is produced is not as complicated as that heard in African music due to the shortness and spacing of stratified rhythmic patterns. One rhythmic pattern may involve all four beats, while a second pattern is heard on beats one and two, another emphasizes beats two and four, while the fourth pattern provides the subdivisions of each beat. In sparsely or unaccompanied songs, the "voice" of the instrument assumes the role of missing instruments. Such substitutions are common to the tradition and illustrate another dimension of African influences within U.S. Black music.

Current research reveals that West African musical concepts form the foundation for the various musical genres Black Americans have created. During each phase of its development, Black music has exemplified the collective attitudes, values, philosophies, and experiences of the Black community. The social organizations as determined by environmental factors encouraged the retention, reinterpretaton, and revival of various African concepts.

In adapting to environmental changes over three hundred years, Blacks have continued to rely on familiar traditions and practices for self-preservation. Musical forms have been recycled through age-old concepts. The musical tradition the slaves established continues to persist in the twentieth century, reinterpreted as the social times demand. Whatever social changes arise in the future, African concepts will continue to form the basis of Black musical expression. The nature of human behavior forces cultural groups to draw on traditional concepts and practices as they united during times of crises.

Inevitably conflict and crises will stimulate new forms of musical expression. Hence, the Black musical tradition will continue to evolve and mirror new values, attitudes, philosophies and lifestyles, but it will never lose its West African essence.

NOTES

1. Studies of this nature include Berlin (1974); Genovese (1974); Blassingame (1972); Mullin (1972); and Haynes (1972).
2. Levine (1977); Epstein (1977); Dundes, ed. (1973); and Whitten and Szwed, eds. (1970).

3. For a summary of theories advanced by three writers see Levine (1973: 153-182). Also, see Johnson (1930).

4. Jordan (1968: 66-85).

5. Jordan (1968: 66); and Litwack (1961: 4-6).

6. See Jordan (1968: 66).

7. See Southern (1971: 31-48); and Maultsby (1975: 402-404).

8. See Genovese (1974: 7-25) and Blassingame (1972: 41-42, 154, 172-177).

9. See Uya (1971); Stampp (1956: 30, 34-36); Genovese (1974: 8-9, 328-365); Blassingame (1972: 155, 158).

10. For further discussion, see Epstein (1977: 8-17).

11. Additional information about these holidays may be found in Epstein (1977: 144-147).

12. For detailed descriptions of this holiday see Southern (1971: 51-52); and Epstein (1977: 67).

13. Comments of this nature may be found in Godwin (1689: 33); and Murphy (1967: 328).

14. For detailed discussions on African derived instruments played by American Blacks, see Courlander (1963: 204-220); and Epstein (1977: 53-60, 144-147).

15. "Praise houses" were places designated for slave worship.

16. For detailed information about Blacks and the Revival Movement see Lovell (1972: 71-374; Epstein (1977: 191-216).

17. Hymn singing became prominent among the colonists in the mid-eighteenth century; for detailed information about this tradition see Chase (1966: 41-64).

18. For descriptions of and discussions about religious services conducted by slaves, see Epstein (1977: 191-237); and Levine (1977: 3-80).

19. See Maultsby (1974a: 182). These performance practices also can be heard on the following recordings: *Been in the Storm So Long*, recorded by Guy Carawan on Johns Island, South Carolina (Folkways Records FS 3842); *Afro-American Spirituals, Work Songs, and Ballads*, edited by Alan Lomax, The Library of Congress Music Division (AAPS L3); *Negro Religious Songs and Services*, edited by B. A. Botkin, The Library of Congress Music Division (AAFS L10).

20. For detailed descriptions of and stylistic trends associated with slave singing see Epstein (1977: 191-237); Murphy (1967: 327-329); Blacking (1973: 209-210); Laubenstein (1930: 379); and Waterman (1943: 41-42).

21. The secular musical tradition of the slaves is discussed in Levine (1977: 15); Courlander (1963: 80-88, 89-122, 146-161); and Epstein (1977: 161-190).

22. Berlin (1974: 66, 89, 187-216); Wade (1964: 64-152).

23. Berlin (1974: 282, 298-299).

24. For discussion about and descriptions of services associated with independent Black churches see Berlin (1974: 284-303); Wade (1964: 160-176); Epstein (1977: 197, 223); Maultsby (1975: 407-418), and Yarmolinsky (1930: 30).

25. For historical information about the status of Blacks after the Civil War see Frazier (1949: 171-272); Levine (1977: 136-170); and Woodard (1966: 11-65).

26. Information relating to legislation that affected the lives of Blacks is included in Frazier (1949: 123-168); Woodward (1966: 11-65); and Haralambos (1975: 50-51).

27. See Frazier (1949: 227-237); and Titon (1977: 3-15).

28. Discussions about musical style or performance practices associated with the blues tradition may be found in Charters (1967); Haralambos (1975: 76-82); Titon (1977); Levine (1977: 217-224); and Keil (1966: 50-68).

29. For discussions on blues instruments see Ferris (1978: 37-38); and Evans (1970: 229-245).

30. Williams-Jones (1977: 23, 25). See also Williams (1974).

31. For descriptions of musical practices associated with the Black folk church see Williams-Jones (1975: 374, 381, 383) and Levine (1977: 179-180).

32. Bontemps (1942: 76-77); and Boyer (1978: 36-38). Bontemps gives the years 1901-1906 as the time period when Tindley wrote his first songs and Boyer believes the period to be between 1900 and 1905.

33. A variety of instruments that are used to accompany early gospel may be heard on *An Introduction to Gospel Song* compiled and edited by Samuel B. Charters (RBF Records RF 5).

34. Many of James Brown's recordings released between 1969 and 1974 illustrate the "Black pride" concept in soul music; see also White (1977: 36).

35. Discussions about the function of Black musicians in the context of the Black community are found in Evans (1977); Keil (1966: 143-163); Haralambos (1975: 104-154); Levine (1977); Nketia (1974: 35-42); and Ferris (1978: 79-80).

36. For discussions about textual themes in Black music, see Courlander (1963); Levine (1977: 11-14, 170-177); Titon (1977: 169); and Keil (1966: 121, 143-163).

37. See Nketia (1974: 139-146); Titon (1977: 28-29); Boyer (1978: 42-43); Maultsby (1976: 54-69); and Burnim (1977: 10-13).

38. Boyer (1978: 42-43); and Maultsby (1974: 222, 259).

39. For melodic traits characteristic of various genres of Black music see Maultsby (1974: 328-335); Titon (1977: 145-165); Nketia (1974: 147-159, 168-174); Courlander (1963); Waterman (1943: 41-43); and Boyer (1978: 42-43).

40. Detailed information regarding instruments used by Black Americans is found in Evans (1977: 11-13); Courlander (1963: 204-220); Epstein (1977: 30-38, 53-58); and Nketia (1974: 67-107).
41. Instrument playing techniques associated with Black musicians are discussed in Anderson (1970: 66, 68); Evans (1977: 12); Oliver (1970); and Wilson (1974: 15-21).
42. Information regarding the rhythmic organization of Black music is included in Wilson (1974: 3-15); Nketia (1974: 111-138); Evans (1977: 17-18); and Williams-Jones (1975: 211).

REFERENCES

Anderson, Thomas J. et al. 1970. "Black Composers and the Avant-Garde." In *Black Music in Our Culture*. Ed. by Dominique-René de Lerma. Kent, Ohio: The Kent State University Press, 62-78.
Berlin, Ira. 1974. *Slaves Without Masters: The Free Negro in the Antebellum South*. New York: Vintage.
Blacking, John. 1973. "Field Work in African Music." In *Reflection on Afro-American Music*. Ed. by Dominique-René de Lerma. Kent, Ohio: Kent State University Press, 207-221.
Blassingame, John W. 1972. *The Slave Community*. New York: Oxford University Press.
Bontemps, Arna. 1942. "Rock, Church, Rock!" *Ground*, 3 (Autumn), 35-39.
Boyer, Horace. 1977. "Contemporary Gospel Music: Sacred or Secular?" *First World*, 1 (January/February), 46-49.
_____ 1978. "Gospel Music." *Music Education Journal*, 64 (May), 34-43.
Burnim, Mellonee. 1977. "Black Song in a Black Sect: Let the Church Say, Amen." Unpublished paper. (Indiana University).
Charters, Samuel. 1967. *The Bluesmen*. New York: Oak Publications.
Chase, Gilbert. 1966. *America's Music*, Rev. 2nd ed. New York: McGraw-Hill.
Cone, James. 1972. *The Spirituals and the Blues: An Interpretation*. New York: Seabury Press.
Courlander, Harold. 1963. *Negro Folk Music U.S.A.* New York: Columbia University Press.
deLerma, Dominique-René. 1970. *Black Music in Our Culture*. Kent, Ohio: The Kent State University Press.
Dundes, Alan, ed. 1973. *Mother Wit from the Laughing Barrel*. Englewood Cliffs, N.J.: Prentice-Hall, Inc.
Epstein, Dena J. 1977. *Sinful Tunes and Spirituals*. Chicago: University of Illinois Press.
Evans, David. 1970. "Afro-American One-Stringed Instruments." *Western Folklore* 29, October, 229-245.

_____. 1977. "African Elements in Twentieth Century United States Black Folk Music." Unpublished paper delivered at the 12th Congress of the International Musicological Society (Berkeley, California).

Ferris, William. 1978. *Blues from the Delta*. New York: Anchor Press.

Frazier, E. Franklin. 1949. *The Negro in the United States*. New York: The Macmillan Company.

Garland, Phyl. 1969. *The Sound of Sound*. Chicago: Regnery Co.

Genovese, Eugene D. 1974. *Roll, Jordan Roll: The World the Slaves Made*. New York: Pantheon Books.

Godwin, Morgan. 1689. *The Negro's and Indian's Advocate* . . . London: Printed by F.D.

Haralambos, Michael. 1975. *Right On: From Blues to Soul in Black America*. New York: Drake Publishers, Inc.

Haynes, Robert. 1972. *Blacks in White America Before 1865*. New York: David McKay Co.

Herskovits, Melville J. 1958. *The Myth of the Negro Past*. Boston: Beacon Press.

Johnson, Guy B. 1930. *Folk Culture in St. Helena Island*. Chapel Hill: University of North Carolina Press.

Jones, Charles Colcock. 1842. *Religious Instruction of the Negroes in the United States*. Savannah: T. Purse.

_____. n.d. *Suggestions on the Religious Institution of the Negroes in the Southern States* . . . Philadelphia: Presbyterian Board of Publication.

Jordan, Winthrop D. 1968. *White Over Black*. Chapel Hill: The University of North Carolina Press.

Keil, Charles. 1966. *Urban Blues*. Chicago: The University of Chicago Press.

Laubenstein, Paul. 1930. "Race Values in Afro-American Music." *Musical Quarterly* 16 (July), 378-403.

Levine, Lawrence. 1973. "Slave Songs and Slave Consciousness." In *American Negro Slavery*, 2nd ed. by Allen Weinstein and Frank Otto Catell, eds. New York: Oxford University Press, 153-182.

_____. 1977. *Black Culture and Black Consciousness*. New York: Oxford University Press.

Litwack, Leon F. 1961. *North of Slavery*. Chicago: The University of Chicago Press.

Lovell, John. 1972. *Black Song: The Forge and the Flame*. New York: The Macmillan Co.

Maultsby, Portia K. 1974a. "Afro-American Religious Music 1619-1861." Ph.D. dissertation, University of Wisconsin-Madison.

_____. 1974b. "John's Island, South Carolina: Its People and Songs." *Ethnomusicology* 18 (January), 181-183, record review.

_____. 1975. "Music of Northern Independent Black Churches During the Ante-Bellum Period." *Ethnomusicology* 19, September 401-420.

_____. 1976. "Black Spirituals: An Analysis of Textual Forms and Structures." *The Black Perspective in Music* 4 (Spring), 54-69.

Mullin, Gerald W. 1972. *Flight and Rebellion.* New York: Oxford University Press.

Murphy, Jeanette R. 1967. "The Survival of African Music in America." In *The Negro and His Folklore,* ed. by Bruce Jackson. Austin: University of Texas Press, 327-339.

Nketia, J. H. Kwabena. 1974. *The Music of Africa.* New York: W. W. Norton and Co.

_____. 1977. "African Roots of Music in the Americas: An African View." Unpublished paper delivered at the 12th Congress of the International Musicological Society (Berkeley, California).

Oliver, Paul. 1970. *Savannah Syncopators: African Retentions in the Blues.* New York: Stein and Day.

Russell, Henry. 1895. *Cheer! Boys, Cheer! Memories of Men and Music.* London: John Macqueen, Hastings House.

Simpson, George E. 1973. *Melville J. Herskovits.* New York: Columbia University Press.

Southern, Eileen. 1971. *The Music of Black Americans.* New York: W. W. Norton and Co.

Stampp, Kenneth. 1956. *The Peculiar Institution.* New York: A. A. Knopf.

Titon, Jeff Todd. 1977. *Early Downhome Blues: A Musical and Cultural Analysis.* Chicago: University of Illinois Press.

Uya, Okon E. 1971. "Life in the Slave Community." Unpublished paper, University of Wisconsin.

Wade, Richard C. 1964. *Slavery in the Cities: The South 1820-1860.* New York: Oxford University Press.

Waterman, Richard. 1943. "African Patterns in Trinidad Negro Music." Ph.D. dissertation, Northwestern University.

White, Cliff. 1977. "After 21 years, Still Refusing to Lose." *Black World* 4 (April), 32-37.

Whitten, Norman E., and John F. Szwed, eds. 1970. *Afro-American Anthropology.* New York: The Free Press.

Williams, Melvin D. 1974. *Community in a Black Pentecostal Church.* Pittsburgh: University of Pittsburgh Press.

Williams-Jones, Pearl. 1970. "Afro-American Gospel Music in Development of Materials for a One Year Course in African Music for the General Undergraduate Student." Ed. by Vada Butcher. Washington, D.C.: Howard University, 201-219.

_____. 1975. "Afro-American Gospel Music: A Crystallization of the Black Aesthetic." *Ethnomusicology* 19 (September), 373-385.

_____. 1977. "The Musical Quality of Black Religious Folk Ritual." *Spirit* 1, 21-30.

Wilson, Olly. 1974. "The Significance of the Relationship Between Afro-American Music and West African Music." *The Black Perspective in Music* 2 (Spring), 3-22.

Woodward, C. Vann. 1966. *The Strange Career of Jim Crow*. Second revised edition. New York: Oxford University Press.

Yarmolinsky, Avrahm, ed. 1930. *Picturesque United States of America: 1811, 1812, 1813*. New York: William Edwin Rudge Inc.

3

GEORGE L. STARKS, JR.

Salt and Pepper in Your Shoe: Afro-American Song Tradition on the South Carolina Sea Islands

Off the coast of South Carolina lie numerous tracts of land that are referred to as the "Sea Islands." These islands, separated from the mainland by water flowing in from the Atlantic Ocean, are a part of many such parcels of land, which stretch from the Carolinas into Florida. Some of the islands in this group are so low that they are unhabitable; others are not only populated but historically have been among the most important examples of an African cultural presence in America.

Amerindians, though rarely found in the region today, were the original residents of these islands. Place names such as Edisto, Daufuskie, and Wadmalaw are among the prominent reminders of the people who once dwelled there.

Spaniards, led by Pedro Quexos in 1521, were the first to encroach upon the islands. They came in search of slaves to sell in the West Indies, in quest of gold and land. Quexas seized 140 Amerindians at Winyah Bay; five years later, in 1526, the first Africans to be enslaved in what is now the United States were brought into the vicinity of North Island, South Carolina, by a group of Spaniards. They had plans to establish a colony in the region, but these were thwarted by Amerindians who attacked them in retaliation for taking their corn and by the Africans who revolted against them.

It was almost 150 years later, with the coming of English settlers in 1670, that slavery became firmly entrenched in coastal South Carolina. Many of the English settlers came from the West Indies—

a significant portion from the island of Barbados—and trans-
planted both their slaves and their system of slavery to South Carolina. Slaves were also purchased in Charleston for servitude on the
Sea Islands, where they worked cultivating rice, indigo, and cotton.

With the onset of the Civil War, slavery on the Sea Islands came
to an end. Many planters abandoned the islands in the face of the
Union presence, some never to return, and thus slaves on Sea
Island plantations were among the first to gain their freedom.
Through the Freedman's Bureau, many became landowners. Although they soon lost much of the property through dispossession,
the former Black slaves were eventually able to purchase small
parcels of land. Some of this land still remains in the possession of
their descendants.

For more than a century, these Sea Islands have been of great
interest to scholars in many disciplines. Historians, anthropolo-
gists, linguists, folklorists, and ethnomusicologists have come to
find the Afro-American presence. The principal reason is that a
large number of cultural traditions, dating back to the early
Africans' arrival in this country—and indeed back to the African
continent itself—have survived here. The relative isolation of the
Sea Islands, coupled with the fact that Blacks have appreciably out-
numbered Whites for most of the time following permanent European settlement, are two important reasons for the retentions that
have been and are now a part of Black Sea Island culture.

Among the most important of these retentions is the dialect
known as "Geechie" or "Gullah." These terms refer both to the dialect and to the people who speak it. Having grown up and lived in
Afro-Amercian communities, I have found that Geechie seems to
be the most frequently used term among Black Americans. Gullah,
though not unknown among Blacks, appears to be used more by
European Americans and in academia.

The source of the word Geechie is sometimes said to be Georgia's
Ogeechee River, along which some speakers of this dialect live. As
for the sources of the word Gullah, popular notions are that it
comes from "Angola," one of the areas on the African continent
from which slaves were brought into South Carolina, and "Gola,"
the name of a group of people in the African country of Liberia.

Early researchers were overwhelmingly critical of the dialect, dis-
avowing its African influence. Many claimed the dialect developed

as the slaves adopted the "baby-talk" their masters used in speaking to them and combined it with peasant or early English (Krapp 1924; Bennett 1908, 1909; Gonzales 1964; Smith 1926; Johnson 1930; Woofter 1930; Crum 1940).

The publication of *Africanisms in the Gullah Dialect* in 1949 by the noted linguist Lorenzo Dow Turner rebutted this theory. Unlike the proponents of the "baby-talk" theory, Turner had extensive knowledge of both African languages and dialects developed in the "New World" by people of African descent. In his research into the origins of the Geechie dialect, he found four to five thousand African words from almost thirty languages.

Largely from Turner's conclusions came another theory that the dialect is a creolized language. As Turner (1949: xiii) explains: "Gullah is a creolized form of English revealing survivals from many of the African languages spoken by slaves who were brought to South Carolina and Georgia during the eighteenth century and the first half of the nineteenth."

Turner's findings raise doubt as to the authenticity of early Gullah transcriptions and the accuracy of details reported in early studies of Black culture on the Sea Islands. The debate continues. Guy B. Johnson (1980) holds to the basic findings of his 1930s research, while Twining and Baird (1980b) align themselves with the creolized school of thought.

Remnants of the early African presence make themselves seen and heard in other areas besides language. For example, rice was the staple in the Sea Island slaves' diet, and it is rare today for an islander to eat a meal that does not include rice. The telling of tales is an important tradition from the days of slavery that extended well into this century (Parsons 1923). Even today one still hears the basic plots of some of the tales. Traditionally, a song has often helped to carry the story line. This practice has its roots on the African continent.

Many facets of Sea Island culture show important relationships to the traditions of Africa and to those in other areas of the "New World" where there is a sizeable number of people of African descent (Twining and Baird 1980a). This cultural relationship and continuity is evidenced in the traditional music of the islands: polyrhythms, multimeter, vocal timbre, heterophony and/or polyphony; the integration of music with other aspects of culture; and the all-

encompassing meaning music has for the people. All these characteristics are integral to African music.

When William F. Allen, Charles P. Ware, and Lucy McKim Garrison published the first book collection of Afro-American songs,
Slave Songs of the United States, in 1867, more songs from the Sea
Islands were included than from any other region, despite the fact
that the book covered songs from the Eastern Seaboard to the Mississippi River. As Allen related in the introduction:

The largest and most accurate single collection in existence is probably that
made by Mr. Charles P. Ware, chiefly at Coffin's Point, St. Helena Island.
We thought it best to give this collection in its entirety, as the basis of the
present work; it includes all the hymns as far as No. 43. Those which
follow, as far as No. 55, were collected by myself on the Capt. John Fripp
and neighboring plantations, on the same island. (Allen et al. 1867: iii)

In that same introduction, Allen presented his views on the
music, commenting: "Still the chief part of the negro [*sic*] music is
civilized in its character—partly composed under the influence of
association with the whites, partly actually imitated from their
music." (Allen et al. 1867: vi)

Allen anticipated that an examination of secular music might
yield different findings: "Indeed, it is very likely that if we had
found it possible to get at more of their secular music, we should
have come to another conclusion as to the proportion of the barbaric element." (Allen et al. 1867: vii).

Even prior to the publication of *Slave Songs of the United States,*
Sea Island songs appeared in several periodicals (McKim 1862;
Garrison 1862; Spaulding 1863; Higginson 1867). Most of these
songs were of a religious nature, as McKim, Spaulding, and Higgin-
son noted the paucity or absence of secular songs on the islands
(Starks 1980).

Not as well known as *Slave Songs of the United States,* but a
very important book, nevertheless, is *Saint Helena Island Spirituals*
by Nicholas George Julius Ballanta, published in 1925. Ballanta, a
native of Sierra Leone and a self-taught musician, was working
toward a degree in music—by mail—when his book was published.
In the introduction (1925: iii), George Foster Peabody describes
Ballanta's academic work in music:

This man of 28 years, Mr. Nicholas George Julius Ballanta of Freetown, West Africa, whose grandfather was baptized as Taylor by Church Missionaries, had taught himself music without other aid than Sir John Stainer's book on harmony, for which he had sent to London. He made such progress that prior to 1921 he was able, through submitting compositions by mail, to pass the intermediary examination of Durham University, England for the degree of Bachelor of Music. He hopes to complete this work and final oral examination during the current year, 1925.

Ballanta's work received its initial impetus in New York in 1922 when Ballanta presented one of his compositions to the Damrosch brothers, Walter and Frank, who were important figures in American music. Impressed with his work, they encouraged him to further his music education. After completing his studies at the Institute of Musical Arts, Ballanta went to South Carolina to conduct field research on the Afro-American music of the region. His book contains the songs he collected at Penn School on St. Helena Island. Many were sung for him by the St. Helena Quartet, and when he transcribed the songs, he did so in the four-part harmony in which the men sang them. (During my field research on St. Helena, a former quartet member—A. J. Brown—also helped me with my work.)

As the title indicates, Ballanta's book is devoted to the spiritual. Like McKim, Spaulding, and Higginson before him, Ballanta felt that the spiritual made up the main body of Afro-American song: "There are several other classes of songs known as fiddle-songs, coon-songs, jig-tunes and devil songs but all these taken together are smaller in number than the spiritual" (1925: v).

An important section of *Saint Helena Island Spirituals* is the foreword in which Ballanta compares the spiritual's characteristic rhythmic, melodic, and formal features with those of traditional African music. He tells us:

A detailed exposition of the relationship between African music and the Negro spiritual would fill volumes instead of a few pages, but enough has been written to show that the Negro spiritual is in many respects identical in the elements of melody and rhythm with the African conception of those elements. . . . Not only is the spiritual allied to African music in those respects but the form or design of these spirituals is the same in Africa,

where the form of the solo and chorus or refrain which is found in most of
the spirituals is in use. (1925: xvii)

His thoughts concerning the harmonic practices of the Saint
Helena Quartet were not as conclusive, although here, too, relationships with African musical practices figure prominently. The
harmonies of the Saint Helena Quartet, he said, are

an evidence of the advance in harmonic conception, that is, the feeling for
definite tonality, attained by the Negro in his new environment. African
part singing is contrapuntal and interestingly so and the feeling for harmony in the sense of harmonic progression is very rudimentary. Though a
conception of tonality, by which is meant a group of chords, having a
definite relation one with another around a common center, exists, yet such
a conception varies with different tribes and is not so pronounced as to
allow of an undisputed conclusion being arrived at as is the case with the
rhythmic, melodic and formal elements; but conclusions as to the
intervallic sense of the African may be drawn from the fact that he sings in
the chord and not in the scale. (Ballanta 1925: xvii)

In 1930, Guy B. Johnson published a work on St. Helena Island's
dialect, folk songs, and folklore. It was part of a three-volume collection, which grew out of a study of Black life on St. Helena that
was jointly supported by the Institute for Research in Social Science
of the University of North Carolina and the Social Science Research
Council. Johnson was a champion of the "white to Black" school of
thought, which claimed that Afro-Americans developed their culture from a Euro-American base. Applying this notion to the origin
of the Afro-American spiritual put him at odds with Ballanta:

Mr. Ballanta's excellent collection entitled *St. Helena Island Spirituals*
makes it unnecessary for me to publish additional spirituals. At the same
time, his work, with its insistence on the African origin of the various characteristics of the Negro spirituals, makes it imperative that someone point
out that there is much to be said for a white ancestry for the music of the
spirituals. This I have attempted to do, the result being somewhat supple-
mentary to Mr. Ballanta's contributions, and at the same time something of
a note of caution to those who are too quick to ascribe to Africa the pecu-
liarities of American Negro folk music. (G. B. Johnson 1930: xx)

Johnson's hypothesis places him in the same "white to Black"
camp as George Pullen Jackson (1943) and Newman I. White (1928),

while Ballanta's theory places him in the "survivalist" school, along with Lorenzo D. Turner (1949) and Melville Herskovits (1941), who emphasize the retentions of African tradition in Afro-American culture.

Another important source on Sea Island music is *The Carolina Low Country*, published in 1931 by members of the Society for the Preservation of Spirituals. This organization grew out of a core of fifteen to twenty white Charlestonians, who started meeting in the 1920s. As their constitution states, "the purpose of the Society shall be the preservation of the Negro Spirituals and Folk Songs, the education of the rising generation in their character and rendition. . . ." (Smythe et al. 1931: vi). Toward this end, the Society gave concerts in Charleston, as far to the north as the state of Massachusetts, and in the state of Georgia to the south. As Smythe (1931: vii) states in his preface to *The Carolina Low Country*, "the primary end of the organization . . . is to reduce to musical notation . . . the songs . . . correctly notating the melodies and . . . to reproduce the words as the negroes [*sic*] pronounce them. . . "

The chapter entitled "The Negro in the Low Country," with its patronizing air, probably tells us more about the author's feelings toward the Black residents of the Low Country than it does about the inhabitants themselves. Indeed, this was a primary purpose of the book, for as Smythe stated the group wanted to "express in one book, the feelings of the members of the Society and of all others of similar heritage, towards the songs themselves, and the black people who sing them. . ." (Smythe et al. 1931: vii).

Robert W. Gordon, in his chapter, "The Negro Spiritual," comments: "Some spirituals seem almost barbaric in their wildness" (1931: 219). While he does not preclude Afro-American contributions to the development of the spiritual, the "white to Black" theory is primary in his thinking on the music's origin. At the same time, for him, one element was primarily Black: "Most important, and most purely African, is the negro's [*sic*] highly developed sense of rhythm. Here he literally has become teacher instead of pupil" (1931: 220). Gordon also made a case for the Black secular repertory: "The various work songs alone, if brought together, would probably far outnumber the spirituals. The negro [*sic*] has special songs for cotton picking, for hoeing, for threshing, for turpentine work, for heavy lifting, for loading and unloading cargoes" (Smythe et al., 1931: 192).

While members of the Society were active song collectors, they decided against publishing a comprehensive collection of spirituals. Their book included forty-nine songs from the Low Country, twelve of which came from the Sea Islands.

The transcribers commented on what they saw as deviations from "the usual rules," ignoring an African origin to the musical practices:

The country Negro, being quite naive in his manner of singing, has little regard for the usual rules. He seldom attacks a note clearly; he slides his intervals up or down; he often wobbles all round a note before deciding where to sing it. . . . There is an indescribable effect of wildness in his singing, due chiefly to inaccuracy of pitch. (Symthe et al. 1931: 225)

Another white, Low Country resident—Herbert Ravenel Sass— while subscribing to the "white to Black" theory for the origin of spirituals, spoke of the Blacks' music with a more favorable tone. In his work, *The Story of the South Carolina Low Country*, Sass (1956: 245) says, "The Negro took the white man's early religious songs . . . [and] created something new and beautiful—something which is now wholly his own."

More recently, Charles W. Joyner has published a book that merits attention (Joyner 1971). While Euro-American songs far outnumber the Afro-American ones, Joyner presents a thoughtful discussion of the spiritual, emphasizing the Sea Islands' form.

(I have concentrated here on the music of the South Carolina Sea Islands, but because of their proximity to and close ties with the Georgia Sea Islands, the music of these islands is relevant as well. See, for example, Francis (Fanny) Anne Kemble's *Journal of a Residence on a Georgia Plantation in 1838-1839* (1863), *Drums and Shadows* by the Georgia Writers' Project (1940), *Slave Songs of the Georgia Sea Islands* by Lydia Parrish (1942), and *Step It Down* by Bessie Jones and Bess Lomax Hawes (1972).

THE DATA

As a native South Carolinian, my interest in Sea Island music is a long-standing one. My home is in the northern, or "upper," part of the state (or the "Up-Country"), while the Sea Islands are off the coast in the "lower" part of the state or "Low Country." I conducted fieldwork on the Sea Islands during the 1970s. I examined both sacred and secular musics—including spirituals, gospel, work songs, blues, and children's songs—from both contemporary and historical perspectives. My data come from six of the most important islands in terms of African presence—James, Johns, Yonges, Edisto, St. Helena, and Daufuskie—all of which are situated between Charleston, South Carolina, and Savannah, Georgia, as well as the community of Red Top, which sits in close proximity to Johns Island, although it is not on a Sea Island. All of the songs included in this paper, with the exception of the text of "Old Lady Come From Booster," were collected by me during my fieldwork.

Although the islands continue to be steeped in tradition, life on them has not been static, as is sometimes thought. Bridge construction to the mainland began in the 1930s, and all of the islands on which I conducted my research now have that link, with the exception of Daufuskie, still accessible only by boat. James Island, for example, is in many ways part of Charleston's suburbs and now has a white population that greatly outnumbers the once numerically dominant Black population. Public school systems, once segregated, are now integrated. Migrant workers now provide much of the farm labor once supplied by islanders.

Music is very closely tied to, and very much an expression of, the lives of the Afro-Americans who reside on the Sea Islands. When we listen to the musical output of the people, we witness the continuation of African tradition as it responds to its new environment. This is true with religious music (Starks 1980), work songs, blues, and children's songs. It is the children's songs that I would like to turn to now.

CHILDREN'S SONGS ON THE
SOUTH CAROLINA SEA ISLANDS

Whether sitting on brownstone steps in the heat of an August night in a big city up north or on the grass in front of a southern rural house, children entertain themselves by singing. Frequently, this singing is, for the children, a practical introduction to the traditions of their musical culture. The songs, with their vocal timbre, pitch concepts, phrasing, and rhythmic patterns created by hands and feet, bear the stamp of their musical heritage.

Sung for the pleasure they bring the youngsters, the songs frequently reflect their private world and the larger world of which we
are all a part. Many of the same songs are heard in rural and urban
settings, but regional or local factors frequently produce variations. For example, a song that accompanies a particular game in a
big city may be sung differently in given neighborhoods of that city
because the varying street dimensions change the way the game is
played which in turn, changes the song's text. Sometimes regional
differences in verbal expression are reflected in the song texts and
frequently give us a clue, if only in a general sense, to the origin of a
particular version.

The sources of the songs are varied. Some are learned from adult
relatives, others from teachers, classmates, or playmates. In addition, young people frequently create their own songs; personal experiences, which can be greatly affected by location, often play a
crucial role in the outcome of these compositions. Thus, in the
music of the youngsters, we find long-standing traditons as well as
recent practices.

The events of everyday life often stimulate Sea Island children to
create songs. This method of composing is the way many early
Afro-American songs originated. As McKim reported in 1862,
when he inquired as to the origins of Afro-American songs in the
area, he was told by a Black Sea Island resident:

Dey make em, sah. . . . I'll tell you; it's dis way. My master call me up and
order me a short peck of corn and a hundred lash. My friends see it and is
sorry for me. When dey come to de praise meeting dat night dey sing about
it. Some's very good singers, and know how; and dey work it in, you
know; till they get it right; and dat's de way. (1862: 149)

A Black Sea Island resident told Higginson (1869: 210) a similar
story about his involvement in the creation of a song:

"Some good spirituals," he said, "are start jess out o' curiosity. I been
a-raise a sing, myself, once."

My dream was fulfilled, and I had traced out, not the poem alone, but
the poet. I implored him to proceed.

"Once we boys," he said, "went for tote some rice, and de nigger-driver,
he keep a-callin' on us; and I say, 'O, de ole nigger-driver.' Den annudder

said, 'First ting my mammy tole me was, notin' so bad as nigger-driver.' Den I made a sing, just puttin' a word, and den anudder word."

Then he began singing, and the men, after listening a moment, joined in the chorus as if it were an old acquaintance, though they evidently had never heard it before. I saw how easily a new "sing" took root among them.

Even today there are still singers on the islands who in the words of McKim's informant, "know how." One such person was a young man called "Boogie," who shared his songs with me. He was a thirteen-year-old eighth grader when he composed "I Met This Girl by the River" (figure 3.1).[1] About its origin, Boogie told me "this song was made when we was going on the railroad track picking blackberries, and Kenneth [a friend] saw a snake and he was scared. And I make Kenneth stay with me, and I tell him a little story."

Boogie has created many songs from everyday situations and taught them to other children. He also collaborated with friends in composing several songs.

In many cultures around the world, song is a means to hand down certain traditions. Afro-American beliefs often find their way into song. Charms that are used in romantic pursuits, for example, are frequently sung about in the blues. In Willie Dixon's composition, "Hoochie Coochie Man," which became a big hit for bluesman Muddy Waters in the 1950s, we find an example of this.

In a children's song called "Here Comes Uncle Jessie" (figure 3.2),[2] which I heard a group of youngsters sing on Johns Island in 1972, salt and pepper are described as love charms.

> . . . if you want a fellow, I'll tell you what to do.
> Just take some salt and pepper and put it in your shoe.

In the city, Uncle Jessie may come "walkin' down the street," but in a rural area such as Johns Island, he would more likely "come riding thru the field."[3]

Because most of the significant writing on the Sea Islands stresses the past isolation of the Islands and the distinctiveness of their culture (Herskovits 1941; G. G. Johnson 1930: G. B. Johnson 1930), it often comes as a surprise that in many ways, life on the

Figure 3.1
"I Met This Girl By the River"

Figure 3.2
"Here Comes Uncle Jessie"

islands is the same as life on the mainland United States, particularly in Afro-American communities. From a musical standpoint,
one element that demonstrates the continuity in culture between
the Islands and the mainland is the songs—gospel, hymns (Starks
1980), disco, or children's game songs—sung in widely scattered
areas.

One song that is popular on the islands is "Little Sally Walker"
(figure 3.3).[4] It is widely known in Afro-American communities on
the mainland. I recorded the following verison on Johns Island.

Figure 3.3
"Little Sally Walker"

While melodically it is not particularly different from popularly known versions, it includes lines not commonly found in them. "Head hanging down with your feet stretching up" is one such unique line. "Put your hand on your kimble" is another. Here, the word, "kimble" is used to refer to the hip, rather than the more familiar word "hip."[5]

By the same token, one of the most distinctive aspects of Afro-American Sea Island culture is the Geechie or Gullah dialect I discussed earlier. Many islanders are interested in preserving the dialect alongside what is called "standard" English. One result is that "switching" or "code-switching" is common; that is, in a song, the text switches from traditional dialect to standard English or vice versa. Although segments of the dialect can be heard among all age levels, older islanders use it more frequently than youngsters. Differences in the employment of dialect in song are evident in the various renditions of "Old Lady Come from Booster." Two versions[6] of the song appear on two separate record albums, which were recorded on Johns Island. One recorded in the 1960s, features a mother and her adult daughter singing the song, the other recorded in the 1970s, features the "grands" (term used on the island to refer to grandchildren) and the children of the singers on the '60s album.

One traditional characteristic of the dialect that has been maintained is the use of singular and plural forms of both nouns and verbs interchangeably. In both the title and the first line of the song, the phrase, "Old lady come," illustrates the use of the plural form of the verb in conjunction with a singular noun.

Another characteristic of the dialect appears in the second line of the song: "He had two hen." In that line, the gender of the pronoun differs from its antecedent in the opening line. Additionally, the singular form of the noun, "hen" is used with the plural adjective, "two." Similar passages occur in other lines of the song.

Below is an excerpt; variations of the youngster's rendition are in parentheses.

"OLD LADY COME FROM BOOSTER"

Old lady come from Booster
He had two hen and a rooster
The rooster died, the old lady cried
He (She) couldn't get (her) egg like he used ta. . . .[7]

"Keeping the beat," as it is called, is as important to youngsters as it is to their elders. The beat is maintained in a number of ways— for example, by playing sticks on a box, by playing spoons on a pan or by using whatever is handy to produce a percussive sound. The most frequent method I encountered in my field work—one that has deep roots in the Afro-American tradition—was hand-clapping.

The following song (figure 3.4), which I recorded on Yonges Island,[8] contains some intricate turns of the hands, which make its performance interesting from a visual as well as a rhythmic stand-point. Entitled, "Batman and Robin," it is named for two fictional comic-book characters, who are well known by youngsters.

I also recorded "Tick, Tock" (figure 3.5) on Yonges Island.[9] Per-formed by a group of young girls who stood in a circle as they sang, "Tick, Tock" brings to the fore two additional traditional musical characteristics: the use of call and response and multimeter. Each girl is called by name (in this example, the girl's name is Sherry) and she answers with the appropriate response. The answers are predetermined, with the exception of the boyfriend's name, which is revealed during the third response (in this example, his name is Johnny Hall). The ease with which the youngsters handle metrical change is very much in evidence in this song.

For the time-honored lore to be maintained, it must be passed on from each generation to the next through the oral tradition. The play songs the youngsters sing for themselves and each other are vitally important to this transmission.

In Afro-American culture this involves more than preserving a song or body of songs per se, for traditional performance practice is crucial to the preservation of the Afro-American musical tradition. While the tradition is not static—in fact, change, itself, is traditional —new developments must be built upon a traditional base. Gospel groups, for example, have adapted melodic and harmonic practices of other twentieth-century Afro-American musics, but they main-tain improvisational techniques and polyrhythms—by clapping their hands and patting or stamping their feet—which give them a direct link to the older shouting spirituals (Starks 1980). Like the older shouting spirituals, gospel songs are quite capable of setting the proper atmosphere for the holy dance.

In Afro-American "jazz," musicians of contemporary styles, known as "be-bop," "hard-bop," and the "new music"[10] have found

Figure 3.4
"Batman and Robin"

Figure 3.5
"Tick, Tock"

it necessary to reassert the importance of improvisation, swinging, and the concept of the talking instrument, once they've seen the existence of these elements threatened in the work of some big bands, in "Progressive Jazz," "Cool Jazz," and "Third Stream" music.

Time has not left the singing and transmission of Sea Island children's songs unchanged either. Radio, television, trips to other places, and contact with children from other locales are among the factors that have brought new elements into the music. The integration of public schools created a means of exchange between Afro-American and Euro-American traditions that had not previously existed in the school environment. Both Black and white students come into contact with new songs and new ways of singing them. They learn new music, both from their teachers and from children their own age, as they sing in the classroom (particularly in younger grades) and during free time on school grounds.

It must be borne in mind that many of the new songs prove attractive to Afro-American youngsters because they have already been widely influenced by Black American music. Like Afro-American adults, the children change the Euro-American songs to suit their concept of melody, harmony, and rhythm.

Girls have been the primary keepers of the play-song tradition. Boys, for the most part, do not take part in the games or singing once they pass the primary grades; they know the songs, but would not be caught playing "girls' games." Football, baseball, boxing, and wrestling are among the pastimes that keep the young boys occupied. In addition, radio and television now claim the time both boys and girls once spent at play.

The songs Sea Island youngsters sing nevertheless continue to serve as a practical introduction to the Afro-American musical tradition and aesthetic. Compositional techniques, which go back to antebellum days; the continued use of "folkways" in song texts; the ability to fashion materials at hand into musical instruments; and intrinsic aspects of performance, such as improvisation, the creation of polyrhythm through the use of the hands and feet as percussive instruments, call and response, multimeter, and polymeter are all deeply rooted and children still preserve them. (Black children throughout the United States are also preserving these and other aspects of Afro-American musical tradition.)

Through traditional songs, children learn about themselves and their heritage and safeguard it as they move through an increasingly complex, fast-paced world. With these songs, they teach all of us, so "take some salt and pepper and put it in your shoe."

NOTES

1. Transcribed by author from field recordings undertaken on John's Island.
2. Transcribed by author.
3. Some other Seas Islanders refer to this song as "Uncle Jessie." A version of "Uncle Jessie" from the Georgia Seas Islands can be found in Bessie Jones (1972: 112-114).
4. Transcribed by author.
5. "Little Sally Walker" is popular among Black and White children; for Afro-American versions, see Jones (1972: 107-111).
6. Refer to *Been in the Storm So Long*, Folkways FS 3842 for the 1960s recording and *John's (sic) Island, South Carolina: Its People and Songs*, Folkways Records, FS 3840 for the 1970s recording.
7. For a musical transcription of "Old Lady Come from Booster," see Carawan (1967: 131). A recorded version of this song is available on the album *Step It Down*, Rounder Records, 8004 and sung by Bessie Jones.
8. Transcribed by author.
9. Transcribed by author.
10. This style has also been referred to as "avant-garde," "free jazz," and "new thing," among other labels.

REFERENCES

This list includes general references as well as works cited in this chapter.

Allen, William; Charles Ware; and Lucy McKim Garrison, eds. 1867. *Slave Songs of the United States*. New York: A. Simpson & Co.
Ballanta, Nicholas G. J. 1925. *Saint Helena Island Spirituals*. New York: G. Schirmer.
Bennett, John. 1908, 1909. "Gullah: A Negro Patois." *South Atlantic Quarterly*, October and January.
Carawan, G., and C. Carawan. 1967. *Ain't You Got a Right to the Tree of Life?* New York: Simon and Schuster.
Crum, Mason. 1940. *Gullah*. Durham, North Carolina: Duke University Press.

Garrison, Lucy McKim. 1862. "Songs of the Port Royal 'Contrabands.' "
    Dwights Journal of Music, November 8.

Georgia Writers' Project. 1940. *Drums and Shadows*. Athens, Ga.: Univer-
    sity of Georgia Press.

Gonzales, Ambrose E. 1964. *The Black Border*. Columbia, South Carolina:
    The State Company.

Herskovits, Melville J. 1941. *The Myth of the Negro Past*. Boston: Beacon
    Press.

Higginson, Thomas Wentworth. 1867. "Negro Spirituals." *Atlantic
    Monthly*, June.

_____ 1869. *Army Life in a Black Regiment*. Boston.

Jackson, George Pullen. 1943. *White and Negro Spirituals*. New York:
    J. J. Augustin.

Johnson, Guion G. 1930. *A Social History of the Sea Islands*. Chapel Hill,
    N.C.: University of North Carolina Press.

Johnson, Guy B. 1930. *Folk Culture on Saint Helena Island*. Chapel Hill,
    N.C.: University of North Carolina Press.

_____ 1980. "The Gullah Dialect Revisited: A Note on Linguistic Accul-
    turation." *Journal of Black Studies* 10.

Jones, Bessie, and Bess Lomax Hawes. 1972. *Step It Down*. New York:
    Harper & Row.

Joyner, Charles W. 1971. *Folk Song in South Carolina*. Tricentennial
    Booklet No. 9. Columbia, S.C.: The University of South Carolina
    Press.

Kemble, Frances (Fanny) Anne. 1863. *Journal of a Residence in a Georgia
    Plantation in 1838-1839*. New York: Harper and Brothers.

Krapp, George P. 1924. "The English of the American Negro." *American
    Mercury*, June.

McKim, James Miller. 1862. "Negro Songs." *Dwights Journal of Music*.
    Boston, August 9.

Parrish, Lydia. 1942. *Slave Songs of the Georgia Sea Islands*. New York:
    Creative Age.

Parsons, Elise Clews. 1923. *Folklore of the Sea Islands*. South Carolina,
    Cambridge, Mass., and New York: The American Folklore Society.

Plair, Sally. 1972. *Something to Sing About*. Mount Pleasant, S.C.:
    Molasses Lane Publishers.

Sass, Herbert Ravenel. 1956. *The Story of the South Carolina Low Coun-
    try*. West Columbia, S.C.: J. F. Hyer Publishing Co.

Smith, Reed. 1926. "Gullah." Bulletin of the University of South Carolina
    No. 190. Columbia, S.C., November 1.

Smythe, Augustine T. 1931. *The Carolina Low-Country*. New York: The
    Macmillan Company.

Spaulding, Henry George. 1863. "Under the Palmetto." *Continental Monthly*, August.

Starks, George L., Jr. *Black Music in the Sea Islands of South Carolina— Its Cultural Context: Continuity and Change.* Ph.D. diss., Wesleyan University, 1973.

———— 1980. "Singing 'Bout a Good Time: Sea Island Religious Music." *Journal of Black Studies* 10, 4.

Turner, Lorenzo D. 1949. *Africanisms in the Gullah Dialect.* Chicago: The University of Chicago Press.

Twining, Mary A., and Keith E. Baird. 1980a. "Preface: The Significance of Sea Island Culture." *Journal of Black Studies* 10, 4.

————.1980b. "Introduction to Sea Island Folklife." *Journal of Black Studies* 10, 4.

White, Newman H. 1928. *American Negro Folk-Songs.* Cambridge: Harvard University Press.

Woofter, T. J. 1930. *Black Yeomanry.* New York: Henry Holt and Company.

SELECTED DISCOGRAPHY

South Carolina Sea Islands

Been In the Storm So Long. Folkways Records FS3842.

John's [sic] *Island, South Carolina: Its People & Songs.* Folkways Records FS3840.

Moving Star Hall Singers and Alan Lomax. *Sea Island Folk Festival.* Folkways Records FS3841.

Georgia Sea Islands

American Folk Songs for Children. Atlantic SD-1350.

Georgia Sea Island Songs New World NW278. (Contains selections from Prestige International INT 25001 and INT 25002.)

Georgia Sea Islands, Volume 1. Prestige International INT 25001.

Georgia Sea Islands, Volume 2. Prestige International INT 25002.

Jones, Bessie. *So Glad I'm Here.* Rounder Records 2015.

Jones, Bessie. *Step It Down.* Rounder Records 8004.

The Black Presence in the Music of Washington, D.C.: 1843–1904

The Black community of Washington, D.C., has always placed great importance upon its music. Although today the musical profile of this community is vastly different from that of earlier times, the emphasis on music has remained constant. Of the various types of music that grew with the community, those which fit into the concert tradition received the most attention in written records. It is the growth of this tradition—from its beginnings in the early nineteenth century to its status at the turn of the twentieth century —that I will examine in this essay.

A discussion of musical activity in the Black community of Washington, D.C., before 1900 is dependent chiefly on information from the Black newspapers of the time. Local newspapers such as the Washington _Colored American_ (1893-1904), the _New Era_— later the _New National Era_ (1870-1875), and the _Washington Bee_ (1882-1922) are most important sources, as is _The New York Age_ (1883-1903), which carried a column about Washington, D.C., in most issues. To some extent, these papers are preserved on micro-film, but not all issues are available. Missing also are local Black newspapers for the decade of the 1860s. Local white newspapers, such as the _National Daily Republican_ (1860-1888), _The Washington Post_ (1877-present), and the _Evening Star_ (1853-1981), while usually condescending in tone, are occasionally helpful. As the nineteenth century drew to a close, however, they devoted less and less space to the affairs of the Black community.

In examining the status of music among the Blacks of Washington, D.C., I used three factors as indices of musical growth within the community: (1) the resources the community has available for producing music, (2) the status of musical instruction, and (3) the variety of musical programs within the community.

THE EARLY PERIOD

Musical Resources

The earliest influence and major resource of record in the development of musical traditions in the city of Washington was the church. In the early nineteenth century, Black worshippers, chafed by the segregation within the white churches, established their own houses of worship. As early as 1820, some Blacks withdrew from the white Ebenezer Methodist Church and eventually established ties with the African Methodist Episcopal (AME) Church, which had its beginning in Philadelphia in 1794. In 1839, the Nineteenth Street Baptist Church was opened as the first Black Baptist congregation in Washington. By 1862, there were eleven Black churches servicing a total Black population of 14,316 (11,131 free and 3,185 slave).[1] Of these eleven churches, seven were Methodist, three were Baptist, and one was Presbyterian.

It is likely that some of the music cultivated in the Black churches followed the style and form of the ethnic music of Afro-America. In fact, Daniel Alexander Payne, a bishop of the AME Church in the nineteenth century, spoke of his efforts to discourage the singing of " 'corn-field ditties' which could produce the wildest excitement among the masses" (Payne 1891: 457).

Payne was interested in formalizing the singing in the church and encouraged the establishment of choirs to accomplish this goal. The choir, he believed, had the potential to enhance the service.

A choir, with instruments as an accompaniment, can be made a powerful and efficient auxiliary to the pulpit. Two things are essential to the saving power and efficiency of choral music—a scientific training and an earnest Christianity. Two things are necessary to make choral singing always profitable to a Church—that the congregation shall always join singing

with the choir, and that they shall always sing with the spirit and the understanding. (Payne 1888: 237)

The first choir of record in the city of Washington was introduced at Union Bethel (Metropolitan) Church around 1843. The
Reverend Charles Sawyer, chorister at Union Bethel, as described
by one parishioner, had a fine tenor voice with a broad range. He
was apparently a gifted musician who trained his choir carefully
using only a tuning fork or a pitch pipe. He was respected for his
ability to detect the mildest discord in their singing. His fiery
singing and preaching, his effectiveness at revivals, and his lively
contribution at prayer meetings marked him as an outstanding
churchman. In time, he resigned his post to become an itinerant
minister, but not before he had become known as the most successful choir leader of his day.[2] (See Payne 1891: 457.)

The writings of Bishop Payne record another event that sheds
light on the early cultivation of music in Washington, D.C. Around
1849, Payne called on Dr. James Fleet of Washington, D.C., to
organize a fundraising concert to aid the Saratoga Street church in
Baltimore that needed money to pay for its new building. Dr. Fleet
played flute, guitar, and piano. He was assisted in the sacred
concert by his wife, Hermion Fleet, a pianist; Eliza Huston, soprano;
Fannie Fisher, alto; and James Wormley, "the best, if not the only
performer on the bass viol." The pastor of the Baltimore church
wrote some lyrics, which Fleet set to music. The audience was "de-
lighted, enraptured, and thanked the Lord that they were permitted
to see and hear instruments always devoted heretofore to secular
purposes now consecrated to God's service" (Payne 1891: 456,
457). Sacred concerts, then, were used to raise money from their
beginnings, as they continue to be used today.

Thus we learn from Bishop Payne's account that in the early
nineteenth century, there were already musicians in Washington,
D.C., who were sufficiently well known to be in demand. Andrew
F. Hilyer, prominent citizen and patron of the arts in nineteenth-
and twentieth-century Washington, adds to our knowledge of pre-
Civil War musicians by giving us the names of H. Yates, a bugle
man for a cavalry company known as the Potomac Dragoons,
James Moody, and Henry Jasper, although Hilyer (1901: 9) does
not identify an instrument for the latter.

Musical Instruction

As for musical instruction, we have very few facts. The Blacks of Washington, D.C., and Georgetown, however, were eager to have schools. Several were established for free Blacks between 1807 and 1862.[3] Many were short-lived, some because of a shortage of resources; more, because of harassment that came with the increased racial tensions of the 1830s and 1840s.

While instruction in the schools mainly covered reading, writing, arithmetic and, later, geographical studies, there was some musical instruction. Arabella Jones, who had studied music, opened St. Agnes Academy and introduced music into the curriculum. Mrs. Wood's St. Aloysius, a school for girls, had an assistant named Elizabeth Brown whose duties included teaching music. Dr. James Fleet founded a music school, but it was burned down in 1843.[4] These were meager beginnings, but they are important. The opportunities for musical instruction in the schools, the possibility of obtaining private instruction from practicing musicians, and the presence of church choirs offering limited opportunities for music instruction were probably influential in producing the musicians and music teachers of the post-Civil War period. Most significant in any case is the fact that while Blacks were beginning to strive toward literacy, simultaneously they made the effort to teach and learn music.

MID AND LATE NINETEENTH-CENTURY DEVELOPMENTS

Musical Resources: Church Choirs

With the freeing of all slaves in Washington by the Congressional Enactment of 1862, Blacks were able to expand more easily upon their musical beginnings and to add steadily to their musical variety. In the gradual unfolding of a concert tradition from 1860 to 1900, church choirs regularly sang hymns and short anthems from the accepted hymnals. We may speculate that these comprised the main musical repertoire that was brought to the public in the early sacred concerts. During the 1860s, three church choirs were especially noteworthy within the Black community of Washington, D.C., partly because of their musical activities and partly because of their ministers' eminence. The Fifteenth Street Presbyterian Church, known for its public spiritedness, was fortunate to have several ministers of national fame. Such a man was Henry Highland Garnet, who was pastor there from March 1864 to July 1865. He attracted much attention as an outstanding speaker and a man interested in racial issues. On the first anniversary of the adoption of the amendment to the U.S. Constitution that abolished slavery, the Reverend William R. Channing, chaplain of the House of Representatives, decided to commemorate the solemn occasion with a public religious service. Garnet was asked by President Lincoln to speak on February 12, 1865. The involvement of the choir was described in this fashion:

The choir of the Reverend gentleman's church, which, by the way, is one of the very best we have in the country, was also invited to serve on this occasion and crowned itself with honor. It was a strange sight, in the presence of the assembled wisdom, and, may I add, if not of the old prejudice, certainly of the feeling which succeeds it—it was a strange sight, I say, to see this little band of vocalists, stand up in places where but one year ago only white persons were allowed to stand, and then chant up hymns of praise to God for his goodness and his wonderful works to the children of men. (Smith 1865: 66)

After the Reverend Garnet read the first hymn, "All Hail the Power of Jesus' Name," "all eyes were turned toward the choir as in sweet and touching melody it warbled forth the beautiful sentiment, 'Arise my soul, shake off thy fears' " (Smith 1865: 66). The first two lines of this Isaac Watts hymn, "Arise my soul, shake off thy fears/And gird the gospel armor on," fit well with Garnet's famous message, "Emancipate, enfranchise, educate, and give the blessings of the gospel to every American citizen" (Schor 1977: 201).

The pastor and members of Israel Colored Methodist Episcopal (CME) Church also took pride in being leaders in civic affairs. During the 1860s, its Israel Lyceum invited congressmen and other knowledgeable figures to speak at regular meetings. Within such a context, the choir of Israel CME could not help occupying a position of eminence.

The choir at Union Bethel (later Metropolitan AME) was also prominent during this period. According to Bishop Payne, an organ was installed in the church in 1864, paid for partially with money earned from choir concerts (Payne 1891: 457). Having the first organ in a Black church no doubt contributed to the fame of the choir and its director, John Simms, at that time. But this church choir also overshadowed all others in musical offerings for at least four decades.

In 1880 the Reverend John W. Stevenson was appointed to Union Bethel for the purpose of building an entirely new and spacious structure for the church which had already been designated by the General Conference of 1872 as Metropolitan AME (Cromwell 1922: 73-75). The church members planned to finance this awesome task by selling property and holding benefit concerts that featured a troupe of musicians. The troupe, sometimes billed as the Washington Harmonic Company, consisted at one point of eight singers and pianist Blanche Washington. They performed in Maryland, Pennsylvania, and New York between 1883 and 1885 and once reported that their earnings reached forty dollars per performance. Of the women in the octet, soprano Amelia Tilghman emerged as a very active musician in Washington, D.C., during the 1870s and 1880s according to reports in the Washington *Bee* and the *New York Age*. She graduated in 1871 from Howard University's Normal School, having been enrolled also in the music department each semester. Afterward, Tilghman taught in the public schools and pursued her interest in music by singing in the Fifteenth Street Presbyterian Church Choir. One of her noteworthy appearances occurred in 1879 when she was featured as soloist assisting Madame Marie Selika. On more than one occasion during her career she was referred to as "Washington's favorite prima donna."[5] Around 1886 she moved to Montgomery, Alabama, where she published the *Musical Messenger*, a newspaper devoted to discussion of music and the welfare of musicians.[6]

Because of its activities, Union Bethel (Metropolitan) AME was often in the news from 1864 through 1883. On many occasions, the musical resources of other churches and organizations called upon Union Bethel (Metropolitan) AME to help raise money and to provide entertainment for special religious services.

The new Metropolitan AME church was dedicated in 1885; the first concert in the new auditorium employing its new organ was given in 1886. This "grand concert" brought in some new performers, along with several already familiar to Washington audiences. Professor Jardine of New York, builder of the organ, Professor Bischoff, the blind organist of the First Congregational Church (white) of Washington, D.C., and Mr. Jarvis Butler, concert organist, all played the new instrument. The church choir performed the "Hallelujah Chorus" from G. F. Handel's *Messiah*. Soloists included Agnes Smallwood and Lena Miller (St. Augustine), John T. Layton (Metropolitan AME chorister) and F. C. Miller (St. Luke's musical director). The new auditorium could seat 1,800 people, conservatively speaking; there was also a lower hall, which could seat 1,000 persons. Together, the large auditorium and the organ made the Metropolitan AME church the Black community's favorite concert hall well into the twentieth century.

The dominance of the Metropolitan AME Church Choir, however, was also a result of its chorister's talent. John T. Layton, chorister from 1875 (or 1876) to 1915, was so important to the musical life of the Black community that he merits a short digression here. Aside from conducting the church choir and performing extensively as a bass soloist, Layton trained and directed other singing ensembles. Many of these were small temporary groups formed to assist in a benefit for a specific cause. More permanent was the Orpheus Glee Club, a well-known male singing group which he trained and directed for about fifteen years. As conductor of the Union Bethel (Metropolitan) AME Choir, he had high standards. A former choir member remembers that he tested new members rigorously and insisted that members be able to read music (McCampbell, 1981). Teaching music played a central role in Layton's life, as he taught in the public schools and served for several years as assistant director of music in Black school divisions. He received training in music from several institutions (he received a doctorate from Wilberforce University in 1906, according to his obituary) and studied voice from a private tutor. Layton was also an arranger and composer, having contributed several items to the Methodist Hymnal of 1897.[7]

Indicative of Layton's popularity among his fellow musicians is the fact that two musical testimonials were held in his honor during his lifetime, each one a major musical event of the season. Participants in the testimonials included the most respected musicians in the city. In the first instance on May 16, 1887, Agnes Smallwood,

Martina Jackson Irving, Eunice Wormley, Lucy Moten, Helen
Handy, Jarvis Butler, J. W. Cole, R. W. Tompkins, William Goins,
F. C. Miller, A. J. Hall, J. Henry Lewis, F. W. Jones, and the
Orpheus Glee Club performed. A choir of 100 voices, mainly from
the Metropolitan AME Choir, was accompanied by Jarvis Butler
(organ) in Haydn's *The Heavens are Telling*. The second testimonial
in 1898 was conceived by the Washington *Colored American* newspaper and was announced in its pages in a letter signed by leading
ministers and fifty-one prominent citizens. Participants again
included local favorites, and the finale, this time on a grander scale,
was sung by a grand union choir comprised of senior and junior
choirs of Metropolitan AME and voices from thirty-five church
choirs of Washington, D.C., Georgetown, and Alexandria,
Virginia.[8]

The Union Bethel (Metropolitan) AME Church Choir's prominence is a product of yet one more factor: its association with the
Bethel Literary and Historical Association. Similar to the Israel
Lyceum, this was one of the most influential organizations in Black
intellectual circles of Washington, D.C. Its importance to this discussion lies not only in the prestige which its national reputation
brought to Union Bethel (Metropolitan) AME Church and to its
choir, but also in the emphasis which the Association placed upon
music.

Founded by Bishop Payne in 1881, the Bethel Literary and Historical Association met regularly at Union Bethel (Metropolitan)
AME Church. Within its first years the Association demonstrated recognition of the importance of music. In 1882, for example, the Bethel Literary (as it was commonly known) sponsored a
program of musical performances and discussions about outstanding Black musicians. The list of musicians discussed—"Blind Tom"
(Thomas Green Bethune), the Lucca family, the Hyer Sisters, the
[Fisk] Jubilee Singers, Nellie B. Mitchell, F. Craig, Henry W.
Williams, Samuel Jamieson, and James Bland—was indicative of
the interest which Bethel Literary took in educating its audiences
concerning achievements of Black American musicians. The first
major program of Bethel Literary was a Symposium and Literary
presentation designed to assist Union Bethel's fund raising effort
(1882). The main speaker was the Reverend Joseph C. Price of
North Carolina, but the major portion of the presentation was a
musical program by local musicians including the Union Bethel

(Metropolitan) AME Choir with John Layton conducting. Throughout its history, Bethel Literary continued to sponsor programs
which included music and continued to promote the finest local
musicians. In addition to major concerts and symposia on music
which it offered to the public during its twenty-five years of
existence, the Bethel Literary often concluded its meetings with a
musical selection or a dramatic reading.[9] John Layton, J. Henry
Lewis, and Will Marion Cook were a few of the local musicians
invited to perform. The Bethel Literary was one of the reasons that
Washington, D.C., was known as one of the most intellectual and
most informed Black centers (Cromwell 1898).

We have described in some detail the musical activities of the
three most influential churches—Fifteenth Street Presbyterian, Israel
Baptist, and Union Bethel (Metropolitan) AME—during the 1860s.
We may assume that other churches also developed choirs at this
time or shortly thereafter and that as new churches were built, new
choirs joined the community resources. During the 1870s, in addition to the three mentioned above, the choirs of St. Augustine
(Catholic), Asbury Methodist Episcopal, Israel Bethel (Colored
Methodist Episcopal), Nineteenth Street Baptist, Shiloh Baptist,
and St. Luke (Episcopal) are frequently cited in the newspapers. Of
concerts by *individual* church choirs, however, we read little until
the 1880s. In the 1870s, we read instead of combined choir ventures. In these a temporary choir was formed from members of
several established church choirs. Occasionally the combined
choirs appeared under a name such as "The Washington Church
Choir" or "The Washington Glee Club."[10] It would seem that
church choirs shared a strong sense of unity which enabled them to
support one another and to join together to perform music that
required superior vocal forces.

From the 1880s onward, the individual church choir concert
became commonplace. The ambitious programs repeatedly featured excerpts from Handel's *Messiah*, Mendelssohn's *Song of
Praise* and *Elijah*, John Stainer's *Crucifixion*, Theodore Dubois' *The
Seven Last Words of Christ on the Cross*, and Rossini's *Stabat
Mater*. Thus, well before the turn of the twentieth century, Washington, D.C., had excellent choirs which tackled the choral master-
pieces, and the city's audiences were appreciative of the skillful
choral singing which they heard.

In addition to the church choirs, a community chorus known

sometimes as the Amateur Glee Club, and other times as the Original Amateur Glee Club, flourished from the early 1880s to the early 1890s. A writer for the *Washington Bee* felt that the Original Amateur Glee Club was the oldest and the most popular musical organization south of Boston.[11]

Musical Instruction

We must not neglect the influence of musical instruction on the status of musical activity in the Black community in the years following the Civil War. A law was passed by Congress in 1862 requiring public school education for Blacks in the city. The law provided for an allocation of ten percent of taxes from property owned by Blacks for support of their schools. This arrangement was found to be ineffective, and, until 1866, when a provision was made allowing trustees of the Black schools to sue for the 10 percent appropriation, public schools had to be supported by private means.

The Black community, zealous for its schools, sought ways to pay for their operation until government funds were available. An artist of national stature did come to the aid of the Black schools. Elizabeth Taylor Greenfield, was visiting Washington, D.C., in 1864 when she heard that support was needed and she offered her services for a benefit concert.[12]

Obstacles to funding were removed by the summer of 1866 (Lewis 1976: 60) and the number of pupils and teachers in public school grew rapidly. The first public school music teacher for Blacks, Letitia Arnold, was appointed in 1869, and vocal music soon became an important part of the elementary school course. This course which *stressed* music reading for every child was greatly enhanced in later years by the work of three teachers, John Esputa, John T. Layton, and Henry Grant. All three were fine musicians and intensely interested in music education. What must have been the first public performance of elementary school pupils took place in September 1872 at the dedication of the Charles Sumner School. Mary Wormley, elementary school teacher, led her charges in the singing of three hymns. In the years following there were many programs of vocal music. At first only elementary school pupils were included, but in 1876-1877 Black pupils from all grades were invited to participate in a choral presentation. From this time on high school students participated on the annual school programs even though vocal music was not introduced officially in the high schools until 1888 and was not made compulsory until 1891. By the turn of the century the high school had both glee club and choir as well as an orchestra.[13]

Minor Normal School, one of the first institutions of higher learning for Blacks in Washington, D.C., included vocal music in each of its four terms beginning in the school year 1874-1875. Howard University, opened in 1867, had a music department by 1870. These institutions of higher learning were the two main sources of music instruction for teachers in the District of Columbia until the Washington Conservatory of Music and School of Expression opened in 1903.

Private instruction was now more abundant. In the late 1890s, The Washington *Colored American* carried advertisements for private music lessons, especially in voice and piano. It was not unusual for one teacher to offer instruction on more than one instrument. For example, William Braxton, organist of the Metropolitan AME Church, advertised lessons in piano, violin, and organ. By 1900 advertisements appeared for Black technicians who gave piano lessons and tuned pianos. Local stores ran advertisements announcing pianos for rental and sale, suggesting that owning a piano was not unusual, if not commonplace, among Blacks.[14] As the nineteenth century came to an end, there was a strong music program within the public school system; there were also other avenues of music instruction that provided the groundwork for the development of a core of well-trained choir singers and a supply of knowledgeable listeners within the Black community.

Musical Programs and Organizations

After the Civil War, the scope of musical performances was widened to include entertainment other than the sacred music which had been dominant in the early part of the century. One such innovation was opera. One of the earliest large-scale productions in Washington's Black community was by the Colored American Opera Company. John Esputa, teacher for more than four years in the public schools, formed the all-Black company in 1872 and presented the *Doctor of Alcantra* by Julius Eichberg in 1873. Esputa, a fine cornetist and teacher of cornet, violin, and viola, appears to have been of Spanish origin (Beirly 1973: 28). He established a conservatory of music in which John Philip Sousa who later became conductor of the U.S. Marine Band and America's "march king" was enrolled (Beirly 1973: 30). Esputa was associated with the Black community as a teacher in the Black division of the public schools from 1874 to 1879 (Elward 1975: 87, 90) and as choir director at Blessed Martin's Chapel (after 1874, St. Augustine). The speculation that the opera company grew from the church choir receives support from the fact that a high proportion of the leading singers and the chorus were members of the church. Further corroboration comes from a historical sketch of St. Augustine Church in the *Washington Post*: "The choir attained its high standing in musical circles under Prof. Esputa . . . in the time of the late Father Barotti. . . . Under Professor Esputa the organization made a tour of a number of cities in opera, and everywhere they went they were received with enthusiasm."[15] The review of the *Doctor of Alcantra* (February 6, 1873) in the *New National Era* states that "Lincoln Hall was packed, and that the company, composed mainly of members of the St. Martin's Colored Catholic Church, was in good form." All reviews described the performance in favorable terms.

The major characters were played by persons who continued to be active musical performers for several decades in Washington, D.C. The most familiar were Agnes Smallwood, soprano, and Henry F. Grant, tenor. Agnes Smallwood later joined the Bergen Star Company and occasionally received top billing in her New York appearances. The roster of the *Doctor of Alcantra* performances provides us with a record of other teachers, singers, and conductors of Washington.[16]

American audiences became very fond of operas by Gilbert and Sullivan during the 1870s and even more in the 1880s. In keeping with this, the Black community of Washington, D.C., took to its heart *H.M.S. Pinafore*, presenting it twice in the same year. A large scale production was mounted at the National Theatre in 1879. Agnes Smallwood was the leading female singer again and her associates—Mary Coakley, William Benjamin, and Richard Tomkins—were all of the *Doctor of Alcantra* cast. Because of this some writers confused the production with the work of the Colored American

Opera Company. A newspaper article[17] attributes to the Colored American Opera Company an extensive repertoire and mentions specifically *H.M.S. Pinafore, Penelope, Haman,* and the *Tragedy of Pizzara,* but there does not seem to be any record of its performing these works. The death of Esputa, circa 1882, probably marked the end of the Company. The *Peoples Advocate* of May 10, 1879, carried the explanation that the *H.M.S. Pinafore* production was sponsored by a Mr. Ford, *formerly* of the Colored American Opera Company. The chorus of sixty voices, largely from St. Augustine Church, won praise. A smaller production of the operetta was performed at Lincoln Hall by the Washington Church Choir as a benefit for St. Luke's Church. There followed in 1899 a production of Gilbert and Sullivan's *Box and Cox.* More than once, an original operetta (usually billed as an opera) was staged. One instance was the production of *Noble Revenge* by Anna M. Savoy of Washington, D.C., with Florence Smallwood as soloist and Will Marion Cook as director.[18] The most ambitious project in the series of operatic ventures was, however, the production of Von Flotow's *Martha* at the Grand Armory Hall in 1890. William T. Benjamin, bass of the Colored American Opera, sang in this production also.[19] Reviews, which emphasized the novelty of grand opera by a Black cast, generally commended the performance.

In the last quarter of the nineteenth century, other types of vocal ensemble commanded the attention of the Black concert-goer. For example, some singers joined in duets and quartets as often as they sang solos. There were also many octets, which were made up of the finest singers that could be gathered together for a particular performance. There were, however, a few stable singing groups. Often such groups were drawn from the church choir, but frequently they sang secular music and fulfilled a more social function than the church choir. The Amphion Glee Club, established in 1891, consisted of sixteen to eighteen men who gave concerts as well as hosted summer excursions down the Potomac River to Notley Hall on the River Queen Steamship. They regularly practiced the American custom of combining a banquet with a small concert. Members of this ensemble, especially John T. Layton, were frequently heard as soloists on other programs. Under their leader, J. Henry Lewis, the group offered assistance to many musical programs in churches and elsewhere. Their activities varied from acting as hosts to the celebrated vaudeville stars Bert Williams and William Walker to singing a concert as featured guests of the prestigious Bethel Literary and Historical Association.

The Orpheus Glee Club organized in 1883 may be considered the rival male organization of the Amphions. The first conductor was Dr. E. S. Kimball, a voice teacher of established reputation who was cited by John T. Layton as one of the most important musical influences in his life.[20] Kimball was succeeded by J. B. Tipton in 1885 and John T. Layton was the conductor from around 1887 to the apparent disintegration of the organization around the turn of the century. The Orpheus Glee Club appeared most often with other artists, bringing several known and unknown artists to the Washington scene. It had the opportunity to appear with Madame Marie Selika in 1886.[21] The Club's activities, also partly social, included special dinners and much publicized visits to the socially prominent at Christmas. The repertoire, consisting mainly of the popular salon classics of the day with the addition of the occasional operatic chorus, was much the same for the Orpheus and Amphion Glee Clubs.

In the late nineteenth century, a resident of Washington, D.C., could enjoy a wide sampling of the current Black artists of national reputation for many came to perform in this city. Actually, the practice of presenting visiting artists started much earlier since by the mid-nineteenth century, Washington had church auditoriums large enough to accommodate large audiences. The earliest record of a visiting artist comes from 1855 when Elizabeth Taylor Greenfield sang a concert at Fifteenth Street Presbyterian Church. Greenfield (the "Black Swan") had just returned in July 1854 from a highly successful concert tour in England, concluding with a command performance for Queen Victoria at Buckingham Palace. Her program in Washington was typical for the prima donna of this era. It included a few operatic arias and ballads sung by the artist herself and several selections sung by assisting artists, drawn from local talent. As was the case for most of the prima donnas, her enthusiastic audience was racially mixed.[22]

Thomas Green Bethune ("Blind Tom") appeared at the Nineteenth Street Baptist Church on January 4, 1884. He had appeared in Washington in 1860, but it is doubtful that any members of the Black community were in attendance then since he performed at

Marini's Assembly Room, which was normally exclusively reserved for white patrons.[23]

Washington audiences enjoyed the singing of college choirs as early as the 1870s. Their appetite for collegiate singers was whetted by choirs which provided music for the first and second commencements of the Howard University College Department in 1871 and 1872. A columnist of the *New National Era* was especially impressed with the quality of the 1872 ensemble which he described as a "fine choir of students."[24] Thereafter the Howard University commencements became a strong attraction in the community, partly because of its great interest in education, and partly because of the unusual speakers and the trained musical artists who could be heard.

The Fisk Jubilee Singers made several visits to the city and were received enthusiastically each time. Their earlier concerts (1872 and 1873) drew audiences so large that even the largest hall available was inadequate. The singers returned in 1881, after a six-year world tour, and were again welcomed by an overflow audience. One of their members, Mattie Lawrence, was a native Washingtonian; her singing of "When 'Tis Moonlight" elicited an ovation, and she was presented with a watch, a watch chain, and an album as a testimonial of her Washington friends' affection.[25]

The choir of the Hampton Normal and Agricultural Institute visited Washington in February of 1873.[26] President Ulysses S. Grant received them in the East Room of the White House where they sang a program of spirituals. The nineteen students, assisted in their Lincoln Hall appearances by a corps of Howard University students, sang to large and well-disposed audiences.[27]

A great favorite with Washington audiences of the 1880s was Madame Marie Selika. She was, of course, one of the most renowned singers in the second half of the nineteenth century, having made her reputation in Europe. She sang many concerts in Washington, with the Orpheus Glee Club in 1886, with several local singers in 1879 and 1881, with her own assisting artists in 1878, and with the Washington, D.C., Selika Quartette and others in 1885. Unfortunately, the Selika Quartette did not measure up to the star to which it had attached itself; reviews were not favorable.[28] In general, however, her appearances were successful.

Flora Batson Bergen, known as the "Queen of Song" or the "Queen of Ballad Singers," was born in Washington, D.C., and had as manager one of the most successful agencies handling Black artists—the Bergen Star Company. These facts may have helped to account for the great excitement that she created in this city. Bergen's audiences were always huge. For example, hundreds were turned away from her concert in 1887, which was termed "more than a success."[29] In March 1896 she sang to the largest audience ever to fill the Metropolitan AME Church.[30] Her supporters were defensively enthusiastic about her, and when Sissieretta Jones was crowned "Queen of Song" on December 24, 1895, at Metropolitan AME Church, a music critic complained that the title belonged only to Flora Batson Bergen, to whom it had been granted by the press and by the Queen of England.[31]

An artist's realization that a White House appearance could materialize from a visit to the Nation's Capitol must have added greatly to the appeal of a performance in the District of Columbia. This honor was accorded to Black artists with surprising frequency. The prima donna, Sissieretta Jones ("Black Patti"), was among those so honored. So great was the interest in this star that many had to be turned away from her concert in the Metropolitan AME Church in February 1892. Two days later, she sang for President Benjamin Harrison and his family at the White House. For the president, she sang "Cavatina" by Meyerbeer, "Swanee River" by Stephen C. Foster, "Waltz" by Pattison, and "Home, Sweet Home" by Sir Henry Bishop. The next season she appeared in Washington in a variety concert with Louise (Lulu) Hamer, contralto; Harry T. Burleigh, basso cantante; Sidney Woodward, tenor; Joseph H. Douglass and Walter Craig, violin; J. C. Alston, cornet; and Bessie Butler, child vocalist. After she abandoned her attempts at an operatic career, Sissieretta Jones began touring with Black Patti's Troubadours, a company of fifty vaudeville performers (Southern 1971: 304). The show came to Washington several times after 1896. Its wide variety of entertainment moved from comedy sketches to cakewalk contests. As the finale and the climax, Jones sang, with the entire troupe—all in elaborate costumes—forty minutes of excerpts from operas and operettas popular at that time. Audiences received these shows just as enthusiastically as they had the earlier concert performances of the prima donna.[32]

The discussion here has centered around *vocal* guest artists. To be sure, Washington audiences were fond of their choruses and prima donnas. But a main reason for the paucity of *instrumental* guest artists was simply that they were fewer in number at the time. One might have expected a sell-out attendance at the concert of Albert F. Mando's New York orchestra, but a newspaper report relates that the audience was very small and was displeased with the four-hour concert and with the fact that four-fifths of the orchestra players were white.[33] Other instrumentalists to appear in Washington were the Boston Brass Band (with thirty artists), W. F. Craig, violinist from Brooklyn, New York, and Professor Jackson of Boston, a guitarist.

Advertisements and other items in the local newspapers reveal that bands and orchestras grew steadily in number and in quality in the last two decades of the nineteenth century. Both orchestras and bands are of interest in an examination of the concert tradition because both types of ensembles were used in the concert setting. Earlier in the century the Marine Band was often used by the Black community on occasions such as the Howard University commencements.[34] The earliest Black bands were marching bands, often used in parades. The main Black parade of the nineteenth century in Washington, D.C., was the Emancipation Day Parade. Celebrated at first by the entire city, Emancipation Day—April 16—soon became an all-Black experience. There were floats and costumes, but the bands received the greatest emphasis. The Washington Cadet Band, Capitol City Band, and Wilson Drum Corps marched along with the bands representing the Elks, Odd Fellows, Masons, and many other organizations. There was also an Emancipation Day concert, which featured vocal as well as instrumental music. As the parades became more expensive, that form of celebration gave way to the concert and/or banquet with speakers.

Orchestras came into being in Washington, D.C., in the 1880s. The Warren Orchestra, conducted by Joseph S. Simms, is the first to be mentioned. It received an honorary testimonial in 1886, launching its beginning. Frederick Douglass was an honorary member. In 1890, the Cook Orchestra advertised for engagements. Its members included Joseph H. Douglass, Will M. Cook, John Cole, Charles Sewell, William Smith, and Robert Brown on the violin; Alexander Lee on the violoncello; Joseph Lee, Stanton Wormley, and James Adkinson on the cornet; George Dickey and W. Ferguson on the French horn; C. Hamilton and G. Grayson on the clarinet; T. Johnson on the flute; Elzie Hoffman on the saxophone; J. Simms on the tambourine; and Charles Lee on the bass violin. The announcement of its 1890 concert indicated that Frederick Douglass would introduce the group and that there would then be a concert, after which the floor would be cleared for dancing. A special feature was to be a saxophone solo, played for the first time in Washington, D.C., with an orchestra that included Afro-American musicians.[35] Around the same time the Washington Monumental Orchestra and the Douglass Orchestra were also available for concerts and other functions.

Just as the nineteenth century was ending, yet another important instrumental ensemble came into being. This was Elzie Hoffman's Standard Orchestra.[36] Hoffman, returning from the study of music in New York, started not only an orchestra but also a new music school and a community chorus known as the Washington Permanent Chorus. Hoffman taught the group the principles of sight-singing each week. They prepared a choral program, which incorporated Hoffman's thirty-piece orchestra. The community chorus was a concept that would be taken up many times in the next century.

THE EARLY TWENTIETH CENTURY

The community's musical resources were extensive by the early 1900s. They included several orchestras and bands, singing organizations of various types, and clubs and societies that supported musical activities. Teachers were available for instruction on any one of the popular musical instruments. The public school system offered music courses and cultivated instrumental and vocal ensembles. Music was taught in several private schools and in institutions of higher learning within the city.

The more than eighty churches in 1901 were prime musical resources for the community. First of all, each had at least one choir. In fact, by this time the Black community of Washington, D.C., was known for its excellent choirs. Second, the churches were the major sponsors of concerts and recitals and often doubled as concert halls for musical events. In surveying the Black community of Washington in 1900, Andrew F. Hilyer, prominent citizen and patron of the arts, identified the most famous church choirs as those of the Asbury Methodist, Fifteenth Street Presbyterian, St. Augustine (Catholic), Vermont Avenue Baptist, Nineteenth Street Baptist, and Metropolitan African Methodist Episcopal (AME) churches. Hilyer also identified some musical clubs which he considered most influential, naming the Amphion Glee Club, the newly organized Dvorak Musical Association, and the Treble Clef Club, an association of married women who wished to cultivate the "better class" of music (Hilyer 1901: 141-147, 153-154).

Another indication of the flourishing state of the concert tradition in Washington, D.C., during the early twentieth century is the variety and quantity of musical events offered by local and visiting artists within a nine-month season. The performances of the Samuel Coleridge-Taylor Choral Society, which stimulated tremendous interest not only in this city but also in other communities of the United States, made the years 1903 and 1904 especially significant for Black concert-goers. The Choral Society presented its first performance of Samuel Coleridge-Taylor's *Hiawatha* on April 23, 1903, at the Metropolitan AME Church. The 160-voice choir was conducted by John T. Layton and the solo roles were sung by guest artists: Kathryn Skeene-Mitchell, soprano, of Cleveland; Sidney Woodward, tenor, formerly of Washington, D.C.; and Harry T. Burleigh, baritone, of New York. The accompaniment was supplied by local musicians Gabrielle Pelham and Mary Europe at two pianos and William Braxton at the organ.

Mrs. Andrew Hilyer, a Washington resident, had met the African-English composer during her travels in England. She had returned to the city with the idea of forming a choral society and with the hope that the composer would one day conduct the society in the performance of his compositions. In 1904, after extensive correspondence with the Hilyer family, Coleridge-Taylor arrived in Washington, D.C., and conducted "The Hiawatha Trilogy" as part of a Coleridge-Taylor Festival, Harry T. Burleigh sang the baritone role, this time with Estelle Pinckney Clough, well-known operatic soprano of Massachusetts, and J. Arthur Freeman, an outstanding tenor of St. Louis, as the other soloists. The Marine Band furnished the accompaniment. Several other concerts were given in Washington and in Baltimore at which Coleridge-Taylor was honored with gifts and other presentations. Perhaps the most impressive aspect of Coleridge-Taylor's Washington visit came with recognition at the

White House by President Theodore Roosevelt a few days after the first concert (Tortolano 1977: 72, 89, 117).

Most of the reviews extensively praised the singing, the chorus's trainer, John T. Layton, and composer-conductor Coleridge-Taylor. The one note of dissatisfaction related to the Marine Band which was found to be inadequate. From time to time, the local press gave recognition to the significance of these concerts. The *Negro Music Journal* called the 1903 concert "one of the most notable events in the musical history of the colored race."[37] Similarly an article in the *Evening Star* described the same performance as "splendid" and designated it as "an event of interest in the musical history of this city."[38] A. Kaufmann remarked that the 1903 concert was "in no sense a pretentious imitation of the established Choral Society but was the expression of musical culture actually attained by a very large part of the colored people of this city."[39] Maud Cuney-Hare, a patron of the arts, understanding well the significance of these concerts, observed that "the Samuel Coleridge-Taylor Society of Washington, D.C., . . . has been one of the most potent aids in the advancement of musical culture in the capital of the nation" (Cuney-Hare 1936: 161, 244).

As already indicated, the Black community had come to expect much from its musicians, even before the first performance by the Samuel Coleridge-Taylor Choral Society in April 1903. The music critic of the *Washington Bee*, writing in January of the same year, expressed his high standards.

With just about one third of the concert season gone, the local Afro-American musicians have done nothing from a musical standpoint to be proud of. With all of what is claimed to be an abundance of talent here, not one first class concert has been given. Note the difference amongst the whites, viz.; the Choral Society has had one big concert and are now about to render the *Messiah*.[40]

This critic was probably satisfied when the Samuel Coleridge-Taylor Choral Society concerts were given later in the season, but in his search for concerts on a grand scale, the critic had overlooked substantial productions of music in the Black community.

There were, for example, numerous concerts of sacred music given by church choirs. It had been the custom for some time for the choir or choirs in Black churches to give several sacred concerts during the year. All of these were major events, but the ones at Christmas and Easter and the closing concert of the season assumed greater significance. One choir concert that received more notice than others, was John Stainer's "Crucifixion" by the Lincoln Temple Choir, with Clarence C. White assisting on the violin and Mary Europe on the piano. There was also a series of recitals at the Israel Colored Methodist Episcopal (CME) Church, which included nationally known artists Harry T. Burleigh, baritone; Estelle Pinckney Clough, soprano; and Melville Charleton, organist. Mme. Azalia Hackney, soprano, appeared at Lincoln Memorial Church in a program of Grieg, Schubert, Mascagni, Rossini, and Dvorak. As was traditional, pupils of both private teachers and public schools presented musical programs.[41]

The year 1903 was also significant because a new music school was opened in the Black community. The Washington Conservatory of Music and School of Expression was founded by Harriet Gibbs, a graduate of Oberlin College and a concert pianist.[42] The new school was unique as it was one of the first private schools to be founded by Blacks for the purpose of providing Black students with college-level education in music. It was conceived as one part of a National Negro Music Center, which would collect and preserve the music of the Black heritage and promote more performances by Black artists in the city. Clarence C. White and Azalia Hackley, both of whom gave recitals in 1903-1904, became faculty members of the Conservatory.

Another dominant personality came to Washington, D.C., in the person of Lulu Vere Childers. She was introduced first in 1902 as a guest soloist in concert with Harriet Gibbs. Three years later, she was appointed to the Department of Music at Howard University. Childers was also a graduate of Oberlin College and was often praised for her beautiful contralto voice. Under her leadership, the Howard University Department of Music (later School of Music) reached full development, offering its first bachelor's degree in 1915. Both the Conservatory and Howard's School of Music contributed significantly to the later growth of the musical life of Washington, D.C., by providing musical training and sponsoring concerts.

The Coleridge-Taylor concerts of 1903 and 1904 constitute a

benchmark in our study of the Washington, D.C., concert tradition, for they were both the culmination of a long period of musical development and the harbinger of an era of expanded musical activities. A choral tradition, which had been nurtured for decades, had culminated in a series of programs that attracted nationwide attention. Of great significance to the Black community was the fact that not only had major choral works been performed but also a Black composer and conductor of international fame had been celebrated. New organizations were being formed to cultivate further the choral tradition, and the Black community was primed to enjoy performances of the choral works of large proportions. In the following years, owing partly to the stimulation offered by the Samuel Coleridge-Taylor Choral Society and similar organizations, the Washington Conservatory of Music, and Howard University, the Black community dramatically increased its musical activities. Visiting artists, whose number grew as the century wore on, were heard more and more frequently and concerts were more numerous. In addition to an expanded concert season, Washington audiences had the benefit of a wider variety of music after the turn of the century, for developments in blues and jazz were reflected more and more in the musical offerings of the city. Nightclubs and theaters gradually became extremely important musical resources and the musical horizons of the community were broadened.

The years preceding the turn of the twentieth century were full of musical activity. At first, choirs, singing groups, and soloists carried the main weight within the Black community. Then, orchestras and bands surfaced and became more numerous by the 1890s. Local artists served their community, but the community also heard some of the most prominent Black artists from around the country. The words of the *New York Age* in January 30, 1866, were indeed true:

Washington is fast becoming a great literary and artistic center. It is no longer the provincial city of a dozen years ago, but it is now in fact as in name the capitol of a Nation, and all that is best in the Nation, sooner or later, comes here—the great preachers, lecturers, actors, capitalists, men of letters and affairs.

These words applied to Washington's musical offerings as much as to any other area.

NOTES

1. The Census of 1860 gives these population figures. For a discussion of the founding of these churches see Cromwell (1922: 64-106).

2. Simms Family Papers, Collection Box 89-1 and Box 89-2, Moorland-Spingarn Research Center, Howard University.

3. See Williams (1971-72: 369).

4. The most comprehensive study of schools for Blacks in Washington, D.C., is *History of Schools for the Colored Population, New York, 1969*, reprint of *Special Report of Commission of Education on the Improvement of Public Schools in the District of Columbia, 1871*. See also Document 315 Forty-First Congress of the United States of America, Second Session, Washington, D.C., 1869.

5. The *Washington Bee*, for July 14, 1883, lists as members of the troupe Misses Tilghman, Washington, Slade, Jurix, and Wallace; Messrs. Layton, Butler, Lane, and Walker. See also the *New York Age*, June 30, 1883, and August 18, 1883. For references to Amelia Tilghman see for example, the *Washington Bee*, November 3, 1879, February 10, 1883, and May 17, 1884.

6. For further discussion see Penn (1891: 401-404).

7. See *African Methodist Episcopal Church Hymn and Tune Book Adapted to the Doctrines and Usages of the Church*, Philadelphia: African Methodist Episcopal Concern, 1947 reprint 1897, p. xvii.

8. See *Washington Bee*, May 16, 1887; Washington *Colored American*, November 5, 1898. Information on Layton can be found in his obituary in the *Washington Star*, February 15, 1916; see also *Washington Post*, April 10, 1904.

9. See *Washington Bee*, February 24, 1883 and January 9, 1886.

10. See *Peoples Advocate*, November 15, 1879.

11. See *Washington Bee*, May 10, 1884, December 1885, and February 28, 1891.

12. See *National Daily Republican*, January 22, 1864.

13. The facts concerning music in the Black schools of the District of Columbia are taken from Elward 1975.

14. See Washington *Colored American*, June 11, 1898.

15. See *Washington Post*, May 20, 1905.

16. See *New National Era*, February 6, 1873.

17. See *Washington Bee*, February 8, 1890.

18. See *Washington Bee*, April 12, 1890.

19. See *Washington Bee*, February 8, 1890, and April 14, 1890.

20. See *Washington Post*, April 10, 1904.

21. See *Washington Bee*, October 4, 1886. The Orpheus Glee Club made its debut on a program with another prima donna, Nellie Brown Mitchell

"Queen of Song": *Washington Bee*, November 29, 1883. Nellie Brown
Mitchell had made her debut in Washington, D.C., in 1874, receiving a
complimentary review in *The National Republican*. See Trotter (1881:
202).

22. See *Daily National Intelligencer*, February 5, 1855.

23. Ibid., December 11, 1860.

24. See *New National Era*, June 13, 1873.

25. See *New National Era*, February 1881, March 7, 1872, and February
16, 1873. Later appearances are given in *Peoples Advocate*, February 5,
1886.

26. See *Evening Star*, February 15, 1873.

27. See *The Capitol*, February 16, 1873; see also *Evening Star*, February
15, 1873.

28. See *Washington Bee*, September 26, 1885, which states that the
church was not acoustically good, that Selika sang well, but her voice
lacked sweetness and expressiveness, and that the quartette sang poorly.

29. See *Washington Bee*, April 16, 1887.

30. See *Washington Bee*, March 7, 1896.

31. See *Washington Bee*, December 28, 1895.

32. See *Washington Bee*, February 22, 1892, and February 28, 1892. See
also Washington *Colored American*, December 5, 1896.

33. In the *Washington Bee*, September 15, 1888, this event was
advertised as the "Grandest event of the Ages." It was discussed as a finan-
cial failure in the October 6, 1888, issue of the paper.

34. For other occasions see *Washington Bee*, May 13, 1893, and March
31, 1888.

35. See *Washington Bee*, September 29, 1890, and October 25, 1890.

36. Washington *Colored American*, May 28, 1898, and June 25, 1898,
Hoffman advertised regularly in this newspaper.

37. See *Negro Music Journal*, May 1903, pp. 185-187.

38. See *Evening Star*, April 24, 1903, p. 13.

39. See *Washington Post*, April 10, 1904.

40. See *Washington Bee*, January 10, 1903. The critic continues by listing
other concerts planned in the white community.

41. For newspaper accounts of musical events for the years 1903-1904,
see Washington *Colored American* for these years.

42. For an extensive discussion of the school and its contribution, see
McGinty (1979: 58-69).

REFERENCES

Beirly, Paul E. 1973. *John Philip Sousa: American Phenomenon*. Englewood Cliffs, New Jersey: Prentice-Hall, Inc.

Cromwell, John W. 1898. *History of the Bethel Literary and Historical Society*. Washington, D.C.

_____. 1922. *Journal of Negro History*. January

Cuney-Hare, Maud. 1936. *Negro Musicians and Their Music*. Washington, D.C.: The Associated Publishers, Inc.

Elward, Thomas J. 1975. "A History of Music Education in the District of Columbia." Ph.D. dissertation, Catholic University of America.

Hilyer, Andrew. 1901. *The Twentieth Century Union League Directory*. Washington, D.C.

Lewis, David L. 1976. *The District of Columbia: A Bicentennial History*. New York: W. W. Norton.

McCampbell, Corinne. 1981. Interview, February 6.

McGinty, Doris Evans. 1979. "The Washington Conservatory of Music and School of Expression." *The Black Perspective in Music*, Spring, Vol. 7, No. 1.

Payne, Daniel A. 1888, rpt. 1968. *Recollections of Seventy Years*. Nashville, Tenn.; rpt. New York: Arno Press.

_____. 1891. *History of the A.M.E. Church*. New York: Arno Press.

Penn, Irvine Garland. 1891. *The Afro-American Press and Its Editors*. Springfield, Mass.: Wiley Co.

Schor, Joel. 1977. *Henry Highland Garnet*. Westport, Conn.: Greenwood Press.

Smith, James M. 1865. "A Memorial Discourse; by Rev. Henry Highland Garnet." Delivered in the hall of the House of Representatives, Washington, D.C., on Sabbath, February 12. Philadelphia.

Southern, Eileen. 1971. *Music of Black Americans*. New York: W. W. Norton.

Tortolano, William. 1977. *Samuel Coleridge-Taylor, Anglo-Black Composer, 1875-1912*. New Jersey: Scarecrow Press.

Trotter, James Monroe. 1881, rpt. 1968. *Music and Some Highly Musical People*. Boston: Lee & Shepard; rpt. Johnson Reprint Corporation.

Williams, Melvin R. 1971-1972. "Blueprint for Change: The Black Community in Washington, D.C., 1860-1870." Records of the Columbia Historical Society, Vol. 48.

5   *IRENE V. JACKSON*

Music Among Blacks in the Episcopal Church: Some Preliminary Considerations

This essay examines historically the musical activities of Blacks in the Episcopal church.

To date, scholarly attention has been given primarily to the religious experience of Blacks who are outside mainline denominations. One is hard-pressed to find adequate discussion of Black religious activities within the principal churches of America. The situation becomes even more critical when the subject is the musical activities of Black people in the larger religious bodies. It is not the intent of this essay to offer an explanation of the paucity of material on Black musical practices in mainline denominations. Rather the attention of this study is given to the musical activities of Blacks in the Episcopal church. An analysis of the social forces which gave rise to Black musical attitudes is an important subject. However, a socio-historical examination of the musical activities of Black Episcopalians will be left for another time.

The larger issue that will be addressed in the course of this essay is the religious musical tradition of Afro-Americans.

Scholarly interest in the religious music of Afro-Americans has been almost exclusively devoted to the study of one genre—the spiritual—and of musical activities among Black independent de-

First published in the *Historical Magazine of the Protestant Episcopal Church,* XLVIV (1980), pp. 21-36. Reprinted with permission of the Historical Society of the Episcopal Church.

nominations where worship modes are covertly or overtly linked to West African modes.

The account of the English musician Henry Russell who visited the United States from 1833 to 1841 is representative of accounts of Black worship patterns. Russell writes:

> I had long taken a deep interest in Negro life, and I wondered whether it was possible that Negroes could originate melody. I was desirous of testing this, and I made up my mind to visit any Negro meetings throughout several of the states. On my entering the chapel at Vicksburg [then a slave town] there was a restlessness about the little congregation—whether it emanated from one or two white people being present I cannot say. There was one peculiarity that struck me forcibly. When the minister gave out his own version of the Psalm, the choir commenced singing so rapidly that the original tune absolutely ceased to exist—in fact, the fine old psalm tune became thoroughly transformed. For a moment, I fancied that not only the choir but the little congregation intended to get up a dance as part of the service. (Chase 1966: 236-237)

The above description is but one example of the many recorded accounts of Black worship patterns. However, these accounts focus primarily on situations that involve the more demonstrative forms of religious behavior such as shouting, dancing, or glossolalia.

The religious music of Afro-Americans must be thoroughly investigated and perceptively conceptualized. Therefore, a discussion of religious music of Afro-Americans—as this essay intends to show—must take into account not only music in Black independent churches but also the musical practices of Blacks in mainline denominations.

It will be demonstrated that Blacks in the Episcopal church have historically regarded the centrality of music in their Christian life.

MUSIC AND THE ANTE-BELLUM CHURCH

The history of musical practices among Black Episcopalians in a formal way begins in the latter part of the eighteenth century in Philadelphia with Absalom Jones and Richard Allen who together formed "The Free African Society." Jones went on to found the first Black Episcopal parish in the United States, St. Thomas African Episcopal Church, which was established in 1794 in Philadelphia.

The minutes of the January 18, 1793, meeting of "The Free African Society," which was attended by Absalom Jones, give the first glimpse of attitudes about music within the "Society." Since Jones was present at the meeting and presumably voted on the "recommended rules" of the "Society," we have some idea about his attitudes regarding music in worship. From the minutes of this meeting, "it was recommended that at the time of singing, the *congregation* shall stand or keep seated as *they* find freedom, and that the *congregation* should supply such books as are necessary to read, *sing*, and praise the Lord in harmony" (Douglas 1862: 54, my italics). We know then that music was an integral part of worship and that *congregational* singing was encouraged. We know also from the minutes that singing should be entered into as a *corporate* act of worship.

In a somewhat less formal sense, the history of music among Black Episcopalians begins in the early eighteenth century with the work of the Society for the Propagation of the Gospel in Foreign Parts (referred to as the S.P.G.), comprising English missionaries who were sent to the Colonies to christianize Blacks and Indians.

The early work of the S.P.G. occurred in Goose Creek, South Carolina, where slaves were reported to have been converted in 1695 under Rev. Samuel Thomas. From 1712, the work of the S.P.G. was spearheaded by the Rev. George Ross who as a missionary put forth an effort to provide slaves with instruction in church catechism. His efforts were largely concentrated in Delaware. Ross, in a letter to the S.P.G., indicated that the Quakers gave little attention to instructing slaves and that the few slaves who were baptized belonged to Churchmen, that is Anglicans.

Probably the most important and well-known name in connection with the S.P.G. was the Rev. Thomas Bray. An early eighteenth century letter to the S.P.G. from a clergyman, a missionary who served in St. James parish in South Carolina, reported that the work among the Blacks was successful because the Lord's day was no longer profaned by dancing. One of the conditions of baptism as set down by the white clergymen was that slaves were required to promise that they would not spend the Lord's Day in feasts, dances and merry meetings.[1]

In addition to being instructed in the church catechism, Blacks were introduced to the music of the Anglican Church in the way of

singing the psalms, as reported by a New York clergyman to the
S.P.G. in a letter dated December 3, 1726 (Pennington 1939: 78).
Missionary activity was moving along full tilt in Savannah,
Georgia and Charlestown, South Carolina. By the 1730s, missionaries requested that the S.P.G. send "Bibles, primers, spelling
books, horn-books, testaments, and *psalters*."[2] Blacks were taught
to sing psalms using a practice referred to as "lining-out." The song
leader or precentor would sing one or two lines of the psalm and
the congregation followed, repeating the lines with some melodic
ornamentation. The practice of "lining-out" was a device used to
teach slaves to read and sing from notes.

Contrary to the popularly held notion that Blacks were not attracted to the formality of Anglican worship style, we learn from
letters dated September 30, 1745, and March 28, 1751 and sent to
the S.P.G. from missionaries in New York that "the singing of a psalm
had produced a good effect: it had engaged many of the Negroes to
a closer application in learning to read," and "that Blacks often
meet in the evenings on a regular basis for instruction in the singing
of the psalm tunes."[3] It seems reasonable to assume from the aforementioned quotes that music was used by Blacks non-liturgically,
as a means of providing group solidarity and identity.

Where Blacks worshipped along with whites, although most
often restricted to a special area, or where Blacks worshipped in a
separate building under white leadership, Blacks were, by the
founding of Black independent churches in the late eighteenth century, beginning to experience musical syncretism within the colonial Church of England. That is, Blacks were fusing certain African
and Afro-American musical practices with Anglo-American
musical practices.

In a history of Black Episcopalians, Robert Bennett suggests how
this musical syncretism manifested itself.

In the south, where the majority of Black Episcopalians were to be found
and where prior to the Civil War the Bishop of South Carolina claimed
more Black communicants than white and where Black churchmen worshipped in separate galleries or chapels, it was this body which described
their plantation Holy Communion services in the spiritual, "Let Us Break
Bread Together on Our Knees." (Bennett 1974: 239)

Bennett presents us with an intriguing conjecture. This passing comment of Bennett's suggests that Blacks within the Episcopal Church contributed to the growing body of Afro-American religious folksong to be known later as spirituals. Bennett seems to imply that the spiritual "Let Us Break Bread Together" originated among Black Episcopalians, possibly since the kneeling stance is assumed in communion and probably because the administering of the Holy Sacraments is central to Episcopalian liturgy. Perhaps what is most intriguing about Bennett's hypothesis is that Blacks other than those who were under the influence of the Methodists and Baptists were not to be excluded from certain musical practices that were popular among the masses of Blacks. These musical practices included the singing of religious folk songs—to be later known as spirituals—and the performance practice referred to as "lining-out."

Before the introduction of the organ in Black Episcopal churches, which occurred in the late 1820s, congregational singing made use of the performance practice of "lining-out."

Most congregations, both Black and white, developed what church authorities called "undesirable" practices in terms of congregational singing before the organ became the standard instrument for accompanying congregational singing. These "undesirable" practices consisted of the use of a highly embellished vocal line. The concerns of the clergy for improved congregational singing gave rise to singing schools which were intended to promote the "regular" or "correct" way of singing as it was called, or "singing by note." The movement toward the establishment of singing schools began in New England in the eighteenth century, and by the second half of the century had become a regular institution in New England. St. Philip's (New York) established a church music school (to teach "singing by note") which held classes twice a week in the evenings, according to *Freedom's Journal*, October 26, 1827. There seemed to be no opposition to "singing by note" among Black Episcopalians, at least not in New York City or Philadelphia; such was not the case in Philadelphia's Bethel A.M.E. church where the older people vehemently resisted "singing by note." Among the more enlightened Black Episcopalians and Black independents the introduction of the choir and organ into the church service as well as musical literacy were viewed as progressive whereas the older communicants in the A.M.E. denomination regarded the new practice of music reading as "having brought the devil into the church" (Payne 1891: 452-453; 1888: 234).

An important musical activity to be noted among Black Episcopalians during the early nineteenth century was church sponsored concerts. St. Philip's (New York) was not only instrumental in establishing church music schools, but also led the way in sponsoring sacred concerts, usually consisting of large choral works often with orchestral accompaniment. Most often, the concerts featured the works of European composers, and occasionally the works of Black composers were presented.[4]

There was a high performance standard placed on music in Black congregations of the Church. Very often on the occasion of institutions and consecrations clergy commented upon the quality of singing. For example Bishop Kemp, who consecrated St. James (Baltimore), made the following comments in recording the events of that day: ". . . the congregation was large and devout, . . . the responses were well made and the chanting and singing quite delightful" (Bragg 1909: 13).

By the 1830s, the organ had become such a tradition at St. Thomas that when the Rev. J. M. Douglas accepted the call to St. Thomas, he described the church in the following way:

She stood alone in favor of education of ministry and people . . . and once spoken of in disparaging terms on account of care for cleanliness, decency in worship house, her carpeted aisles, her pews and *organ*, now closely imitated in all respects." (Douglas 1862: 130; my italics)

In the south, it is not known whether many Black communicants were actually able to read music. It is probable that they learned the chants and hymns by rote. However, in instances where singing was done without instrumental accompaniment, the singing was still commented upon as being "acceptable" and "well rendered." Probably, then, careful instruction was given in singing; probably instruction was given in reading music as well as its performance.

It seems that music within Black Episcopal churches maintained its high quality during the 1840s. Most often, the quality of the music in Black congregations was the subject of comment by clergy who visited these congregations. Such was the case at Christ Church, Providence, Rhode Island, which was admitted as a parish in June of 1843 and was originally led by Alexander Crummell. One of the white clergy who had charge of the parish submitted the following in his annual report:

This is the only colored church in New England, though there are several meeting-houses of different sects in the city of Providence. The services, the church and the worshippers, present an appearance of order, neatness and regularity which are seldom equaled, and can hardly be surpassed. The organist is a colored girl under twenty years of age and the music is excellent.[5]

During the 1850s, church music among Black Episcopalians continued to be given careful attention and thus was well performed, particularly since trained Black musicians and composers were often Episcopalians. For example, at St. Philip's Church, Newark, which was instituted circa 1856, Peter P. O'Fake, a notable musician of Newark and a baritone, served as choir director beginning in 1856. Under O'Fake's leadership, the choir received favorable comments.[6]

While Peter O'Fake was active in Newark, William Brady and Thomas J. Bowers, both Black musicians, concertized in New York and Philadelphia during the 1850s. Little is known about William Brady, who died in 1854, except that James M. Trotter described him as a "composer of a musical service for the Episcopal Church." In addition to his musical activities in New York, Brady performed in Philadelphia from the 1820s through the early 1850s. It has not been disclosed whether Brady was a musician in one of the Black Episcopal churches in New York City. However, it is likely that he was a musician at St. Philip's (New York) or at least an Episcopalian as evidenced by his composing music for the Episcopal service.

Thomas J. Bowers, his brother John C. Bowers, and his sister Sarah Sedgewick Bowers were prominent musicians in Philadelphia beginning in the 1850s, and were members of St. Thomas, where their father was senior warden. St. Thomas has a distinctive history of musical activity beginning in the nineteenth century. Maude Cuney-Hare in *Negro Musicians and Their Music* (1936) mentions that much of the sacred music written about 1800 was composed

for services at St. Thomas. Both Thomas Bowers and his brother
John served as organists at St. Thomas. The music historian James
M. Trotter provides some informative insights into the Bowers
family and sheds light on the quality of music in Philadelphia
among the Black "elite." By extension then Trotter gives some idea
of the quality of music at St. Thomas—at least during the period
from the 1840s through the eighties:

The parents of the subject of this sketch [Thomas J. Bowers], although
highly pleased with the natural musical qualities and with the accomplishments displayed by their children, were such strict church people as not to
wish them to become public performers. Recognizing the pleasing, refining
influence of music, they desired its practice by their children in the home-
circle, for the most part; but were not adverse, however, to hearing its
sweet and sacred strains issue from choir and organ in church service, not
to having their children take part in the same (Trotter 1880, rpt. 1969: 132).

By the late 1850s, the use of the organ in worship among Black
Episcopalians had influenced Black independent denominations to
introduce instrumental music into their worship services as well.
The following is an account of the influence that St. James (Baltimore) had on other Black churches in that city, in terms of the
introduction of the organ into the worship service:

This was a real novelty and invited strong denunciations from the colored
churches of the city. Reproachful and sneering terms were applied to the
church because of this introduction into the public services of the church of
the "devil's music box." Thus, the Church was an early witness for musical
accessories in divine services, as well as for order and decorum in public
worship. The indirect influence of St. James has been very great in this city,
as the marvelous changes in the conduct of services in colored churches
witnesseth. (Bragg 1909: 30)

By the middle of the nineteenth century, Black Episcopal
churches in the north had thriving music programs. In the south on
the plantations, musical practices among Black Episcopalians tended
to be within the folk tradition, that is, songs were sung unaccompanied.
    The account of musical activities on a North Carolina plantation
belonging to Ebenezer Pettigrew and Josiah Collins, which reported

100 Black communicants, is probably representative of performance practices among southern Black communicants. Bishop Ives, who worked among Blacks on this North Carolina plantation, commented on "being struck by the beauty of the singing which is done without instrumental accompaniment."[7] Singing a capella was also the case at Calvary Church in Charleston, South Carolina, where it was reported that "a choir of Negroes sang the chants and hymns without accompaniment," on the occasion of the consecration of the building in 1849.[8]

Less wealthy parishes were not always able to purchase organs and thus sang without accompaniment. The oral tradition prevailed in parishes such as St. Paul's in Wilmington, North Carolina, which was organized in 1858. It was unlawful to teach reading to Blacks; music was provided by "a choir of colored persons who were *orally* taught the catechism and to sing the psalms and hymns."[9]

Even when Blacks were taught the hymns and psalms by note or by oral tradition, "undesirable performance practices—as they were called by educated white and Black clergy—did not seem to develop in Black Episcopal churches as they did in Black independent churches.

The mode of worship among Black Episcopalians became a distinctive feature of worship, so much so that a Swedish visitor to Cincinnati, Ohio, Frederika Bremer, made the following comments in a letter she sent to Sweden from Cincinnati, dated November 27, 1850:

I had in the forenoon visited a negro *Baptist church* belonging to the *Episcopal creed*. There were but few present, and they were of the negro [sic] aristocracy of the city. The mode of conducting the divine service was quiet, very proper, and a little tedious. The hymns were beautifully and exquisitely sung.[10]

With regard to the "undesirable practices" that developed in Black independent churches, some Black clergy such as Daniel Alexander Payne warned his A.M.E. congregation against "clapping and stamping feet in a ridiculous and heathenish way."[11] Such clergy as Payne seemed to associate demonstrative forms of religious expression with the "unenlightened."

Influenced by St. James (Baltimore) to introduce the organ into his church service, Payne did so in 1867. At the same time, he introduced the choir as well. This event met with no opposition because, Payne says, "the membership of our Church in the enlightened city of Boston was so intelligent that they regarded the introduction of the choir and the organ as an advanced step in their religious public worship" (Payne 1891: 458).

By the close of the Civil War, a foundation had been laid in Black Episcopal churches for music that was performed according to high standards. St. Thomas had led the way in this regard. By the mid-1860s, St. Thomas owed only a small balance on its organ, which was a significant achievement. And in the south, by the close of the War, school children were regularly drilled and given instruction in music and singing the chants (Bragg n.d.; Jackson 1975).

THE POST-BELLUM PERIOD

Music in Black Episcopal churches had become, by the post-bellum period, a "cultivated" or "genteel" tradition, as distinct from a "folk" or "vernacular" tradition.

Black Episcopal churches persisted in providing quality music in the worship service. The Rev. Calbraith B. Perry, a white clergy, worked in Black congregations in Baltimore from the late 1860s through the late 1870s. Having visited St. Philip's mission, established as a Black congregation in 1868, he informs us that "it was a small structure but when the service began the small size of the mission was forgotten because of the sweet music." Perry (1884: 22) goes on to add that "despite infrequent clergy leadership, the colored folks had loyally and persistently maintained services."

Even in small congregations, Black Episcopalians apparently viewed the organ as a vital component of worship, so much so that at St. Philip's-St. Luke's (New Orleans), organized in 1878, a pipe organ was purchased in 1880 for a congregation of three men and ten women (Duncan 1883: 227-228).

Black Episcopal churches were most often noted in accounts of the musical activities of Blacks in urban areas. St. Thomas (Chicago) is notable in this regard. The first rector of St. Thomas, the Rev. James E. Thompson,[12] was apparently critical of the music there and it is likely that he guided its direction. St. Thomas

(Chicago) was probably one of the churches to which the music historian James M. Trotter refers in discussing the music situation in Black churches in Chicago in the 1870s: "Besides several fine church-choirs, there is a large organization of well-trained vocalists, the performance of which have been highly spoken of by journals of Chicago . . . (Trotter 1880, rpt. 1969: 321).

While Black Episcopalians primarily sang hymns from the Anglican tradition, in at least one instance sources indicate that Methodist hymns were sung by Black Episcopalians. This was an interesting development. And perhaps the most illuminating discussion in this regard is offered by Calbraith B. Perry in his book, *Twelve Years Among the Colored People* (1884), in which we are provided with a glimpse of the musical activities at St. Mary's Chapel, Baltimore (established in 1878). Perry (1884: 75) writes that "a choral service was regularly held on Friday nights and also at 4 p.m. on Sundays after the close of the Sunday School session when people gathered for short musical services."

Perry's descriptions about musical life at St. Mary's indicate that at least one Black Episcopal church had been influenced by Methodist hymnody. The hymns that are mentioned were, as Perry indicates, "familiar hymns" to the congregation of Black Episcopalians. Perry describes the evening service as being held at eight o'clock—a shortened form of evening prayer—Perry says that "the chants were sung," and "the hymns were set to inspiriting [sic] tunes which were interspersed with familiar Methodist hymns: 'Coronation,' 'There Is a Fountain,' and 'Nearer My God to Thee' " (Perry 1884: 78). These comments are revealing for several reasons: it is likely that the musical practices among Black Methodists, at least in the city of Baltimore, had affected Episcopalians; and it is not too far-fetched to conclude that the hymn tradition among Blacks was interdenominational, as it continues to be.

It was not unusual for Black congregations of Episcopalians to spawn notable musicians. Often these musicians were formally trained. Musical people in Baltimore during the 1880s "worthy of mention" include certain choir members of St. Mary's Episcopal Church:

Mr. H. C. Bishop, general director; Mr. W. H. Bishop, precenter; J. Hopkins Johns, who has a very pleasing voice; Mr. J. Taylor, a fine basso, who has been a member of a meritorious concert-troup; Mr. C. A. Johnson, organist; and Mr. George Barrett, tenor. (Trotter 1880, rpt. 1969: 329)

The music historian Trotter adds: "C. A. Johnson, the organist, has on several occasions been the director of excellent public concerts in Baltimore and its vicinity, and is deserving of much praise for his activity in promoting the music-loving spirit. The same may be said of Mr. George Barrett, another member of St. Mary's Choir" (Trotter 1880, rpt. 1969). C. A. Johnson was also the leader of an association of musicians called "the Monumental Cornet Band," which furnished instrumental music for festive occasions at St. Mary's and in the city of Baltimore (Perry 1884: 78). It should be noted that St. Mary's choir members, the organist at the Bethel Methodist Church, and members of the Sharp-Street Church choir were apparently the most musical Afro-Americans in Baltimore at that time. The point is that during the 1880s, music at St. Mary's was more noteworthy than the music at St. James, if Trotter's comments are an actual account of the musical situation in Baltimore at that time.

The musical legacy of St. Mary's (Baltimore) was maintained by the Rev. Hutchens G. Bishop, who was the fourth rector of St. Philip's (New York) and whose older brothers and sisters were among the pioneers of St. James (Baltimore). Bishop established the second congregation in Baltimore, St. Mary's. Bishop was confirmed at St. Mary's and sang in the choir there. Upon his coming to St. Philip's (New York), Bishop was attentive to the music performed, given his nurturing and the musical activities in which he engaged as a youth.[13] The men and boys choir at St. Philip's became a recognized concert group under Bishop's rectorship.

Bishop's interest in music extended beyond the church. He was a member of the board of directors of the Negro Music School Settlement (New York City).

Other notable musicians included Mrs. Arianna Cooley Sparrow who was a member of the Handel and Haydn Society in Boston during the 1880s, and who because of "excellent training retained the natural sweetness of her voice and purity of tone that enabled her to sing acceptably in St. Augustine Episcopal Church (Boston) when over eighty years of age" (Cuney-Hare 1936: 221). By the 1890s, we know for certain that women had been admitted to church choirs. At St. Matthew's (Detroit) where women were admitted to the choir in 1892, they were not allowed in the choir stalls but had to occupy the front pews.[14] (Women, however, had historically served as organists in Black Episcopal churches.)

By the turn of the century, Black Episcopal churches were still recognized for their music. Writing in 1897 about Black life in Philadelphia, W.E.B. Du Bois discussed various Black Episcopal churches in that city and went on to add that the Church of the Crucifixion (which was over fifty years old in 1897) was "perhaps the most effective church in the city for its benevolent and rescue work and it [made] especial feature of good music with its vested choir" (Du Bois 1899: 217).

In a history of St. Philip's by the Rev. B. F. DeCosta, published in 1889, we are informed that "for the benefit of those who never enjoyed literary privileges, it was the custom, as in many churches *long before*, and *even afterwards*, to line off the psalms and hymns, in order that all might join in the praise of the Almighty God" (DeCosta 1889: 15; my italics).

The aforementioned quote by the Rev. DeCosta is important for several reasons. Although DeCosta's comments are about a specific Black congregation, by extension we perhaps are provided with some idea about the extent of musical practices in Black Episcopal congregations during the late nineteenth and early twentieth centuries. Contrary to the commonly held notion that all Black Episcopalians were literate, we know from DeCosta's comments that this was not entirely the case, at least not by the beginning of this century. From DeCosta's insights, we can conclude that an oral musical tradition persisted to a degree in Black Episcopal churches into the twentieth century.

From the turn of the century through the early twenties several events are worth mentioning that directly or indirectly influenced music in Black Episcopal churches. For instance, by 1910, St. Athanasius School, an Episcopal Church School for Blacks, was founded. It started as a mission in 1884 and developed into a high and training school; among its "efficient department" were domestic science, manual training, and music (Bragg 1922: 222).

Sources disclose that it was not uncommon for priests to be trained musicians in the early twentieth century. For instance, at St. Augustine's (Atlantic City), which was spawned by St. James

(Baltimore), the vicar was the Rev. James Nelson Denver, whom Bragg describes as a person with "a fair high school education" and "a musician and general 'hustler' " (Bragg 1922: 174). The Rev. Maximo Duty, vicar of St. Philip's (Richmond) from 1901 to 1903, was also a musician, while the Rev. Issac A. McDonald, rector of St. Philip's from 1938 to 1942, served also as the choir director.[15]

A "cultivated" musical tradition characterized Black Episcopal churches in urban areas by the early twentieth century—except in some instances where the psalms and hymns were still "lined-out." It has been reported that at a mission in Burroughs, Georgia, communicants employed the practice of "lining out" during the early twentieth century.[16]

THE CONTEMPORARY SCENE

Church-sponsored concerts that began in the 1820s and continued full swing into the twentieth century in Black Episcopal churches had always provided performance outlets for Black musicians. Marian Anderson gave her first Detroit concert on November 1, 1926, at St. Matthew's to raise funds for the rectory.[17]

In the twentieth century, Black congregations of the Church also produced musicians of note. This continued a tradition that had been set in motion during the nineteenth century. For instance, Carl R. Diton (1886-1969), composer and teacher, served as organist at St. Thomas (Philadelphia) during the 1920s. Diton is famous for his organ fantasy, based on the spiritual, "Swing Low, Sweet Chariot." He is also well known for his choral arrangements of Afro-American spirituals. Melville Charlton, who was born in New York in 1883, was perhaps the leading organist of the race at that time and was the first Black to become a member of the prestigious American Guild of Organists. He was organist at St. Philip's Episcopal Church (New York) (Cuney-Hare 1936: 340-341).

An interesting musical activity developed during the 1930s at St. Ambrose (New York), under the rectorship of the Rev. E. E. Durant. Durant, a West Indian, was concerned that services were "bright and that people entered heartily into singing," and held singing contests to promote congregational singing. One such contest involved the singing of six hymns; the competition occurred between the men and the women and between the congregation and the choir. Durant was so concerned about the quality of music at St. Ambrose that he always attended all choir rehearsals when he was in the city. About Episcopal churches, he says: "Some people complain about the dullness of some churches, all people like a bright, spirited service. I love it myself" (Durant n.d.: n.p).

St. Ambrose, under Durant's leadership, spawned at least one musician of note—an organist. Clarence E. Whiteman, presently professor of organ and theory at Virginia State College, served as an acolyte at St. Ambrose and credits this exposure and experience as having influenced his becoming an organist. Whiteman's formal musical education includes degrees from Manhattan School of Music, Guilmant Organ School and the School of Sacred Music, formerly at the Union Theological Seminary (presently at Yale Divinity School), and from Trinity College in London. He served as organist and choirmaster at St. Philip's (New York), where in 1973, for regular worship, he featured music composed by Blacks (Southern 1978: 168-187).

By the 1960s, the state of congregational singing in many Black Episcopal churches was critical. It is likely that the comments given in the parish profile of St. Philip's (Richmond) are representative of the state of music within Black Episcopal parishes: "The congregation is passive in participating in the service, both in singing and in prayer response."

Presently, there is real effort underway to revitalize and rejuvenate the worship experience among Black Episcopalians. Much of this effort involves the appropriation of traditional materials from the Afro-American experience to the Episcopal liturgy. Perhaps the Rev. Arthur Myron Cochran led the way in his arrangements of music (largely based on Afro-American spirituals) for the Communion Service. The Cochran Mass was published in 1925 and revived by the St. Augustine's College Choir in a recording produced by the Rev. Robert B. Hunter (presently rector of Church of the Atonement, Washington, D.C.).

There is present-day concern about the relationship of Word, music and Mass. One priest maintains that "the key to bringing Episcopalians [i.e., Black Episcopalians] together is to break down the separateness between the choir, the congregation and the minister. The Word, the music and the Mass must move toward wholeness." "This is achieved in several ways: by altering the Mass

into contemporary language, and by experimenting with spatial relationships in terms of the choir, congregation and the minister and
passing from a strictly hymnbook tradition to one which is oral in
the sense that the music and text become so familiar that people are
able to enter into the worship experience without being bound to
the printed page."[18]

Mainline denominations have begun to recognize the power of
Black song and Black worship style and are finding ways of
utilizing this music, i.e., Afro-American music, within the framework of their liturgies. Such a movement is underway in the Episcopal church. For example, the Rev. William James Walker, a
Black priest, commissioned Lena McLin, an Afro-American who is
a music educator and a composer, to compose a Mass for the Episcopal liturgy in which one cannot help but note the Afro-
Americanisms in the compositional style. In 1982 the Office of
Black Ministries of the Episcopal Church published a hymnal, "Lift
Every Voice and Sing," which is a collection of Afro-American reli-
gious songs and other hymns that are traditional among Afro-
Americans.

The activities—music being one—of Blacks in the Episcopal
Church need further documentation. This, of course, is a challenge
to scholars.

This essay will hopefully provoke more study and research into
the musical activities of Black Episcopalians. In the course of this
essay, attention was given to highlighting these activities and in an
indirect way topics for future research were illuminated.

What are some of the questions that have been raised from this
discussion? For this writer, several. For instance, what is the possibility of an Episcopal source for the Afro-American spiritual, "Let
Us Break Bread Together on Our Knees"? Or to what extent were
the religious folk songs of Afro-Americans used in Black parishes
with Black or white leadership? How were these songs performed?
Another question that comes to mind is: What are the cultural and
social factors that gave rise to music-making among Black Episcopalians? These examples must suffice.

Hopefully this essay demonstrates the validity of the study of the
music of Blacks in the Episcopal church and demonstrates that
further study of this area is imperative.

NOTES

1. Pennington (1939: 25) quoting *S.P.G. Series A*, V., #49 (October 20, 1709); see also Clifton (1970: 63-64).

2. Pennington (1939: 17) quoting the "Minutes of the Meetings of the S.P.G. (1729-1735)," pp. 62-65; my italics.

3. Pennington (1939: 82) quoting *S.P.G. Series B*, XIII, #219 and *S.P.G. Series B*, XIX, #68.

4. For further discussion see Southern (1977: 306); she quotes the concert program as it appeared in *Freedom's Journal*, September 23, 1827.

5. Bragg (1922: 102-103) quoting the AME Magazine, 1845.

6. See Southern (1971: 122); and Trotter (1880, rpt. 1969: 306). O'Fake also had the distinction of being the first Black to conduct the Newark Theatre Orchestra.

7. See Franklin (1944: 221) quoting the *Journal of the North Carolina Convention*, 1943.

8. Durden (1965: 82) quoting *The Charleston Gospel Messenger and The Protestant Episcopal Register*, 19 (1852).

9. Jackson (1975) quoting *The Church Messenger* (Winston, North Carolina) July 21, 1881. St. Paul's was a mission of St. Marks which was consecrated on June 18, 1975; my italics.

10. Quoted in Southern (1971: 112-113); my italics.

11. See Southern (1971: 26-64; 68-70).

12. It is also interesting to note that all three of Thompson's children were musicians. One son, J. DeKoven Thompson, composed a song which was sung at the funeral of President William McKinley. See *The Thirty-Sixth Anniversary Tea Program Bulletin* (St. Thomas, Chicago) Sunday, June 18, 1844; and Cuney-Hare (1936: 227).

13. See Bragg (1922: 88); and Bishop (1946; 298-317).

14. From *Centennial Celebration Bulletin 1846-1946*, St. Matthew's Episcopal Church, Detroit.

15. From "Parish Profile," St. Philip's Episcopal Church, Richmond, Va., October 1975, unpublished MS.

16. Personal Interview, Dr. Tollie Caution, April 1978, New York City.

17. *Centennial Celebration Bulletin*, 1846-1946, St. Matthew's Episcopal Church, Detroit.

18. Personal Interview, Reverend Kwasi Thornhill, New York City, March 1978.

REFERENCES

Bennett, Robert A. 1974. "Black Episcopalians: A History from the Colonial Period to the Present Day." *Historical Magazine of the Protestant Episcopal Church* 43 (September).

Bishop, Shelton. 1946. "A History of St. Philip's Church." *Historical Magazine of the Protestant Episcopal Church* 12 (March).

Bragg, George F. n.d. *The Story of Old St. Stephens, Petersburg, Va.* Baltimore: Church Advocate Press.

———. 1909. *First Negro Priest on Southern Soil.* Baltimore: Church Advocate Press.

———. 1922. *History of the Afro-American Group of the Episcopal Church.* Baltimore: Church Advocate Press.

Chase, Gilbert. 1966. *America's Music.* New York: McGraw-Hill.

Clifton, Denzie T. 1970. "Anglicanism and Negro Slavery in Colonial America." *Historical Magazine of the Protestant Episcopal Church* 39 (March).

Cuney-Hare, Maude. 1936. *Negro Musicians and Their Music.* Washington, D.C. Associated Publishers.

DeCosta, B. F. 1889. *Three Score and Ten: The Story of St. Philip's Church, New York City.* New York: printed for the parish.

Douglas, William. 1862. *Annals of the First African Church.* Philadelphia: Kerg and Baird.

Du Bois, W.E.B. 1899. *The Philadelphia Negro.* New York: Schocken Books.

Duncan, Herman Cope, Reverend. 1883. *History of the Diocese of Louisiana.* New Orleans: A. W. Hyatt.

Durant, E. Ellio. n.d. (1946?). *The Romance of an Ecclesiastical Adventure.* N.p.

Durden, Robert F. 1965. *The Establishment of Calvary Church.* Charleston: Dalcho Historical Society.

Franklin, John Hope. 1944. "Negro Episcopalians in Ante-Bellum North Carolina." *Historical Magazine of the Protestant Episcopal Church* 13/3 (September).

Jackson, Allen J. 1975. "100th Anniversary Bulletin of St. Marks," Wilmington (North Carolina).

Payne, Daniel Alexander. 1888. *Recollections of Seventy Years.* Nashville: Publishing House of the A.M.E. Church.

———. 1891. *History of the A.M.E. Church.* Nashville: Publishing House of the A.M.E. Sunday School Union.

Pennington, Edgar. 1939. *Thomas Brays' Associates and Their Work among the Negroes.* Worcester, Mass.: American Antiquarian Society.

Perry, Calbraith. 1884. *Twelve Years Among the Colored People.* New York: James Patt and Co.

Southern, Eileen. 1971. *Music of Black Americans.* New York: W. W. Norton and Co.

_____. 1977. "Philadelphia and New York, ca. 1800-1844." *Journal of the American Musicological Society* V. 30, no. 2.

_____. 1978. "Conversation with . . . Clarence E. Whiteman, Organ-Music Collector." *Black Perspective in Music* (Fall).

Trotter, James M. 1880, rpt. 1969. *Music and Some Highly Musical People.* Boston: Lee and Shepherd; rpt. Chicago: Afro-American Press.

A Comparative Analysis of Traditional and Contemporary Gospel Music

For the last several years, gospel music aficionados have been bombarded with articles on the changing style of the genre.[1] If a consensus can be gathered from these articles, it is that gospel music is moving away from "the church" and toward "the world." In other words, a large amount of gospel music is now more secular than sacred.

The present reaction against secularization is not the first to surface. Surprisingly, the first reactions came in the 1930s in Chicago, when the ministers of that city told Professor Thomas A. Dorsey who is recognized as the Father of Afro-American gospel music that they did not want his "rocking" kind of music in their churches. The objection to the so-called jazz licks and riffs performed by Sister Rosetta Tharpe on her guitar in 1945 drove her to move her concerts from the church to the ballparks, while twenty years later church people expressed shock at the appearance of Clara Ward and the Ward Singers at clubs in Las Vegas. When Art Reynolds incorporated "jazzy" rhythms into his 1968 album *Tellin It Like It Is*, gospel music lovers became a little suspicious of him. And in 1969, they responded to Edwin Hawkins' gospel ballads with, "Are these gospel songs?"

The latest protests against changes in gospel music seem to be directed principally at Andrae Crouch, who is regarded as a gospel innovator. He justifies his gospel style with the comment: "If a cat needs to be funkafized, or if they need something sweet, you've got

to give it to them, and then you lay your message over it"
(Doerschuk: 1979: 10).

The music of Andrae Crouch is considered the "new" gospel
sound. "New" gospel always signifies a physical and intellectual
move from the rural—or what has come to be considered rural—to
the urban. In some instances, this means a deeper plunge into the
mainstream of secular *practices, sound,* and *acceptance.* The most
important of the three is *sound.* How then, do the sounds of "old"
and "new" gospel music differ? Let's begin by defining the types of
gospel music.

Two styles of gospel music are heard today. The older style is
referred to as "historic," "classical," or "traditional," while the
newer style is called "pop," "contemporary," "progressive," or
"modern." In this essay, I will use the terms "traditional" and
"contemporary."

If the sound, devices, and accompaniment of the gospel music
prove to be an extension of the established tradition—that is, the
tradition as established by Thomas A. Dorsey, Mahalia Jackson,
Roberta Martin, the Pilgrim Travelers, and Brother Joe May, it is
called *traditional* gospel music. If the sound, devices, and accompaniment of the music are distinctly, recognizably "borrowed"
from another already established tradition—that is, jazz, soul, or
blues, and it is difficult to translate the music into the *traditional*
gospel sound, it is called *contemporary* gospel music.[2]

Generally speaking, contemporary gospel is rejected by the
mainstream Black church, though Andrae Crouch has successfully
developed a Black church following—only, however, after first
building an audience of white people, high school- and college-age
Black students, and jazz lovers. Crouch was able to attract a large
following in both races through a "split-compositional" personality.
His white and jazz audiences delight in such compositions as "I've
Got the Best," performed in an advanced disco style, and "Dream
Medley,"[3] a group of soft-soul style ballads, while the Black audi-
ence responds to his traditional compositions, such as "Through It
All"[4] and "Soon and Very Soon."[5]

Crouch's duality of style has secured for him a name as a multi-
racial composer and performer, but it has also inadvertently contributed to a prominent confusion about gospel music. Many persons who have not grown up with gospel or who do not know it

well cannot always recognize contemporary gospel as gospel music, for often it is extrinsically not very different from secular music. If they do recognize the music to be gospel, they tend to label all gospel music "warmed over" secular music, citing as proof the elements that gospel "borrows" from blues, jazz, and soul.

THE LEADERS OF THE TWO STYLES

Today, the traditional style is represented by such singers as James Cleveland, Shirley Caesar, Mattie Moss Clark, the Nightingales, J. C. White, the Institutional Choir, the Williams Brothers, and the Jackson Southernaires. The contemporary school is led by Andrae Crouch, Danniebelle Hall, Rahni Harris, Jessy Dixon, Edwin Hawkins, Rance Allen, the New York Community Choir (NYCC), the Dixie Hummingbirds, and the Mighty Clouds of Joy. Walter Hawkins stands midway between the two traditions, employing elements of each.

ELEMENTS OF COMPARISON

The musical elements with which we distinguish gospel music from other Black musics are melody, harmony, form, rhythm, accompaniment, vocal timbre, vocal combinations, vocal background, and the texts of the songs. To differentiate traditional from contemporary gospel, we have to examine each of these elements within the music.

Melody

A cursory discussion of three of the most frequently performed and respected older gospel songs provides a summary of the traditional melodic style.[6]

The melody in James Cleveland's "Grace Is Sufficient" lies within the range of a major sixth, with principal portions placed within the interval of a third. The motion is basically conjunct (stepwise melodic motion), with very few skips, tending to revolve around the first and third degrees of the scale. Thomas A. Dorsey's immortal "Precious Lord, Take My Hand," with its tremendous similarity to the hymn "Must Jesus Bear the Cross Alone?" is an example of the "rocket" melody, with a range of a tenth. The melody begins on c^1 and reaches its peak at E^{b-2} and descends again to A^{b-1}, though there is no skip larger than a fourth. In Albert Goodson's "We've Come This Far by Faith," there is a relatively small range—a major sixth—with basically conjunct motion and no interval larger than a fourth.

Of particular interest in the foregoing examples are two facts. (1) All of the melodies are diatonic, that is, they are based on the scale of the key in which the song is written. What appears to be a chromatic[7] tone in "We've Come This Far by Faith"—the B-flat[8] in the sixth measure of the melody line is called a "blue" note in Black music, particularly traditional church music. It is used to soften the bright edge of the third degree at the beginning of the phrase. (2) Interior cadences, or the last tones in each phrase, tend to fall on one of the principal triadic tones, that is, tones 1-3-5 of the key tone, with a preference for the third degree, creating an "open" as opposed to a "closed" sound.

Generally, in newer music, melody undergoes a radical change. Three contemporary gospel melodies are discussed to illustrate the practices of the newer style.

"Tell Them," one of Andrae Couch's most popular gospel "ballads," occupies no more than an octave or eight tones with the extremes, c^1 and c^2 used sparingly, and with the climax occurring at c^2. There is no chromaticism and the contour ascends and then descends for the final cadence, though several of the interior cadences fall on tones that are extensions of the harmony, rather than on primary tones of the harmony. For example, the first phrase ends on g^1 creating on F^9 chord (1^9).

"Perfect Peace" has a range of an eleventh, though there are no intervals larger than a fourth or a fifth, for conjunct motion characterizes the melody. The rocket principle is again apparent in the melody.[9]

"Be Grateful" is a bifocal composition, that is, certain portions are momentarily in one key (e-flat minor) while other portions are in another key (G-flat Major). The complete melody stretches over a range of eleven tones. (However, on the recording, the soloist, Lynette Hawkins Stephens, expands the range two octaves.[10]) There are fewer skips than stepwise motion, no chromaticism, phrases generally end on triad tones, and the melody is of the ascending variety.

Although this sampling is extremely small, the selections represented are ones that have influenced the entire gospel music community. There have indeed been a few innovations, such as extending the melodic range and using non-triad tones on interior cadences, but these innovations have not been sufficient to create a new style.

Lyrics

The lyrics in gospel music are of three variations: (a) scriptural quotes or paraphrases of the scriptures, exemplified in such songs as "You Must Be Born Again," "Peace, Be Still," and "He'll Understand and Say, Well Done"; (b) praise/adoration of the Saviour, represented by such songs as "He's the Joy of My Salvation, Yes He Is," "God Can Do Anything But Fail," and "You Can't Beat God Giving"; and (c) supplication, as in "Touch Me, Lord Jesus," "Give Me a Clean Heart," and "Precious Lord, Take My Hand."

Composers of gospel songs seek a perfect marriage between lyrics and melody. Andrae Crouch, for example, reports that he received this admonition from his father: "If you have to hymn it, hymn it. If you have to rock it, rock it. If you have to funk it, funk it" (Doerschuk: 1979). This admonition, which Crouch apparently followed, raises the question of whether contemporary lyrics have leaned toward conveying "message" or perhaps giving social commentary, an area gospel music has for the most part neglected.

But on the whole, lyrics have not changed. Crouch's "I Will Give You Perfect Peace, If You Keep Your Mind Stayed On Me"[11] is a scriptural quote, as is Danniebelle Hall's "All Things Work Together for Good to Them That Love the Lord,"[12] while "Take Me Back"[13] is a supplication; Walter Hawkins' "Be Grateful"[14] is indirectly a song of praise.

Although this is the lyrical material from which most gospel songs emerge, we should take note of the practice begun some fifteen years ago of adapting secular songs for the gospel catalogue. This is done by substituting the words, *Christ, God, Lord,* and *Saviour* for the original nouns and pronouns. Ironically, in the 1940s, there was a reverse trend: Popular musicians adapted gospel to pop. For example, the Guy Lombardo Orchestra adapted Dorsey's "My Desire" for its popular music catalogue. As early as 1938, Sister Rosetta Tharpe transformed Dorsey's "Hide Me in Thy

Bosom" into "Rock Me," but this song, among others adapted by
her, did not create a trend.

Gospel singers reversed the practice in the 1960s. James
Cleveland recorded "I Can't Stop Loving (You) God," followed by
"I Had a Talk with (My Man) God Last Night." Some others
adopted the practice and the field witnessed the Edwin Hawkins' arrangement "His Way" of Paul Anka's "My Way." In the seventies,
both Cleveland and Crouch recorded gospel versions of the Irish
folk song, "Danny Boy," with Cleveland calling his version "The
Love of God" and Crouch calling his version "Amazing Grace."
Cleveland created a sensation at a Carnegie Hall recital a few years
ago with a recasting of the Barry Manilow arrangement of "I Write
the Songs," in which he alternated the original refrain with such
gospel and hymn standards as "What a Friend We Have in Jesus"
and "Lord, Help Me To Hold Out." Cleveland has also given us a
gospel version of "(You're) Jesus Is the Best Thing That Ever Hap-
pened to Me," as well as the Bernard Ighnar composition and
Quincy Jones arrangement of "Everything Must Change." Lately,
gospel music has sustained such selections as Isaac Douglass' "You
Light Up My Life"; "Something About God's Grace," based on the
John Lennon composition, "Something," performed by the St.
James Choir of Detroit and Andrew Rowe and the D.C. Choral
Ensemble, as well as the Maceo Woods Choir's rendition of the
Anne Murray hit, "(You) Jesus Needed Me." One of the popular
gospel recordings of the day is the Supreme Highlights gospel
version of "Then Came (You) God," adapted from the 1974 record-
ing by Dionne Warwick and the Spinners.

If melody were the sole concern of gospel compositions, gospel
music lovers could take the view of General William Booth, the
founder of the Y.M.C.A.: "Why should the devil have all the good
tunes?" (Etherington 1965: 191). But "gospel" practitioners seem to
agree that gospel music means "good news" and that good news
must come through the lyrics.

Although a general evaluation of the lyrics of traditional gospel
compared to contemporary gospel reveals no overwhelming
change, there has been some advancement. Once again, the leader,
Andrae Crouch, has stepped out with some rather unique lyrics. In
one of his latest albums, *I'll Be Thinking of You*,[15] he includes what
he calls "Dream Medley." While the first stanza expresses general
affection: "I'm dreamin'/Dreamin' about You . . . ," the last line of

the refrain gives some direction to the lyrics: "Oh Lord, I keep dreamin' about you." Thus the lyrics, along with Crouch's singing style—shades of Stevie Wonder's influence; Stevie Wonder actually plays harmonica on this album—initially suggest a sensual relationship until the word "Lord" appears in the last line. Crouch sees no problem with this kind of lyrical development in gospel expression. In an interview in *Contemporary Keyboard*, speaking of another of his gospel "love" songs, he says: "I see Him [God] as somebody who really digs me . . . so I write songs about Him which someone might direct to somebody else they love" (Doerschuk 1979).

The contemporary infusion of social commentary into gospel comes to light in Henry Jackson's album, *The Henry Jackson Company*,[16] in a composition called "What's the Matter?" The lyrics are explicit in talking about a pervasive problem—drugs and youth.

Since the lyrics, themselves, usually are not enough to qualify a song for "advanced" status, attention must be directed as well toward the rhythm.

Rhythm and Meter

Traditional gospel has thrived on a rhythmic style that includes the basic 2/4 and 4/4 patterns for "fast" songs, and the 12/8 pattern for "slow" songs in which beats one, four, seven, and ten receive the major pulses. Any symmetrical or asymmetrical divisions of the beat are clearly felt by the listener; the background beat is always accented.

What new rhythmic elements could be brought to the tradition? For one, we could have asymmetrical meters for an entire song or a prolonged section in asymmetrical meter such as 5/4, 7/4, or 9/4 or alternation of symmetrical and asymmetrical meters or layered meters, where such diverse meters as duple, triple, quadruple, quintuple and septuple are used simultaneously.

To date, however, no asymmetrical meters have penetrated gospel style. Listeners have come to expect an unchanging pulse, a unifying element in the song. The feet *pat* on a regular pulse and the hands *clap* on a regular pulse. An asymmetrical pattern, which would require the hands and feet to change beats, might reduce the level of emotion a gospel song is designed to elicit.

There is, however, a new element that has infiltrated gospel—the practice of placing all instruments and/or voices on the same rhythmic motif so that for a few beats, the constant pulse (provided by the voices and/or instruments) is sacrificed for a particular rhythmic motif, not unlike that employed in soft soul music. For example, eight bars into the vocal portion of "Never Alone,"[17] performed by Walter Hawkins and the Love Center Choir, the choir, which has been pulsing on sixteenth notes, shifts without warning to superimposed quarter note triplets for the last part of the measure. This superimposition is heightened because all of the accompanying instruments (drums, piano, organ, clarinet, and bass guitar) join in to accentuate this rhythm.

Of additional interest is the fact that the melody in "Never Alone" is placed in a rhythm called "back-phrasing," where the beginning of the phrase is delayed beyond the written or metrical point but catches up before the next phrase or portion of the phrase is due by rushing parts of the phrase together so that no beats are lost.

"Never Alone," with a tempo of 74 to 125 (using the standard Maelzel metronome) is normally considered a "fast" song today. Yet, in the fifties and sixties, fast songs were performed at a metronomic marking of 74 to 200 for the quarter note in 2/4 or 4/4 meter. Thus, while the tempo of "Never Alone" is considerably slower, in contemporary gospel, 74 to 125 is considered the "fast" tempo (in 2/4 and 4/4 time) and called the "rock" beat, bearing a scant relationship to the dance of the same name, popular a few years ago. The most popular song set in this tempo is Crouch's "Soon and Very Soon."[18] Faster tempos that range between 100 and 150 are now called the "shout" tempos.

While asymmetrical meters are still absent from the tradition, mixed meters are making an entrance. The most outstanding example to date is the revised "church" song, "Too Late" by the Jackson Southernaires.[19] In Part II, the meter shifts from the gospel 12/8 to 9/8. Closer analysis reveals this 9/8 to be a pulse of 6 + 3, creating a *mixed* meter of six pulses, alternating with three pulses. Later in the recording, the tempo moves to a traditional three pulses, adding yet another variation to gospel rhythm and meter:

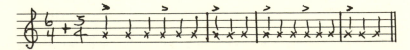

In general, because percussive instruments accompany the singer today, there is much more accentuation of rhythm. Still, notwithstanding the new elements discussed above, the mode of rhythm does not sharply separate the traditional and the contemporary styles. So, let's proceed to the formal structure of gospel music.

Form

As a rule, form in gospel music has traditionally been completely controlled by performance practice. Although the song may be of the verse-chorus variety (A-B), repetition is still an important feature and the number of repetitions of any portion of a song depends entirely upon the inspiration of the audience or the performers or the performer's desire to "get over." For example, when the Roberta Martin Singers performed the composition, "I'm Sealed,"[20] the soloist sang four verses consecutively (A-A-A-A) and then as many choruses as the audience insisted upon (B-B-B-B), while when they performed "Grace," they alternated between chorus and verse (A-B-A-B) for the lengh of the "spirit."

Traditional gospel music exhibits several standard forms: The one-part or period form ("Just A Closer Walk with Thee,"[21] "Precious Lord, Take My Hand"[22]); the A-B or two-part form ("He'll Understand and Say, Well Done")[23]; and the A-B-A form, usually created by the addition of a "vamp" (a harmonic progression) at the return of the A section ("Oh Happy Day").[24]

Contemporary gospel has introduced the five-part song form, in which there is a chorus and *two* different verses that vary melodically and harmonically, thereby constituting a diagram of A-B-A-C-A. The most text-book like example is the Crouch composition, "Take Me Back."[25] The macroform of his rendition is A(A + A)-B-A^1-C-A^1. Crouch insures the integrity of each part by giving each section different textual treatment. For example, the A sections are sung by an ensemble in the direct manner (where all voices sing in the same rhythm), the B section is sung by a solo performer with intermittent vocal punctuations on the syllable "ooh," A^1 gets a call-and-response treatment, while the C section is sung in the direct manner.

Crouch has also introduced a few schematic compositions, that is, compositions built on a carefully arranged idea—or "scheme"— which is used throughout the section or composition as a unifying element. The four most popular schemes are the ground, passacaglia, chaconne, and "twelve-bar" blues. The ground and passacaglia are "fixed" short bass lines of four to eight measures in length which are repeated over and over, with varying melodies added above each time the selected number of measures are repeated. The chaconne and the twelve-bar blues differ from the aforementioned "schemes" in that they are actually a series of recurrent harmonies with or without a recognizable ostinato. Close analysis of Crouch's "Take a Little Time,"[26] also known as "Thank You Lord," reveals that while there is a definite melody in the voices, it is guided by a harmonic progression of four measures, appearing twice during the refrain and three times during the verse. The harmonic scheme is as follows:

While most pianists perform this song with this harmonic scheme, Crouch enriches his harmony with chord extensions and mixtures.

Contemporary gospel makes great use of the vamp (in actuality a succession rather than a progression, since the series of chords does not progress). In the vamp, there are two or more relatively simple chords of indefinite duration. These are employed as fillers until the soloist is ready to start or continue. Or the soloist may add a number of undetermined extemporized solo statements—variations —as these chords are played. The most popular example of the vamp in gospel music is the extended chorus in the Edwin Hawkins arrangement of "Oh Happy Day," though it has been a cherished device since W. Herbert Brewster's "Surely, God Is Able," popularized by the Ward Singers of 1950 and even before. In such famous examples of the vamp as "Surely, God Is Able," "Peace, Be Still" (popularized by James Cleveland), and "Oh Happy Day" (by Edwin Hawkins) the soloist provides all the variety.

There have been three new adjustments to the vamp, two of which come from the exponents of contemporary gospel. The most popular of these is the *chain vamps* (chain of vamps). With this device the background group sets up a textual and harmonic statement, which is repeated. But, after a number of repetitions, the group moves to another textual and harmonic statement and, on occasion, even a third statement is added, constituting a chain of vamps. The Andrae Crouch recording of "Power in The Blood"[27] provides a well-known example, for when Crouch proceeds to the "development" of the song, the background group sings the following vamps:

Vamp I	Lord, Send Your Power (*Several times*)
Vamp II	Power (*as one syllable*) (*Several times*)
Vamp III	Pow-uh (*Several times*)

Each of the vamps is repeated enough to cause the listener to believe that the singers have found the "answer." They then move to a new vamp. On his recording of "Jesus Is Lord,"[28] Crouch again employs the *chain vamps* in the following way:

Vamp I	Every knee shall bow, every tongue shall sing for Jesus is Lord
Vamp II	Jesus is Lord

Notice that in both examples, the successive vamps are extractions from the first vamp. There are few examples of *chain vamps* where additional text is added.

The most sophisticated adjustment to the vamp is making it polyphonic so that several vamps are stated simultaneously. At the conclusion of Walter Hawkins' "I'm Going Away,"[29] while one group sings a vamp on "It Won't Be Long," another group sings a vamp on "Soon and Very Soon," while a third group sings "Someday We'll Meet." To compound the issue further, on occasion, two voices sing the same vamp, so that they offer an alternation of two and three simultaneous vamps.[30]

Another adjustment to the vamp involves additions of harmonic parameters, rather than new text or melody. Usually, a vamp is harmonized in three or four voices first. Once it has impressed itself upon the listener, a contrasting section is inserted and the vamp returns; however, on its return, only one voice enters at a time so that by the time all of the voices are singing, there appears to be a new vamp.

An outstanding example of this practice, called *additive vamp*, is found in James Cleveland's rendition of "I Don't Feel No Ways Tired."[31] After Cleveland exposes the changing material of the song, the vamp or contrast section is introduced by the altos, with the words: "I don't believe He brought me this far." After a while, the tenors join in on the same text, but with a different harmonic line. They are later joined by the sopranos singing the same text, with yet another harmonic line. Cleveland then provides variations on top of this *additive vamp*. The effect is overwhelming.

The addition of a different musical section to constitute a second verse in the five-part form is a radical departure from the gospel of the fifties—the golden age of gospel. The inclusion of schematic compositions (this same device is employed in the traditional gospel staple, the gospel "blues," a sixteen measure composition with a form of A-A-B-A, of which a popular example is "I Know the Lord Will Make a Way, Oh, Yes He Will"),[32] as well as "adjusted" vamps gives us an important clue for differentiating between traditional and contemporary gospel music.

Let us now turn to accompaniment.

Accompaniment

The instrumental ensemble that accompanies gospel singing is a restricted one, and even this limited ensemble developed slowly. The first gospel singers, such as the Golden Gate Quartet, working in the tradition of the Fisk Jubilee Singers, used no accompaniment. Sister Arizona Dranes, a gospel pioneer, used the piano as her basic instrument of accompaniment, but added the mandolin and guitar on recordings.[33] In the thirties, Elder Utah Smith began using the guitar, becoming a star guitarist in the forties. Mahalia Jackson acquired a string orchestra when she moved from Apollo Records to Columbia, and James Cleveland used a trombone solo on one of his recordings in the sixties. Yet the basic ensemble for most gospel recordings and concerts has remained the so-called rhythm section —piano, bass, and drums, joined by the organ as often as possible. These instruments have been treated as additional voices, supplying an accompaniment that supports the melody and background voices in chordal fashion.

In contemporary gospel, this rhythm section is augmented by strings, woodwinds, and brasswinds. Once again, Andrae Crouch leads in this field, usually with the rhythm section aided by one trumpet and two saxophones during "live" performances, and full orchestra on many of his recordings. One of Crouch's latest albums, *I'll Be Thinking of You*,[34] features Crouch accompanied by a harp in one song; in another Stevie Wonder plays a harmonica solo. Likewise, James Cleveland's album, *Live at Carnegie Hall*,[35] and one of his most recent albums, *A New Day Dawn*,[36] feature a full orchestra with strings. The Mighty Clouds of Joy usually use an orchestra on their recordings, and Henry Jackson uses trumpets, flutes, and strings on his album, *The Henry Jackson Company*.[37]

The main addition that leaders of contemporary gospel have contributed, however, is a battery of keyboards. While actually tonal instruments, these keyboards are often employed percussively. They have the advantage of being able to approximate the sounds of the full orchestra. Whether traditional gospel music lovers accept the contemporary instrumentation depends on how the instruments are used. For example, they have embraced the saxophonist Vernard Johnson because he *sounds* like a "church" saxophonist.

The disco age has taught many young musicians a new approach to using orchestral sections. Most disco recordings offered first a motif on the bass, followed by a complementary, yet different, rhythm on the drum. The guitar then settled into a short riff, the horns established a counter-riff and, on top of this, the soloist and background group added yet another layer of sound and rhythm. This style of orchestration has been adopted by Crouch. An example is provided in the opening selection, "Perfect Peace" on his recording, *Live in London*.[38] It is noteworthy too, that on many contemporary gospel recordings the congos have also become a staple feature of the percussion section.

While it must be admitted that contemporary gospel has expanded the orchestral palette, the major difference between the two gospel traditions has yet to be established.

Vocal Timbre and Background Groups

Whereas once it was unusual to see a twenty-year-old gospel singer, it is now more unusual to see a forty-year-old gospel singer. The age of the gospel singers and the sophistication of their musical experiences have produced a vocal timbre unlike any the field has ever experienced. While traditional gospel singers still prefer the "full-throated, strained" sound of James Cleveland, Dorothy Love, and Shirley Caesar, contemporary sound, with its lyrical quality, requires a "pure" voice, evidenced by the soloists in the Edwin Hawkins group of 1969 and 1970. Gentle and often sedate gospel-ballads, such as "Tell Them,"[39] "Changed,"[40] and "Be Grateful,"[41] which are the basis of much contemporary gospel, require the vocal quality of a Tramaine Hawkins or a Sara Jordan Powell. (We should note, however, that these singers are simply extending the style pioneered by Myrtle Scott, Little Lucy Smith, Marion Williams, and Delores Barrett.) It was natural for the young singers to adopt the pure sound, for by the time they began singing, all churches and auditoriums had rather sophisticated sound systems. Additionally, vocal restraint enhances the effect of the harmonic character in contemporary gospel songs.

A pure voice also makes it possible to alternate effectively between unison and harmonic singing, giving diversity to the texture of contemporary gospel. The "bass" voice, which was never as important to gospel as to quartet singing, has all but disappeared from groups and choirs. It is not used by the Hawkins Brothers, Cleveland, or Crouch.

The quality of contemporary voices has affected the type of "response" used in call-and-response selections. While only a few years ago, the background group provided response from the beginning of the song to the end, contemporary gospel employs a background group much the same way as Gladys Knight uses the "Pips," that is, to punctuate and comment. In Crouch's *Live in London* recording of "Perfect Peace," the entire group sings the first sixteen measures in unison, while harmony is reserved for the last sixteen measures. In the Walter Hawkins recording of "Be Grateful," the response is used for a short period as an echo. Hawkins also uses a pseudo-Baroque device in the "response" in this recording. The choir opens the selection with a four-measure motif. This motif returns at the end of the first verse (mm. 16-19 of the printed score), at the end of the second verse (mm. 28-31), and again just before the cadential phrase (mm. 42-45). This motif then serves as a "ritornello," an interlude of at least four measures, that recurs throughout the composition for purposes of unification.

Also a part of the contemporary gospel style is a device resurrected from the past: the practice of dropping the instruments for a few phrases or choruses, so that the performance is both accompanied and a cappella.

Contemporary gospel singers tend to be less active during a performance, often delivering an entire song in one spot, rather than moving through the audience as traditional singers do. In regards to body rhythm, both traditional and contemporary singers use hand-clapping, though contemporary singers have begun adjusting clapping patterns so that while traditionally a singer clapped on beats two and four in a 4/4 pattern, they might clap only on beat four. Contemporary singers also employ the "perpetual" clap, clapping on each beat in a 4/4 pattern.

Let us now turn our attention to the one element that truly appears to separate the traditional and the contemporary gospel.

Harmony

Traditional gospel harmony comprises a set of progressions, designed to support a fairly conjunct and diatonic melody. In most cases, regardless of the melody, the harmony has traditionally had a slow rhythm:

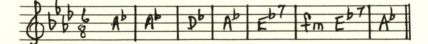

Contemporary gospel is now passing through the "fast harmonic rhythm" stage that jazz experienced in the fifties and sixties. What was once a nonharmonic tone is now an accented chord, so that a passing tone or appoggiatura is harmonized, placed *on* the beat, and sustained for several pulses. Edwin Hawkins used this pattern in the late sixties in his selection, "I Was Glad When They Said unto Me."[42] In this song, the use of a group of chord mixtures is best expressed as bitonality—the combining of two different harmonies. Bitonality is usually considered dissonant to one degree or another; however, because the two tonalities involved in these chord mixtures are not perceived as dissonant by exponents of contemporary gospel, I have termed these mixtures *consonant bitonality*.

The question arises as to why B-flat/C, Em⁷/G-flat, and A-flat/B-flat are not considered "tall chords" or chords of the ninth, eleventh, and thirteenth. This is because in contemporary gospel, the bass voice has been dissolved so that the pianist/composer/arranger thinks of the treble portion of the keyboard as voice parts, and the bass as a "support," thus attaining two distinct harmonies. For example, B-flat/C could be realized as a C^{11}; however, the tones of the chord would be C-E-G-B-flat-D-F, while the only desired tones are C-B-flat-D-F. The gospel composers drop the E and G, build a triad on the B-flat, and write (or think) B-flat/C, since these two chords were originally "heard" and not an incomplete C^{11}.

The most constant bitonal chord in contemporary gospel music is one in which the bass tone is selected, and then supported by a chord in the treble clef, located one whole-step below it. If the bass tone selected is C, a B-flat chord would be placed above it. Other examples are: E-flat/F, F/G, and A-flat Maj 7/B-flat. When tall chords are employed or notated, all of the tones are used. In the printed version of Crouch's "Soon and Very Soon,"[43] he has employed and notated chords such as Gm^9 (b5) and C^9, while the printed and performed version of Walter Hawkins' "Be Grateful"[44] makes great use of the A-flat13.

In the popular version of a few years ago, "Give Me a Clean Heart" by Margaret J. Douroux[45] replaces the subdominant chord with a ii^7 over a tonic pedal in the climax of the first phrase.

Traditionally, the performer moved from I to V by inserting the V/V. Now progression I-V/V-I has been replaced so that the performer moves directly from I to V_6, while the progression IV-V-I, when employed outside of a cadence, has become:

$$IV-V^7-iii^7_{\substack{4\\2}}$$

Most cadential formulae in contemporary gospel avoid IV-V-I and substitute IV-flatIII-V-I or flatVI-flatVII-I.

While interior modulation is still rare, cadential modulation, generally involving third relationship, is becoming popular (for instance in Walter Hawkins' "Be Grateful"). This example also illustrates the possible demise of exclusive root movement by fifths in favor of root movement by seconds and the substitution of another chord for the tonic or home key in which a song has been rendered.

These harmonic innovations show that the greatest difference between traditional and contemporary gospel lies in the discovery and use of a harmonic vocabulary never before witnessed in Afro-American gospel music.

How has the audience reacted?

Congregational Response

Traditional gospel audiences have always come to a gospel concert seeking an extension of the church service: an opportunity to deliver spirit-generated ejaculations, such as "Amen," "Sing it," "You better sing it" and the like; to experience the prerequisite fainting; to shout and clap their hands. Such behavior is not the norm at a concert of contemporary gospel music. Where once a subtle, yet honest, vocal nuance was met with a spiritual evocation expressed through verbal and physical utterances of recognition and encouragement, such a nuance is now met with applause and a standing ovation. The style of singing, the stage deportment, and the dress of contemporary gospel singers discourage traditional kinds of behavior.

It has been my observation that congregational response during many contemporary gospel concerts consists of smiling, soft weeping, and clapping, most often on a primary, rather than a secondary beat; where a section of a song would have previously elicited a moan, shout, or vocal utterance, the audience response is only applause at concerts of contemporary gospel. While such behavior makes it possible to hear the singer's every nuance, it robs the audience of an opportunity to "participate" in the event. And participation is the essence of gospel.

While melody, rhythm, and lyrics have undergone little change in the transition from traditional to contemporary gospel music, harmony, accompaniment, vocal timbre, and background function have changed a good deal as performers are taking advantage of the great variety of musical resources now available. Traditional gospel distinguished itself by refusing to be influenced by many of the newer musical practices, particularly the newer harmonies and full battery of orchestral instruments. After all, Afro-American gospel music is *folk music* and as such is not expected to change rapidly or radically. Critics accuse contemporary gospel of being so rigidly arranged and rehearsed that it takes on a *slick* quality, not unlike that of Las Vegas acts. While such thorough preparation assures the listener of a well thought-out show, gospel singing and concerts are, in fact, an extension of the Black religious worship service and cry out for spontaneity—a quality seemingly absent from contemporary gospel.

While the holiness church always found comfort in using any musical instrument in the service of God, the "mainstream public" considered this "primitive," preferring the piano and organ. (Ironically, the public is generally unaware of the difficulty musicians had in introducing the organ into religious services in the United States.) In contemporary gospel, the entire orchestra is complementary and, at times, necessary to produce the contemporary sound. It would be almost impossible for a contemporary gospel group to render a concert using only the piano and organ. As a matter of fact, the organ is a relatively unimportant instrument in contemporary gospel music for it has been replaced by the synthesizer.

For many years, secular music was greatly influenced by gospel music, adopting not only its singing and piano styles but also its group makeup and movements transformed into stylized dancing. Secular music adopted gospel's penchant for "getting in the *spirit*." Now, an opposite trend has taken hold. Contemporary gospel is incorporating the harmony, instrumentation, background sound and style, and dress of secular music. Many contemporary gospel singers perform in jeans and hats, instead of the choir robes and business suits traditional gospel singers wear. Just how far the influence of secular music extends in the future will be determined by gospel music lovers who make their desires known.

The distinction between *traditional* and *contemporary* gospel has not come about because gospel singers have advocated it. Rather, these labels are affixed by record producers and critics. Very often, the people who are being described have to read the record jackets and reviews to determine their status. Unfortunately, once they are aware of their labels, they feel compelled to match their styles to those labels to please their audiences.

The gospel music of the Black American community need not respond to such crass commercialism. Whatever external labels are imposed, let us hope each new and different gospel singer continues to carry the "good news."

NOTES

1. Among the most significant of these are "Can Gospel Rock?" (*Jet* Magazine, April. 26, 1976), "Andrae Crouch, New King of Pop Gospel" (*Sepia* Magazine, December 1976), "Contemporary Gospel Music: Sacred or Secular?" (*First World*, January/February 1977, reprinted in *The Black Perspective in Music*, Spring 1979), "New Signs On The Gospel Highway" (*The Nation*, May 10, 1980), and "Some Perceptions of Gospel Music," (*Black Perspective in Music*, vol. 10, 1982).

2. For a discussion of standard devices employed in gospel music, see Boyer (1979: 22-58).

3. Light LS-5760.

4. *Soulfully: Andrae Crouch* Light LS-5581.

5. *This Is Another Day: Andrae Crouch* Light LS-5683.

6. All transcriptions are by the author. Musical scores to all examples may be secured from Martin and Morris, Inc., 4312 S. Indiana Avenue, Chicago, Ill., 60653; Lexicon Music, Inc., Waco, Texas, 76701.

7. The use of the term "chromatic" means intervals (tones) which are not common to the standard major or minor scales, producing a melody with as many as twelve different tones as opposed to the standard "diatonic" melody of only seven tones.

8. This B-flat is, in fact, the seventh of the subdominant chord which, several years earlier, would have supplied the harmony for that tone, rather than the bVI^7 which had become a chord in gospel music by the time this song was composed in 1965.

9. *Live in London*. Light LS-5602.

10. *Walter Hawkins: Love Alive II*. Light LS-5735.

11. *Live in London*. Light LS-5602.

12. *Together*. HRB Music and Daydream Productions DD-1010 (LCS-514). Lexicon Music.

13. *Take Me Back*. Light LS-5637.

14. *Love Alive II*. Light LS-5735.

15. Light LS-5763.

16. *The Henry Jackson Company*. Stax GTS-2719.

17. *Walter Hawkins: Love Alive II*. Light LS-5735.

18. Score available from Lexicon Music Inc./Crouch Music and on recording, *This Is Another Day*. Light LS-5683.

19. *Jackson Southernaires: Too Late*. Malaco 4357-B.

20. *The Original Roberta Martin Singers: Here This Sunday*. Kenwood LP-480.

21. *Mahalia*. Columbia CL-2452.

22. *Precious Lord*. Columbia KG-32151.

23. *Take Your Troubles to Jesus*. The Boyer Brothers. Savoy MG-14143.

24. *Edwin Hawkins Singers*. Buddah BDS-5070.

25. *Andrae Crouch: Take Me Back*. Light LS-5637.

26. *Andrae Crouch: Live in London*. Light LS-5717.

27. Ibid.

28. *I'll Be Thinking of You*. Light LS-5763.

29. *Love Alive II*. Light LS-5735.

30. For illustration, the reader should listen to *Walter Hawkins: Love Alive II*. Light LS-5735.

31. *I Don't Feel No Ways Tired*. Savoy DBL-7024.

32. The reader is referred to "I Know the Lord Will Make a Way, Oh Yes, He Will" a composition featured by Eugene Smith of the Roberta Martin Singers, but not associated with any particular artist. The song was featured mainly by male quartets, but some people may remember an old recording of Albertina Walker's, on States Records No. 128, recorded in 1952.

33. *Historical HLP-34* (1928).

34. Light LS-5763.

35. *James Cleveland: Live at Carnegie Hall*. Savoy 7014.

36. *James Cleveland: A New Day Dawn*. Savoy SGL-7035.

37. *The Henry Jackson Company*. Stax GTS-2719.

38. Light LS-5602.

39. *Take Me Back* Light LS-5637.

40. *Love Alive* Light LS-5686.

41. *Love Alive II* Light LS 5735.

42. The performed version is available on the album *Edwin Hawkins: Let Us Go into the House of the Lord*. Pavillion BPS-1001.

43. Score available from Lexicon Music Inc./Crouch Music, 1976.

44. *Love Alive II*. Light LS-5735.

45. *Give Me a Clean Heart*. Savoy 14270.

REFERENCES

Doerschuk, Bob. 1979. "Backstage with Andrae Crouch." *Contemporary Keyboard* (August).

Boyer, Horace C. 1979. "Contemporary Gospel Music: Characteristics and Style." *The Black Perspective in Music* (Spring).

Etherington, Charles L. 1965. *Protestant Worship in Music*. New York: Holt, Rinehart and Winston.

The Black Gospel Music Tradition: A Complex of Ideology, Aesthetic, and Behavior

Scholarship in Black gospel music has already succeeded in confirming the significance of this tradition within the domain of Black religion. As a genre strongly entrenched in the Black church tradition, gospel music still attracts many supporters who identify with it as much for its expression of Black values, experiences, and beliefs as for its pure religious content. In other words, a member of a Black culture whose aesthetic frame of reference lies outside the boundaries of the religious tradition can nonetheless identity with and respond to the same significant aspects of gospel performance as Black Christians do.

This study aims to delineate the concepts that shape and regulate gospel music. As the analysis will show, gospel music is far more than a mere musical genre; it is a music complex, which embodies ideology, aesthetic, and behavior (see figure 7.1).

Primarily, two church populations provide the data for this analysis: Mercy Mission Apostolic Church in Bloomington, Indiana —a small predominantly female congregation—and Grace Apostolic Church in Indianapolis, a five-hundred member collective situated in a large urban center. As part of my doctoral work (Burnim 1980), I conducted intensive research at Mercy Mission from February through May 1976, and at Grace from March through August 1979. I compared and contrasted the data from these two settings and then compared them with information I gathered during short-term field excursions to: (1) the monthly

Figure 7.1
The Black Gospel Music Complex

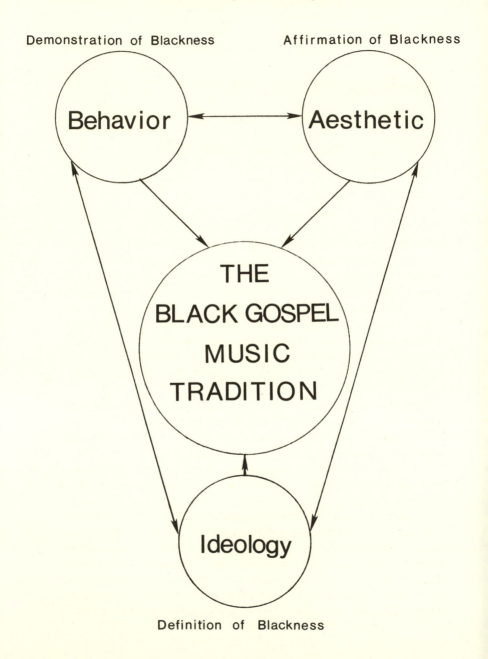

Demonstration of Blackness

Affirmation of Blackness

Behavior

Aesthetic

THE
BLACK GOSPEL
MUSIC
TRADITION

Ideology

Definition of Blackness

Federation of Choirs in Teague, Texas (June 1979); (2) The Twelfth Annual 20,000 member James Cleveland Gospel Music Workshop of America, with its 2,000 voice mass choir in New Orleans (August 1979); (3) the annual National Black College Gospel Choir Workshop in Atlanta, Georgia (November 1978); and (4) the meeting of Pentecostal Assemblies of the World (PAW), the national Black Pentecostal body, in New Orleans (August 1979). This methodology enabled me to establish behavioral and conceptual norms which govern gospel tradition, norms that have implications beyond a single group, locale, or denomination.

Whereas previous studies of gospel music have taken either the song or the musical system as the basic analytical frame, my investigation bases itself on the actual performance event. I elicited from tradition and nontradition bearers critiques of videorecorded performances. I used the feedback interview—a technique that triggers the interviewer's recall by having the interviewer view or listen to tapes of performances previously recorded. Any questions that were generated by these experiences, I explored further in informal discussions and personal interviews. In this way, I determined the significant aspects of gospel music performance.

As many students of Black religion have pointed out, the Black church has historically represented the one and only cultural institution which enabled Black people to express themselves freely and without constraint (Mays and Nicholson 1933; Edwards 1970; Lincoln 1974; Clark 1967; Nelsen and Nelsen 1975). It was in the context of religion that the Negro spiritual was created—a personal and collective response to the slave experience in the United States. When Blacks migrated to urban centers in the North and South during the aftermath of World War I, they created gospel music, a music which reflected their changing ideas and ideals in this new sociocultural environment (see Ricks 1960: 131-143; Levine 1978: 180-189).

The development of gospel music, however, does not represent a complete break with the musical past; rather it is a juncture in an ongoing Black music continuum. In its earliest stages, gospel music, through the innovative use of instrumental accompaniment, represented both a reinterpretation and an expansion of existing musical traditions. In fact, many of the standard gospel songs so characteristic of congregational singing in Black churches today are identical to the Negro folk spiritual, both in form and in function. One such example is "I'm a Soldier in the Army of the Lord," popular in the repertoires of both Mercy Mission and Grace Apostolic. Pearl Williams-Jones (1970: 206) identifies this song as a "holiness shout," created sometime around 1910. Like folk spirituals, it is characteristically accompanied by hand-clapping and the "holy dance" and sung in a call/response pattern:

Call: I'm a soldier

Response: In the army of the Lord

Call: I'm a soldier

Response: In the army.

Call: I believe I'll die

Response: In the army of the Lord

Call: I believe I'll die

Response: In the army.

Because of its demonstrative delivery style and instrumental accompaniment, which closely parallels that of Black secular musics, virtually all Black denominations except the Pentecostals initially scorned and rejected gospel music as "worldly." Mahalia Jackson, who was a renowned gospel contralto, bears out this point in recounting her initial experiences singing gospel music in Chicago during the late twenties and early thirties:

In those days the big colored churches didn't want me and they didn't let me in. I had to make it my business to pack little basement-hall congregations and store-front churches and get their respect that way. When they began to see the crowds I drew, the big churches began to sit up and take notice (Levine 1978: 183).

Thanks to Mahalia Jackson's persistent efforts and those of other gospel pioneers like Thomas Dorsey and Sallie Martin, who together cofounded The National Convention of Gospel Choirs and Choruses during the 1930s, gospel is now the music that distinguishes every major Black denomination in the United States. As Joseph Washington (1973: 78) indicates, "few Black congregations today do not engage in gospel music, even if only by inviting special groups for special occasions."

But despite the increasing interest in and continued development of gospel music, there are still those, both white and Black, who view gospel music with disdain. Washington (1973) contents that "those Black churches that see gospel music as 'low culture' are generally members of communions in which the number of Blacks is small." It is likely that Blacks who disdain gospel have fallen victim to the traditional white attitude that is still common today.

As a result of these attitudes, gospel music has been greatly misunderstood throughout its history and, therefore, gone largely unheralded. Yet, as my data will show, gospel music is indeed an important form of expressive behavior, having "sequence, pattern, and process" (Danielson 1977: 4). In order to understand how these components are conceptualized and manifested, however, it is crucial to view the gospel tradition within a Black perspective —that is, as a medium created by Blacks, for Blacks, and subject only to meaningful criticism and analysis from the vantage point of a Black aesthetic.

IDEOLOGY

Students of the Black church agree that prior to the mid-eighteenth century, relatively few Blacks were converted to the Christian faith (see Frazier 1963: 15; George 1973: 10-11; Jones 1971: 9; Woodson 1945: 1-19). There are several reasons: (1) slaveowners feared that the doctrines of love and equality, fundamental to the Christian faith, would undermine the institution of slavery; (2) English-speaking missionaries found it difficult to communicate with African slaves, who were fluent only in their foreign tongues; (3) only a relatively small number of missionaries took an active interest in the conversion of slaves; and (4) the slaves strongly preferred their own gods and wanted to maintain their own religious rites and practices (Epstein 1977: 101-103).

Most writers contend that it was not until the Second Great Awakening (1795-1840) that proselytizing proved successful among a significant number of Black slaves. By this time, many denominations were openly preaching accommodation to the institution of slavery. Planters, therefore, no longer feared Christianity; rather they began to view it as a viable tool for exerting social control over their slaves (Genovese 1974: 186).

As pro-slavery sentiments became more firmly entrenched in the South, racism against Blacks manifested itself more and more strongly and openly in the North. While Joseph Washington (1973: 63) talks of an intensification of efforts by Methodists and Baptists on the southern frontiers to convert Blacks to Christ, Winthrop Jordan describes for the same period an intensification of racially segregated institutions throughout the United States. According to Jordan (1974: 162) "the trend toward racially separated churches was well under way in the 1790s." Indicting American Christianity and what he called a professed American commitment to "life, liberty, and the pursuit of happiness," Jordan (1974: 159) reports: "At least two independent Negro congregations had been founded in the South before the end of the war, but the rush of blacks into 'African' churches began in the same year and in the same city as the Constitutional Convention."

Jordan is referring here to the creation in 1787 of the Free African Society in Philadelphia. Indeed, the controversy surrounding the formation of the Society attests to the racist forces that permeated the very structure of the Christian church in America. The Society's founder Richard Allen refused to accept the treatment Blacks received at the St. George Methodist Church in Philadelphia. Allen, a minister who began his ministry at St. George's, attracted a significant number of Blacks to the Church. When the number of Blacks in the congregation was small, their movement was unrestricted, but as Allen began to draw large numbers of Blacks to the church, white church members proposed that Blacks be relegated to the church balcony (Southern 1971: 83; Woodson 1945: 63-64; Wesley 1935: 52-53). Rather than submit to this indignity, Richard Allen, Absalom Jones (who later founded the first congregation of Black Episcopalians), and the entire Black congregation withdrew their membership from St. George. In 1794, Allen founded the African Methodist Episcopal (A.M.E.) Church, which eventually severed all ties with the national, white Methodist governing body (Woodson 1945: 63-65; Wesley 1969: 78).

Two years later, another group of Blacks began the process of establishing independence—this time from John Street Methodist

Episcopal Church in New York City. By the year 1800, this collective had officially formed the African Methodist Episcopal Zion Church (Woodson 1945: 67-68).

The first African Baptist church was formed in Philadelphia in 1809 when Black members of the First Baptist Church sought a more congenial atmosphere in which to worship. Thus, the pattern of racial segregation in religious worship during the so-called Second Great Awakening was clearly established.[1]

It should be noted that the Black population responded to white discrimination with action rather than passive acceptance. Blacks consciously *chose* to form an independent Black church rather than be relegated to special pews in St. George Methodist Church. Blacks willfully *chose* to remove themselves from the First Baptist Church of Philadelphia so they would be free to worship in a manner suited to their own tastes and needs. Of even greater significance was the decision among founders of these independent churches to incorporate the word "African," or some designation of Blackness, into the titles of their churches. Theologian James Cone interprets this act as a statement by Blacks about their view of the world and God's involvement in it. He contends:

If they [Blacks] thought it important to define the meaning of their spiritual community by focusing on their racial identity, this meant they believed that either the God of Jesus Christ must meet them at the point of Blackness of their existence, or he is unrelated to reality as they know it to be. (Cone 1970: 248)

By affirming Blackness as "the primary datum of his humanity" (Cone 1970: 244), the African-American gained the power to reject the rites, beliefs, and values of the white society and, particularly, the white church. As a result, Black people were free to adopt an ideology that recognized the historical viability and dynamism of Black culture. Furthermore, this ideology was a continual reinforcement of Black cultural traditions, which represented the very antithesis of those traditions associated with the larger society. The creation of a separate Black church, then, was not merely a convenience for whites; it was a necessity for Blacks if they were to have a religious institution that met their own specific needs, reflected their own particular ideology, and had "relevance and dignity" for a people simultaneously a part of and apart from the larger American society (See Lincoln 1974: 3; Genovese 1974: 281).

Gospel music is a concrete example of how Blacks expressed their unique ideological perspective.

THE BLACK GOSPEL MUSIC AESTHETIC

An analysis of the data I compiled during my field experience yielded three primary areas of significance in Black gospel music performance:

1. Sound quality
2. Delivery style
3. Technique or mechanics of delivery

The operational validity of these three basic conceptual categories (see figure 7.2) is upheld by data from a variety of settings and locales. The concepts are supported further by accounts of performances in the literature on gospel music. The existence of each of these three conceptual components as an integral part of gospel indicates that gospel music is a multidimensional construct.

Sound Quality

Critics of gospel music hold the common misconception that because the predominate sound quality of gospel violates virtually every ideal associated with Euro-American vocal production, gospel music is, therefore, devoid of a rational system. Further, critics claim that those who insist upon performing gospel music are destined to destroy their voices and, consequently, ruin any chance of ever learning to produce tones correctly. When Mahalia Jackson decided in 1932 that voice lessons might provide the boost she needed to set her career in motion, she auditioned for the concert tenor, "Professor Kendricks." This was his reaction:

You've got possibilities, but you, young woman, you've got to stop that hollering. That hollering. That's no way to develop a voice, and its no credit to the Negro race. White people would never understand you. If you want a career, you'll have to be prepared to work a long time, to build a voice (Goreau 1975: 61).

Figure 7.2
Dynamics of Interaction in Black Gospel Music Performance

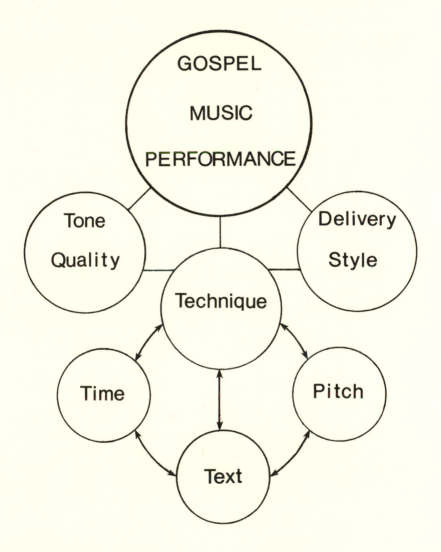

Fortunately for the gospel world, Mahalia Jackson's first lesson was also her last. She left the professor's house unintimidated and more committed than ever to singing in a style that had *cultural* relevance for her. The following was her response to the warning she received from Professor Kendricks: "I'm not studying about this high-class stuff! I'm not singing for white people! I'm singing in the church, for myself!" (Goreau 1975: 61).

Mahalia Jackson expresses well what many gospel music critics have continually failed to see: Gospel music is a product of Black culture. Just as the music of *any* culture is bound by its own qualitative standards, such is the case with the music of Black people in the United States. Gospel music symbolizes Blackness and has neither the intent nor the interest to reflect Euro-American norms and values.

When one attempts to impose the values of the Western European musical aesthetic on an audience of gospel adherents, the reaction is likely to be polite, but reserved. As one respondent states:

L: My God, you know, they [a Black congregation] will acknowledge you with awards, and listen and all that. And [you can be] all over the floor [as if to say,] "Ya'll see, I'm singing as high as I can." . . . And she [the singer] just finishes, just like that. It's no toting off dead bodies [shouting].[2]

When performances contradict the rules of the Black aesthetic, audiences respond accordingly. But when a performer demonstrates the knowledge and skill to maneuver and manipulate the principles of Black performance style, the presentation is immediately rewarded with resonant audience response. In two different feedback interviews covering a performance of the gospel "He Looked Beyond My Faults" at the 1979 Gospel Music Festival at Grace Apostolic, respondents initially commented on the *quality* of the singer's voice. For example, one said: "Oo, this girl can sing— her voice!" Another commented, "Crying time," as the singer began to moan.[3]

A concrete picture of the vocal quality Blacks desire and expect from performers is difficult to formulate because no one definition could encompass the multiplex possibilities. Over and over again, though, respondents indicated to me that the voice must transmit intensity, fullness, and the sense that tremendous energy is being expelled. The singer must convey complete and unequivocal absorption in the presentation, thereby *compelling* the audience to respond. Phrases commonly used by respondents to indicate that a singer successfully met this prerequisite include:

> "She's blowing!"
> "She's jamming; she can't *help* it!"
> "[The] girl is burning."
> "Now that's gettin' in it, boy."
> "She's tough."
> "Sing!"
> "She's gettin' down."[4]

When the expectations of the Black congregation or audience are met, performer and audience merge; they become one. The personalized interpretation of a given gospel selection generates a sense of ethnic collectivity and spiritual unity. The feelings of empathy which flow interchangeably from audience to performer are evident in the comments the respondents voiced about the same performance by the singer at Grace Apostolic Church:

> "The girl needs to sit down and rest a while!"
> "I guess after *that* song that's all you need to do."[5]

Lorraine Goreau (1975: 75) cites a quote from one member of the audience at a Mahalia Jackson concert, who was overwhelmed by the excitement generated during the performance: "That woman sing *too* hard; She going to have TB!"

Although the basis of sound quality is the communication of intensity and the observable release of energy, these effects can only be eloquently achieved through the manipulation of the principles of subtle shading and contrast. The performer must express emotion, but he or she must also prepare the audience properly for musical and emotional climaxes by alternating peak phrases with periods of relaxation. Herein lies the basis for extreme and often sudden dynamic vocal contrasts and the juxtaposition of different vocal textures so characteristic of gospel music. Note this critique

of the same singer's (Grace church) rendition of "He Looked
Beyond My Faults."

> See, I was watching for a pattern; I watched how she had a raspy sound;
> then she went into a real smooth, melodic type thing. Then she went right
> back into it, so I was trying to see if she was going to do it this time. I was
> waiting for her, and she said "Yap!" and got real percussive with it, you
> know. So I was just laughing.[6]

The gospel artist is expected to demonstrate versatility in producing a myriad of vocal sounds—yells, screams, shouts, moans,
grunts—all mechanisms through which the singer conveys the
totality of personal involvement in the performance. In the same
way, the instrumentalist, particularly the organist, is expected to
vary the tonal qualities which are produced by changing playing
techniques. To achieve the highly desirable percussive sound, it is
necessary to rely on a very flexible wrist (a distinctly different
technique from the one I was taught when learning to play the organ
during my undergraduate study in music at North Texas State
University). In order to make the instrument "talk"—to imitate the
voice (another admired gospel technique)—it is sometimes necessary to make adjustments on the instrument itself. The success
with which musical contrasts can be effected on the Hammond
organ makes this instrument one of the trademarks of gospel music.

Finally, the concern for tonal contrast is evident in the way
voices and instruments are combined. Much to the dismay of technicians on the "Ed Sullivan Show," Mahalia Jackson persisted in
her demands for organ and piano accompaniment, instead of full
orchestral accompaniment for her June 17, 1948, performance
(Goreau 1975: 153; Duckett 1972: 40-42). It is common to hear
instruments ranging from the vibraphone to the soprano saxophone used as accompaniments to gospel singing. Virtually any
instrument can contribute to the overall tonal complexity that is
sought in this musical tradition.

The concept of color contrast is also evident in the qualitative
differences among the voices in small gospel groups or ensembles.
Solos or lead singing parts may be exchanged frequently—even
within a single song—to highlight such contrasts. The desire to
achieve these contrasts is also the impetus behind a cappella singing
within any given gospel selection.

DELIVERY STYLE

Sound quality is really only the first step in the total gospel matrix. The most respected artists in the field not only possess a "good voice" but also have the ability to combine with that voice a culturally prescribed mode of presentation that affirms their immersion in Black culture. Equally important as *what* the performer communicates is *how* the performer communicates, that is, the physical mode of delivery. Gospel performance, as all other aspects of the religious ritual, demands total immersion of mind and body. The performer is expected to use every means available —hands, feet, face—to convey the all-consuming, compelling force of gospel music.

In the early stages of her career, Mahalia Jackson, in committing herself to the concept of total involvement, sometimes found herself the object of derision and criticism. When she was seventeen years old, a minister once denounced her from his pulpit, declaring "O shame! This shouting, and bouncing, and clapping [is] unseemly in church." Mahalia retorted unabashedly: "I am serving God! You read the *Bible*—you'll see right there in Psalm 47: 'O clap your hands, all ye people; shout unto the Lord with the voice of a trumpet.' I'm doing what the *Bible* tells me to do!" (Goreau 1975: 57).

The account Levine (1977: 184) cites of the same incident quotes Mahalia as continuing with:

How can you sing of Amazing Grace? How can you sing prayerfully of heaven and earth and all God's wonders without using your hands? I want my hands, . . . my feet, . . . my whole body to say all that is in me. I say, "Don't let the devil steal the beat from the Lord!" The Lord doesn't like for us to act dead. If you feel it, tap your feet a little—dance to the glory of the Lord.

Mahalia's defense of her mode of presentation highlights a central concept. Performance in Black culture symbolizes vitality, a sense of aliveness. Whether singer, instrumentalist, preacher, or conductor, the "performer" must be overtly demonstrative if a Black audience is to be convinced. Accordingly, bearers of the gospel tradition invariably describe the essence of gospel music with dynamic language: One "cooks," "burns," "tears up" or "gets down."

The performer's dynamic use of the body reflects the Black perception of music as a unification of song and dance. Choirs do not merely "walk in" randomly during a processional; they "march" into the choir stand, using synchronized movements. The movements may be as simple as the alternation of right and left feet (a march used by virtually all gospel choirs) or as complex as moving three steps forward and two backward, followed by a turn to the side and a waving of the arm.

Once in the "choir stand," the ensemble often moves in step with the music, beginning only when signalled to by the conductor. When the music has "jelled" and the group begins to "get into it," the director signals the group to start hand-clapping. Clapping patterns, like the processional movements, range from simple to complex. Groups most commonly incorporate the ♪♪ pattern, but the ♪♪♪ pattern is characteristic of 6/8-meter. Today's groups frequently employ ♪♪♪ but virtually any pattern that contributes to the complex layering of sound and the maintenance of tension is permissible. At its level of greatest expression, whether in choir or in congregational singing, gospel music incorporates a multiplicity of complementary, yet contrasting clapping patterns. When combined with foot-stomping and tambourine playing, these often produce an effect reminiscent of the West African drum ensemble. (See Boyer 1979: 31 for other examples of clapping patterns.)

Body motion, facial expression, and foot movements are all major contributors to the ultimate state of religious ecstasy, symbolized by the shout. It is in the shout that the unification of song and dance is most apparent.

The following comment by Nathan Hall, an informant in my 1980 study, reveals how sacred ritual behavior mirrors secular aspects of Black culture since it provides an avenue for individual expression. In fact, individual expression underlies every facet of this musical tradition, creating a medium for both unity and diversity.

Now I'm gon' tell you. I done seen 'em all now, and my church, it's like goin' to a dance. [You see] what dance is in style. Now they're not out there bopping and all that stuff here. They got their *own* dance they do. Like I know there's one fellow in our church, he's a deacon. And the kids in the choir call him 'Steps' 'cause that dude got some steps. He be spinning, splitting—but he ain't doing that to show off, though.[7]

Michael Woods (1979) a performer and a composer of gospel music and a Pentecostal, interprets the use of dance as one of the main distinctions between white and Black religious practice. He explains that dancing in the church is distinguished from "worldly" dancing only by intent, not by design. As he states:

Whites feel that they should just let the spirit overcome them. Blacks *dance* in the spirit because they got saved out of the disco. When you join the Black Pentecostal church, you don't stop dancing, you just change partners [from the devil to the Lord].

Concern for delivery style also manifests itself in the attire that gospel music performers choose. Choirs are exceedingly concerned about their outward appearance because they realize that the visual image they project precedes any auditory contact with the audience. For this reason, choirs choose robes that will distinguish them as a group. Both color and design are important; not only must the robes allow for flexibility of movement, but also the design must complement the flow of the choirs' movements.

The choice of color is not determined by any written liturgical prescription, as often is the case among whites; rather, color and style are purely a matter of personal taste. A particular overall color scheme is chosen for the members of the group. Then, color reversal or alternate design establishes contrast and reveals the group's hierarchical structure. For example, the Bishop's Choir at Grace purchased robes of rose and mauve in 1980. The women wore rose with mauve trim and pleats. The men's robes exhibited the reverse color pattern. The Minister of Music was further distinguished by stripes on the sleeves.

As most gospel groups, the Bishop's Choir has several different outfits, allowing the group to vary its appearance according to mood or occasion. Members of the Bishop's Choir first wore their new robes publicly during their 1979 Anniversary Concert; however, they did not put them on until the second half of the concert. In this way, the group demonstrated a clear-cut desire to create visual contrast in the performance. The change of outfits generated a sense of movement from the simple to the complex— from "good" to "better" to "best."

Technique: Mechanics of Delivery

At the heart of the Black aesthetic is the acceptance of and, more important, the expectation of individual interpretation or personalization of the performance (most commonly referred to as "improvisation"). In other words, even though a well-defined Black aesthetic frames the boundaries of gospel music performance, the principles of this aesthetic simultaneously generate variation, both from song to song and from performance to performance. The skill with which one manipulates the basic rules yet remains within the prescribed boundaries of acceptability determines the degree to which he achieves respect and admiration from other adherents to the gospel tradition. The listeners themselves are the final judges of the relative success of a performance and when a performer meets the challenge, their evaluation is both immediate and vocal.

In judging the technical aspects of a performance, the gospel tradition-bearers I interviewed referred to three basic factors: time, text, and pitch. These factors form the basis of a unified structural network, subject to constant interpretation and reinterpretation by individual performers. Through immersion in Black culture, a performer learns how to determine which structural, rhythmic, textual, and melodic units are potentially expandable, and then demonstrates this knowledge in a personal way during performance. There are a myriad of possible combinations, one of the main characteristics that makes gospel music such a vibrant tradition.

Time. The unique concept of time applies not only to rhythmic aspects of gospel performance but to structural elements as well. The entire Afro-American religious music tradition is based on the creative manipulation of expandable units of time. What appears as unsystematic and unstructured to the outsider is actually a well-conceived and well-executed concept of logically moving units within an organizational whole from one point in time to another.

For example, the Black Pentecostal worship services I attended completely discredit the "erratic" billing they so frequently receive. By the same token, though there is no formal "order of worship" printed in the weekly church bulletin at Grace, members of the congregation nonetheless have a clear-cut understanding of the standard worship format. Just as in gospel songs, there is a well-defined concept of which elements are fixed and which permit latitude for expansion or contraction.

The structures of both the worship service and the gospel song have built-in mechanisms for moving subtly from the simple to the complex. Traditionally, Black church services begin with periods of devotional prayer, testimony, and congregational song; later, they move to the choir processional and the singing of special selections. They then culminate with the sermon. In this way, time is effectively manipulated to build intensity. Likewise, a gospel song itself moves from the simple to the complex by gradually adding layers of hand-claps, instrumental accompaniment, and/or solo voices.

In order to allow for the element of individual interpretation and personalization, soloists and conductors use their knowledge of potential expandable units to lengthen a given gospel selection at will. The performer may choose to emphasize a specific word by repeating it over and over or, if particularly "in the spirit," may repeat entire sections of a certain selection or even add a vocal cadenza at the end of a song. The call-response structure, in which the chorus is a stable unit and the solo sections are highly variable, not only permits, but actually encourages, improvisations.

The gospel conductor exercises creative abilities for and understanding of a Black concept of time by extending the length of notes at climactic points, repeating phrases or sections of a song, signalling instruments to "drop out" temporarily or adding a reprise at the end of a song that has been especially well received. These possibilities may occur to the conductor at any given moment; the conductor communicates the desire to put them into effect by using a core of specialized signs and symbols that are familiar to the group. The spontaneity with which these options are projected make the critical difference between a performance which is simply well executed and one which is "inspired."

Time is further manipulated through the juxtaposition and layering of rhythms and through the effective use of tempo. Using the polyrhythmic concept, gospel music incorporates both vertical and horizontal time contrasts. Not only do various instruments play different rhythms, but soloists may continually shift rhythmic phrases, either by lagging slightly behind the accompanying instrument or by anticipating the beat. The Reverend James Cleveland, founder of the Gospel Music Workshop of America, brings this point home in his description of the intrepretative abilities of Aretha Franklin, Grammy Award winner: "She's such a thinker as she sings and she's not going to perform the same way twice, because of her extensive gospel background. You get little tones here and there to make you know it's the same song each night." (Lucas 1965:22)

In addition, time assumes linear prominence as varying rhythms are relegated to different parts of the body. Iris Rosa, a dance instructor at Indiana University, made this observation while viewing a videorecording of the Grace Apostolic Bishop's Choir:

That syncopation on the "Hallelujahs" has thrown me off. You almost have to move your body to keep the rhythm going. So you really have three distinct rhythms going—one in what you're saying [Hallelujah]; your body's keeping one movement, like the metronome; and then you have the clapping.[8]

Black audiences are not only aware of the complexities of these rhythmic combinations but, in fact, expect them—and thrive on them.

Text. Through the text of a gospel song, a performer communicates his understanding of Black survival in America and his awareness of the contribution religion has made to that survival. Expressing this point of view, one respondent commented: "In my choir, we learn the words. The song must mean something, or we wouldn't be singing it, you know. To put yourself into a song, you gotta live what you're saying."[9]

Whether old, like spirituals, or newly composed, songs are many times incorporated into the gospel tradition on the basis of their text alone. Words of a song are invariably personalized and thereby assume special meaning for each individual who participates in the performance event.

When a performer decides to manipulate time by repeating a phrase in a gospel selection, the performer must take into account both the musical phrase and the textual phrase; this is critical in achieving the desired effect. As one observer commented: "To me, the repetition has a hypnotic effect. As you repeat, you get off into it more and more."[10]

Once the peak experience of shouting is reached in the Black religious ritual, the climax is maintained through the music—often exclusively through the rhythm itself. To the uninitiated, it would appear that the text has absolutely no importance at this point. But, in fact, the text has already done its most significant part in producing the spiritual climax. As the large structural units of text (verses, choruses) are repeated, spiritual involvement intensifies. Thus, what appears to be a subordination or insignificance of text in gospel performance at climactic points may actually be a misunderstanding of a song's sequential development.

In Black gospel music, pitch is valued not as an absolute, but as an element of contrast. This contrast is achieved by juxtaposing voices of different ranges *or* by highlighting the polar extremes of a single voice. Pitch can be manipulated further with the use of bends, slides, melismas, and passing tones—literally any factor of melodic embellishment—in order to achieve the continuous change, extreme latitude, and personalization that characterizes gospel music.

The Black gospel music tradition is a very complex cultural system, which simultaneously transmits uniformity and contrast, collectivity and individuality, unity and diversity. There are definite, identifiable beliefs and practices associated with gospel music, which Blacks begin learning during childhood. Most important, however, is the Black aesthetic, which undergirds the gospel tradition and operates both as creative stimulus and as controlling mechanism.

Gospel music springs from a concrete conceptual base. It is not, as many in the past have contended, the mere feeble attempt by the "untrained" and "unlearned" to express themselves by whatever haphazard means possible. The principles at the foundation of gospel music form the cornerstone of all aspects of Black culture. Gospel is, indeed, a conglomerate of Black modes of speech, music, and dance, all under the influential veil of religion.

NOTES

1. For further accounts of the creation of separate Black churches, see Woodson 1945: 73-86; George 1973: 145.

2. Feedback interview with L. Davenport, N. Thompson, and J. Foster, Indiana University, Bloomington, IN, 17 October 1979.

3. Feedback interview 17 October 1979; feedback interview with K. Scott, N. Hall, C. Keys, and G. Middleton, Indiana University, Bloomington, IN, 19 October 1979.

4. Feedback interview 17 October 1979; feedback interview 19 October 1979; feedback interview with forty members of course A219 (Black Dance), Indiana University, Bloomington, IN, 6 December 1979, 14 December 1979.

5. Feedback interview 17 October 1979.

6. Ibid.

7. Feedback interview 19 October 1979.

8. Feedback interview 6 December 1979, 14 December 1979.

9. Feedback interview 19 October 1979.

10. Feedback interview 6 December 1979, 14 December 1979.

REFERENCES

Boyer, Horace A. 1979. "Contemporary Gospel Music." *The Black Perspective in Music* 7, No. 1 (1979), Pt. I, 5-11, Pt. II, 22-58; Pt. I rpt. *First World*, Jan.-Feb. 1977, 46-49.

Bryant, Margaret. 1979. Personal interview. 4 August 1979. Indianapolis, Indiana.

Burnim, Mellonee. 1980. "The Black Gospel Music Tradition: Symbol of Ethnicity." Ph.D. dissertation, Indiana University.

Clark, Kenneth. 1967. *Dark Ghetto 1965*; 2nd edition. New York: Harper and Row.

Cone, James H. 1970. "Black Consciousness and the Black Church." *Christianity in Crisis* (November), 244-50.

Danielson, Larry. 1977. "Introduction." *Western Folklore* 36, No. 1 (January), 1-5.

Duckett, Alfred. 1972. "I Remember Mahalia." *Sepia* 21 (April), 36-41.

Edwards, G. Franklin. 1970. "Black and White Americans Face Each Other." In *Racial and Ethnic Relations*, ed. by Helen MacGill Hughes. Boston: Allyn and Bacon, 27-36.

Epstein, Dena. 1977. *Sinful Tunes and Spirituals*. Chicago: University of Illinois Press.

Frazier, E. Franklin. 1963. *The Negro Church in America*. New York: Schocken.

Genovese, Eugene D. 1974. *Roll, Jordan, Roll*. New York: Pantheon Books.

George, Carol V. R. 1973. *Segregated Sabbaths: Richard Allen and The Emergence of Independent Black Churches, 1760-1840*. New York: Oxford University Press.

Goreau, Laurraine. 1975. *Just Mahalia, Baby*. Waco, Texas: Word Books.

Jones, Lawrence. A. 1971. "They Sought a City: The Black Church and Churchmen in the Nineteenth-Century." *Union Theological Seminary Review* (Spring). Rpt. in *The Black Experience in Religion*, ed. by C. Eric Lincoln. New York: Anchor Press, 7-23.

Jordan, Winthrop. 1974. *The White Man's Burden: Historical Origins of Racism in the United States*. New York: Oxford University Press.

Levine, Lawrence W. 1978. *Black Culture and Black Consciousness*. 1977; rpt. New York: Oxford University Press.

Lincoln, C. Eric. 1974. "Black Religion and the Black Church: Mode, Mood and Music—Humanizing the Social Order." In *The Black Experience in Religion*, ed. by C. Eric Lincoln. New York: Anchor Press, 1-3.

Lucas, Bob. 1972. "Gospel Superstar." *Sepia* 21 (May): 21-26.

Mays, Benjamin, & Joseph Nicholson. 1933. *The Negro's Church*. New York: Institute of Social and Religious Research.

Nelsen, Hart M., & Anne Kusener Nelsen. 1975. *Black Church in the Sixties*. Lexington, Kentucky: University Press of Kentucky.

Southern, Eileen. 1971. *The Music of Black Americans: A History*. New York: W. W. Norton.

Washington, Joseph R. 1973. *Black Sects and Cults*. 1972; 2nd ed. New York: Anchor Books.

Wesley, Charles H. 1935. *Richard Allen: Apostle of Freedom*. Washington, D.C.: The Associated Publishers.

Williams-Jones, Pearl. 1970. "Afro-American Gospel Music: A Brief Historical and Analytical Survey (1930-1970)." In *Development Materials for a One-Year Course in African Music for the General Undergraduate Student*, ed. by Vada E. Butcher. Project of Fine Arts Department Howard University, Washington, D.C.: U.S. Department of Health, Education and Welfare, 1970, pp. 201-19.

Woods, Michael. 1979. Telephone interview. November 9, 1979.

Woodson, Carter G. 1945. *The History of the Negro Church*. 1921; 2nd ed. Washington, D.C.: Associated Publishers.

Relationships Between Black Males and Females in Rhythm and Blues Music of the 1960s and 1970s

This paper is an exploratory investigation of the functionality of Rhythm and Blues music in Afro-American culture, specifically emphasizing the treatment of Black male-female relationships and familial formation in Rhythm and Blues music. Several phenomena, and in particular the rapid expansion in the number of Black single-parent families, have led to intensive scrutiny of the Black family by social scientists in recent years.[1] It is the contention of this writer that content analyses of Black Rhythm and Blues music are important complements to purely analytical research in the search for a comprehensive understanding of the dynamics of the Black family.

The general frame of reference employed here parallels that expressed by Leroi Jones, who suggests that ". . . if the music of the Negro in America, in all its permutations, is subjected to a socio-anthropological as well as musical scrutiny, something about the essential nature of the Negro's existence in this country ought to be revealed, as well as something about the essential nature of this country, i.e., society as a whole."[2] In a previous study, a foundation for the present investigation was established through a com-

Reprinted by permission of the Author and THE WESTERN JOURNAL OF BLACK STUDIES, Black Studies Program/Washington State University Press, Pullman, Washington, Vol. 3, No. 3 (Fall 1979), pp. 186-196.

parative study of the treatment of contemporary mate-sharing (polygamous relationships) among Blacks. In that study the content of interviews with Black women involved in polygamous relationships was compared with the treatment of such relationships in the lyrics of songs sung by Millie Jackson.[3] In contrast to that investigation, the present study will eschew detailed comparisons with the work of social scientists and concentrate instead on the articulation of two relatively distinctive pictures of Black male-female relationships which emerge from Rhythm and Blues.

The principal thesis which will be defended is that one perspective, roughly associated with the decade of the sixties, which attempts to extend the traditional American notions of romance and courtship portrayed in the popular media to the Black experience with little appreciation of the extent to which social, political, and economic forces can present barriers to romantic love for Blacks. Corresponding to this view is the idea that the nuclear family represents an ideal type tending toward stability. In contrast, it will be argued that in Rhythm and Blues music of the seventies, which projects similar themes, an appreciation of the realities of the Black experience would lead to a rejection of the assumption advanced in the sixties. However, a larger issue which will be addressed is the changing function of Rhythm and Blues music in Afro-American culture. In particular, it will be contended that largely because of technological developments contemporary Rhythm and Blues no longer displays intensive ties to the Black experience.

Prior to discussing these contrasting perspectives on Black male-female relationships, the writer will present a rudimentary framework for appreciating the role of Rhythm and Blues in Black culture in the next section. The third and fourth parts of this paper examine the view of Black male-female interactions reflected in the music of the 1960s and 1970s.

BLACK RHYTHM AND BLUES MUSIC
AND BLACK CULTURE

Historically, various Black musical formats have displayed a dual functionality affecting the relationship between Black people and the white American society. One of these functions has been the articulation of the socio-political thought of Blacks during a given era. Given the perpetual oppression associated with the Black experience in America, the explicit or implicit theme of much Afro-American music has been a collective protest for social change. This function of Black music has been clearly identified by several authors. As an example, Kofsky argues that, as a rule, Black music "will either anticipate or reflect the mood, concerns, and aspirations of Afro-Americans" (Kofsky 1970: 55). Similarly, Jones concludes that "the most expressive [Black music] will be an exact reflection of what the Negro himself is. It will be a portrait of the Negro in America at that particular time" (Kofsky 1970: 102).

At the same time, however, some of the most expressive forms of Black music have discouraged active protest against social oppression. This function has resulted from the provision of a means for a psychological adjustment that encouraged acceptance of the status quo and/or attributed misfortune to forces other than oppressive social structures. The work songs sung by Black slaves are one case in point. These songs shielded the psyches of the slaves by breaking the monotony of work. One result was that worker efficiency was increased, thereby contributing to the perpetuation of economic organizations using slave labor. The slave master recognized the importance of slave songs and often excused the song leader from other forms of work (Southern 1971: 153). This practice introduced an incentive for the work song to become co-opted and to lose its psychological adjustment function.

Another example, more directly relevant to the concern of this analysis, is provided by the Blues. Springer has suggested that the Blues "represented the secular side of a necessary form of release for Blacks, which had its religious equivalent in the spirituals and gospel songs" (Springer 1976: 279). Cone has argued that being able to use an artistic outlet for their troubles enabled Blacks to maintain a certain distance from those troubles (Cone 1972: 125). The picture of male-female relationships in the Blues ignores the social forces that operate to inhibit positive interactions. As will be shown, a similar myopia is reflected in the Rhythm and Blues music of the 1960s. The emphasis on the sexual dimension of male-female interactions in the Blues has its parallel in the Rhythm and Blues music of the 1970s. The absence of a sexual emphasis in the Rhythm and Blues music of the 1960s reflects a reintegration of the sacred and the secular, remedying a dichotomy that was institutionalized with the growth of the Blues.

In part, the decline in the popularity of the Blues reflected its declining functionality within the Black community given the new Black awareness of the 1960s and the emergence of the musical form which is the subject of this investigation. As Springer notes, "the emergence of soul music as the official vehicle of the new Black awareness . . . left the Blues with a depleted audience (Springer 1976: 286).

Other contemporary Black musical forms have also experienced a change in functionality as a result of separation from previous ties with mass Black social consciousness. As an example, jazz has lost much of its folk orientation and become much more of a classical art form. As Kamin notes, "a by-product of jazz becoming an art form . . . was that it no longer fulfilled its former social functions in the Black community" (Kamin 1978: 256).

The "social control" function of Rhythm and Blues music vis-à-vis the white society is not limited to the embodiment of characteristics of the Blues and gospel music. Social control is also exercised via the direct impact of the structure of the music industry and technological developments on the content of Rhythm and Blues music. The result is that economic gains are siphoned off to the white community by the dilution of the content of the music, thereby increasing its audience. Applying a Hegelian framework to describe the emergence of rock-and-roll music, Kamin suggests that following the appearance of the esthetic innovation of Rhythm and Blues in the early 1950s, eventually some modernists blended elements of traditional music with Rhythm and Blues to produce early rock and roll (Kamin 1978: 285). In Kamin's perspective this situation paved the way "for people from the traditionalist camp to form a more moderate synthesis (rock-and-roll) which is generally accepted, and there is a falling away of both extremes" (Kamin 1978). It seems appropriate, to a large extent, to brand this evolutionary process as a distortion of the expression of Black social consciousness because much of the stimulus producing the evolution came from the music industry. Kamin notes that "Rhythm and Blues was a product the major record companies couldn't control. . . . A major impetus for the changes was the industry's aim of reaching the widest possible audience with the most controllable product . . . it changed the lyrics (and) another important element that was lost in translation was the rhythmic organization that had made the original Rhythm and Blues so exciting. The only elements that passed into white culture were those which were not offensive, not too hard to duplicate, and not too foreign to white cultural perceptions" (Kamin 1978). Of particular importance to this investigation are the following observations by Kamin:

The eventual development of Uptown Rhythm and Blues, primarily by Atlantic and Motown records and their subsidiaries, can be seen as the end result of the processes, wherein producers for independent Rhythm and Blues labels learned to produce a formula pop music using Black artists acceptable to the pop market. (Kamin 1978)

In a similar vein Greil Marcus suggests that the dynamic of Motown (Black-owned record company) was the imposition of order "on the risky spontaneity of gospel music" (Marcus 1976: 88).

A principal argument of this analysis is that even the diluted and distorted expression of Black social consciousness in Black Rhythm and Blues music of the 1960s performed a unique social function in the Black community that has been lost in the music of the 1970s. Central to this argument is the hypothesis that, at least in respect of images of Black male-female relationships, writers and performers were able to exercise sufficient power to counter the distortive effects of commercial pressures in the 1960s. The sociopolitical climate of the 1960s, coupled with the prevalence of an integrationist ideology during the early years of the decade, led to an implicit acceptance of general societal values in regard to the desirable characteristics of male-female relationships, the dominance of the nuclear family, and the inevitability of the formation of a stable family unit. In particular, as will be seen in the next section, consistent with the American ethos Black Rhythm and Blues music of the 1960s projects a highly romantic and Platonic view of male-female relationships especially when economic and political forces did not impinge on familial formation and the stability of the familial unit.

This ideological perspective performed a social-control function similar to the ideology embodied in the Blues. Unlike the period during which the Blues gained popularity, it can be reasonably argued that the Civil Rights gains beginning with the 1954 *Brown* decision created a rational expectation that structural integration into the larger society was a real possibility. Moreover, the Rhythm and Blues music of the sixties was a collective product and not an individualized form of expression as was the Blues, attaching greater generality to the ideology embodied in it. In contrast, as will be shown in the fourth section, the changing political climate of the late 1960s and the 1970s, coupled with the pressures emanating from the music industry and technological developments, produced a view of Black male-female relationships that is questionable in terms of the extent to which it reflects the sentiments of the majority of the Black population.

BLACK MALES AND FEMALES IN THE 1960s: TOWARD AN IDYLLIC MYTH

The socio-political message embodied in Rhythm and Blues music of the 1960s was the joint product of the writer, producer, and performer. The collaborative effort that was involved, coupled with the popularity of a song as reflected in sales, certified a specific song as a legitimate expression of communal sentiment. The collective nature of the product makes it difficult to attribute the success of a message to any particular subset of the contributing persons. While the lyrics convey a good idea of the writer's intent, the additional dimension of the message added by the performer is hard to recount. Fortunately, in the case of singers who performed for Motown and its subsidiaries in the 1960s, recorded interviews are available which indicate the perspective which the artist brought to bear in interpreting particular songs.[4] In the case of the writer-performer-producer-artist, who may be considered in some respects to be an analog to the traditional Blues singer, the impact of particular individuals is easier to gauge.

No writer or performer had more impact on the image of Black male-female relations in the Rhythm and Blues music of the 1960s than William "Smokey" Robinson. The love ballads which he wrote and performed with the Miracles are classics and give credence to the view expressed by rock artist Bob Dylan that Smokey Robinson is the best poet in America (Marcus 1976: 81). To a large extent he was responsible for the idyllic view of Black male-female relationships which was projected. He indicates that during the early 1960s he was oriented toward sad songs dealing with love, an orientation consistent with the Blues tradition. An early example of the mystique which Smokey Robinson projected is provided by the lyrics of the song "I'll Try Something New."

The celebration of the Black female through an oath of undying loyalty was the standard Smokey Robinson style during the early sixties and is evident in songs written by Smokey, including "Way Over There" and "You've Really Got a Hold on Me." This same theme is projected as late as 1967 in the song "More Love," in which he promises "more love and more joy than age or time could ever destroy." As a writer for Motown and its subsidiaries, Smokey Robinson made the love ballad and the celebration of the Black female a recurring theme in Motown records. One example is the song "My Girl," performed by the Temptations.

The songs that Smokey Robinson wrote and produced for the female Motown artists also were celebratory in nature, with the obvious object of celebration being the Black male. In the 1964 song "My Guy," sung by Mary Wells, the notion of an unbreakable bond again appears. A metaphor identified with doctor-patient relationships was used by Smokey to create an analogous picture in the Marvellettes' song "You're My Remedy."

Smokey Robinson was, of course, not alone in purveying the Black love ballad in the 1960s. Curtis Mayfield also popularized this format, writing and performing on the ABC Paramount label. The lyrics of "I'm So Proud," performed by Curtis Mayfield and the Impressions, provide evidence of the celebratory theme. Other permutations of the love ballad by Curtis Mayfield include "Talking about My Baby" and "Grow Closer Together."

The celebratory theme was also evident in the records produced by smaller companies. The lyrics of a song, written by Gordon and Wilson and recorded on the Modern Records label by the Ikettes, entitled "I'm So Thankful," are an example. The theme of female devotion reached its epitome in a song written and performed by Barbara Mason on the Artist label entitled, "Yes, I'm Ready."

In the Rhythm and Blues music of the 1960s the source of the dynamic which brings Black males and females together was the perception of incompleteness held by an individual without a partner. The refrain from the song written by Holland, Dozier, and Holland, performed by the Four Tops on the Motown label in 1964, entitled, "Baby I Need Your Loving," illustrates this point.

This theme also emerged in the records produced by smaller companies as exemplified in the song written by Davis and Davis and sung by Emanuel Lasky on the NPC label entitled, "I Need Somebody" and in "You Were All I Needed," written by Van

McCoy and performed by the DC Playboys on the Arock label. Many of the songs performed by Jerry Butler on the Mercury label also projected this theme, including "Lost," written by Butler, Huff, and Gamble.

The ultimate result of a mutually reinforcing loving relationship in the Rhythm and Blues music of the sixties is marriage. Smokey Robinson suggests this in the lyrics of "What's Easy for Two Is So Hard for One," performed by Mary Wells. The need for both parties to contribute to the development of a loving relationship also comes across in the 1966 song performed by Martha Reeves and the Vandellas, entitled, "My Baby Loves Me." In a recorded interview, Martha Reeves indicates that she was originally attracted to this song because she had just undergone a difficult period with a boyfriend and the lyrics had special meaning to her. This experience provides an example of how the artist contributes explicitly to the particulars of the story embodied in the lyrics.

Writers of the sixties recognized that the road to marriage is not always smooth, and, in particular, there is competition for eligible males, but as expressed, for example, in "Keep Loving," written by Smith, Davis, and Milner and performed by Billy Stewart on the Chess label, true love will weather such storms and produce a viable matrimonial state. Moreover, one is immediately aware when true love has arrived as a result of the unique feelings that are generated, as suggested in the lyrics of the song "Heatwave" written by Holland, Dozier, and Holland and performed by Martha Reeves and the Vandellas on the Motown label, which had a beat reminiscent of the Charleston era. This view is also expressed in a number of other Motown songs, including "I Hear a Symphony," performed by the Supremes, "Ain't Nothing Like the Real Thing," written by Ashford and Simpson and performed by Marvin Gaye and Tammie Terrell, and "For Once in My Life," performed by Stevie Wonder and written by Miller and Murden. A recorded interview with the Supremes, in which they discuss the song "I Hear a Symphony," shows how Rhythm and Blues music was influenced by other musical forms in that they indicate that the idea for the song developed from their appreciation for other musical formats, and in particular classical music.

True love conquers all in the Rhythm and Blues music of the 1960s. It can obliterate class lines, as in Stevie Wonder's Motown hit, "Uptight Everything's All Right"; or it can break up tightly knit male peer groups, as for example in the song entitled "One by One," written by Rudy Clark and performed by James Ray on the Congress label. Not all relationships are, of course, true love, and a primary reason for the break up of what had initially appeared to be an unbreakable bond in the Rhythm and Blues music of the 1960s is the appearance of someone else who provides a closer approximation of true love. Competition for mates takes on a rather pristine character as a sort of neutral sorting device destined to achieve some optimal configuration of couples.

The problem which continually reappears is the failure of one of the two original lovers to realize that the relationship was not really true love. The relationship ceases primarily because the accommodations of the party who is still in love are insufficient to counteract the decline in emotional attachment of the other party. Several Motown songs explored the shattering psychological experience associated with the eventual realization that efforts to salvage the relationship are doomed to failure, including "Just Ain't Enough Love," performed by Eddie Holland and written by Holland, Dozier, and Holland, the Supremes' 1965 hit, "Stop in the Name of Love," written by Holland, Dozier, and Holland, the 1966 Temptations' classic "I Know I'm Losing You," written by Whitfield, Holland, and Grant, the all-time best-seller, "I Heard It through the Grapevine," performed by Marvin Gaye and written by Whitfield and Strong, and "Standing in the Shadows of Love," one of the premiere Four Tops songs written by Holland, Dozier, and Holland. An analogous picture emerges from several songs written by Curtis Mayfield and performed by the Impressions, including "I Loved and Lost," "Can't Satisfy," "She Don't Love Me," "You've Been Cheatin'," "I've Been Trying"; and Curtis Mayfield also projects this theme in a song entitled, "It Ain't No Use," sung by Major Lance.

Terminating a love affair is portrayed as being a very difficult and trying experience even if one knows that the other party has found someone else, as in "You Keep Me Hanging On," performed by the Supremes, and even more clearly in the song written by Curtis Mayfield and performed by Walter Jackson on the Okeh label entitled, "It's All Over."

The party who might be described as the victim may grieve

temporarily as in the Fifth Dimension's "One Less Bell to Answer," contemplate extreme action as in the Marvelettes' "Locking Up My Heart," or develop a perception that total detachment from society has occurred as in Jimmy Ruffin's "What Becomes of the Broken-hearted"; but generally when all is said and done, there is always someone else out there to pick up the pieces. The Four Tops' song, "Reach Out For Me," written by Holland, Dozier, and Holland, is an example of the assurance provided to a distraught ex-lover that comfort is available. In a recorded interview Levi Stubbs, lead singer for the group, indicates that the Four Tops were able to project the message of the song effectively because it dovetailed neatly with their personal experiences, again emphasizing the mass base for the themes which emerged during the 1960s.

Breaking up is easier for the party who has found someone else if a prolonged separation from the original lover has ensued. If not, lingering love may inhibit the development of a new relationship, an idea conveyed in Martha Reeves and the Vandellas' "Come and Get These Memories," and in the Supremes' "You Keep Me Hanging On." An early expression of this theme is found in the Tamla recording, "Strange I Know," performed by the Marvellettes and written by Holland, Dozier, and Gorman, and in the 1966 song performed by Martha Reeves and the Vandellas on the Motown label written by Holland, Dozier, and Holland entitled, "Jimmie Mack." It should be noted that both of these records were produced during the Vietnam era, in which a disproportionate number of Black males were drafted. It might be inferred that war, and in particular the Vietnam War, was an important cause of breakups between Black males and Black females.[5] This picture can, of course, be contrasted with the unbridled expression of loyalty in the song "Soldier Boy." An interesting comparison can be drawn between the combined themes of loyalty and implicit patriotism in "Soldier Boy" and one of the themes of "Color Him Father," a song performed by the Winstons and written by R. Spencer, recorded on the Metromedia label. Thus, when patriotism leads to the sacrifice of life, there is someone there to redeem the sacrifice. There is no conception of the relative scarcity of males in the Black community.[6] In fact, an implicit idea in the Rhythm and Blues music of the 1960s is that every female can find a true love, but she must avoid the subset of males who have no good intentions. Songs in this genre include the Marvelettes' "Playboy," written by Horton, Bateman, Holland,

and Stevenson, and "The Sly, the Slick and the Wicked," performed by the Lost Generation and written by Simon and Brownlee, recorded on the Brunswick label.

The song "Color Him Father" also highlights a number of additional themes which allow this writer to end the survey of the 1960s with a discussion of the view of family life which is projected. The importance of the Protestant ethic and Biblical convictions, the idolization of the child for the male parent, and the importance of education are all suggested in the lyrics of "Color Him Father."

It is important to note that this idyllic view of Black family life in the city is projected on top of an ambivalent picture of the viability of the Black family in the rural South. The most classic statement of the effects of Southern deprivation on Black family life is found in Jerry Butler's heart-render "Got to See If I Can Get Mommy (To Come Back Home)," written by Miller and McCoy and recorded on the Mercury label, which chronicles the despair experienced by a Black woman which drives her to leave her family and commit suicide.

Both "Color Him Father" and "Got to See If I can Get Mommy (To Come Back Home)" concretize the primordial theme of the American familial myth, the idea that male-female interactions invariably produce a monogamous marital relationship which lasts until death.

REALISM IN THE 1970s: A RESPONSE TO THE "BALL OF CONFUSION"

As indicated previously, one of the working hypotheses of this analysis is that there was an observable shift in the content of the themes relating to Black male-female relationships between the Rhythm and Blues music of the 1960s and that of the 1970s. Nevertheless, it must be acknowledged that the ideology described in the previous section developed a momentum of its own which has allowed it to survive in a slightly altered form. Consider, for example, the 1972 record performed by the Stylistics, written by Tom Bell and Linda Creed and recorded on the Avco label, entitled, "I'm Stone in Love With You," which displays direct parallels to Smokey Robinson's "I'll Try Something New," discussed at the beginning of the preceding section.

The basic difference between "I'm Stone in Love With You" and

"I'll Try Something New" is that the acts that the male is willing to perform as a testimonial of his love take on a materialist, earthy character in contrast to the flights of fancy in Smokey Robinson's ballad. The survival of themes of the 1960s Rhythm and Blues music has been accomplished principally, however, by the influx of artists with reputations established working with other musical formats into the contemporary Rhythm and Blues arena. There are, of course, exceptions as, for example, in the case of the song performed by the Commodores entitled, "Three Times a Lady," Al Green's sensual renditions of "Tired of Being Alone," and "Let's Get Married," but the influence of Jazz and Blues artists in perpetuating the 1960s themes cannot be overstated. A good example is provided by George Benson's "The Greatest Love of All," but the song, written by Gray and Marshall and recorded on CBS records, entitled, "Lady Love," performed by Lou Rawls, illustrates the point even more clearly. Despite the basic celebratory theme, realism intrudes as Lou Rawls thanks his lady for sticking with him through his "ups and downs" and through his acknowledgment that "it's not easy to keep love going smooth." A final example of the perpetuation of the basic themes of the 1960s music in the seventies by "converts" to the Rhythm and Blues format is the song performed by Roberta Flack and Donny Hathaway on the Atlantic label, entitled "The Closer I Get to You," with lyrics that point, in a manner highly reminiscent of the music of the 1960s, to the inevitability of the emergence of true love.

Few of the writer-performer-producers of the Rhythm and Blues music of the 1960s continued to explore the same themes in the 1970s. One who did is Stevie Wonder, who, in fact, extended the celebratory format to include the progeny of a viable Black male-female union—the Black child—in "Isn't She Lovely" and "Ebony Eyes."

The pressures which forced the writers, artists, and performers to abandon the old themes in the 1970s were numerous, with most of these pressures having their roots in the late 1960s. Most important was the fact that contradiction after contradiction assaulted the foundations of the integrationist ideology which had created the illusion that the American dream was within the grasp of the masses of Blacks. Instead, the Black community at the end of the 1960s was being subjected to another bitter dose of social-economic exploitation. This development itself became subject matter for song-writers and performers in the early 1970s, with the 1970 tune "Ball of Confusion," written by Whitfield and Strong and performed by the Temptations, leading the way.

In addition to the import of the societal pressures of the late 1960s, changes in lyric themes and their functionality also resulted from personnel changes within groups of artists and technological developments. As an example, "Ball of Confusion," discussed above, was reflective of the new format of the Temptations, neces-sitated by the departure of lead singer David Ruffin. The Temptations' transition began with "Cloud Nine," which, one of the group's members indicated in a recorded interview, represented an attempt to exploit the technology of psychedelic sounds and driving beats. Similarly, the song "Reflections," the first song which was released following the transition from the Supremes to Diana Ross and the Supremes, also had a psychedelic beat.

The ultimate result of this complex of pressure was to expose contradictions in the idyllic myth projected during the 1960s. The image of the hardworking father was attacked in the Temptations' "Papa Was a Rolling Stone." The myth of the city as the place where the American dream can be lived out was utterly destroyed in Stevie Wonder's "Living for the City." The difficulty of raising children comes out in Sly and the Family Stone's "Family Affair," the "Band of Gold" sung by Freda Payne, and "Going to Walk Away from Love," performed by David Ruffin, which raised the possibility, respectively, of marriages occurring without sufficient knowledge on the part of both parties to what it actually entails, and the refusal to make a complete commitment to another person. Breaking up is no longer a painful experience as expressed, for example, in Diana Ross's, "Remember Me."

As neatly as the Winston's "Color Him Father" synthesized all of the idealistic themes of the 1960s, David Ruffin's 1969 song "I've Lost Everything I Ever Loved," written by Bristoll and Kemp, exposed the collective fallacy inherent in the myth. In this song the protagonist is an orphan raised by his grandmother, after his parents are killed in a fire on the fourteenth floor of a housing project. Thus, in David Ruffin's song the death of one's parents does not lead to reintegration of the offspring into a new nuclear family as was the case in the Winstons' "Color Him Father." Moreover, the way in which the protagonist's parents died in "I've Lost Everything" conveys the idea of death being unnecessary and without justification in contrast to the patriotic death of the original father in the Winstons' song. At the age of ten, following his grandmother's death, his only friend is his dog, Jeff. There is no new family for him with a grinning male face to guide him. Nevertheless, he is able to attend college where he finds a girl, whom he thinks is his true love. Her parents refuse to sanction the relationship, and the love affair ends, providing the final shattering blow to his attempts to escape the structural violence waged against him. His formal education is not the liberating force which it was projected to be in "Color Him Father." The themes of "I've Lost Everything I Ever Loved" reflect the experience of many Black males from central city environments following the opening up of predominantly white colleges to Black students in the 1960s who were unable to cope with the new environment without the support of the Black female.

The most extensive attack was made on the idea that a strong underlying sense of community existed that mitigated against intense cutthroat competition for mates and respected Black womanhood and the sanctity of the marital state. One result was that the victimization of the Black female by the Black male becomes a recurring theme in the Rhythm and Blues music of the 1970s. Nowhere does this theme emerge more clearly than in the 1972 O'Jays song, "Backstabbers," written by Huff, McFadden, and Whitehead.

Other examples of the sexual exploitation theme are provided by "Me and Mrs. Jones," performed by Billy Paul, the Ohio Players' "Sweet Sticky Thing," and the Commodore's "Brick House." In the first song, although there is no explicit sexual reference, marital infidelity is treated with no more than a passing reference to the conflict in values which such relationships may exacerbate, which is still more consideration than appears in Rufus Thomas's "Who's Making Love?" In contrast to the music of the 1960s, the latter two songs celebrate the Black female in a highly suggestive manner, with the implicit theme that the basis of a relationship is primarily the sexual attraction of the two parties, a theme which becomes embedded in the disco format of Johnnie Taylor's "Disco Lady."

There are two reactions to the sexual exploitation theme found in the Rhythm and Blues music of the 1970s. The first is an attempt to implore the parties in such relationships to cease and desist from exploitative behavior. Illustrative of this direction is a song written by Mitchell and Ivey and performed by Bobby Womack entitled, "If You Can't Give Her Love." Another example of this theme, but directed toward the Black female, is provided by Betty Wright's "Girls Can't Do What the Guys Do," written by Reid and Clarke. The rationale for this reaction is provided in a song performed by the Persuaders entitled, "Thin Line Between Love and Hate," which raises the prospect of retaliatory violence by the Black female against psychological, emotional, and physical abuse by the Black male.

The second response to the theme of exploitation of the Black female has been to portray the Black female as having developed psychological adjustment mechanisms which allow her to practice a parallel form of exploitation. The perspective that females bring to bear in evaluating liaisons and potential relationships with males in the music of the seventies differs markedly from the male focus on sexual attractiveness. In particular, females are increasingly projected as taking a highly pragmatic line in this regard, applying particular scrutiny to the male's capacity to provide material support. This viewpoint is articulated, in respect to cohabitation between unmarried partners, in the monologue that preceded Marlena Shaw's remake of the classic: "Go Away Little Boy." In the case of mate-sharing involving a married male and wife and mistress, in her early "concept albums," Millie Jackson conveyed the idea that sexual/emotional and pragmatic considerations intertwine to make such triangular relationships unstable. Buoyed by commercial success, however, her later albums endorse and celebrate such relationships. One of the progenitors of this particular theme was Betty Wright's 1971 song "Clean Up Woman," written by Reid and Clarke.

There are more disturbing themes that are associated with this second type of response to the sexual exploitation theme, however. In the song "Babysitter," a sixteen-year-old babysitter captures the affections of her employer's husband. Thus, the picture of Black male-female relationships in the Rhythm and Blues music of the 1970s had reached the point where adolescent females were not celebrated as Stevie Wonder would hope, but had instead become full-fledged competitors for the mates of older, mature women. It was virtually predetermined that this theme would emerge in an environment characterized by increasing numbers of adolescents bearing children out-of-wedlock, as depicted in Diana Ross's "Love Child."[7] The song performed by La Belle entitled, "Lady Marmalade," which is a far cry from the standard style of the group Patti La Belle and the Blue Bells of the 1960s, totally reverses the sexual exploitation theme. This record explores the world of a New Orleans streetwalker and the lasting memories which she leaves with a particular John. As La Belle hammers home the refrain, the listener is forced to ponder what this message has to say about the emerging configuration of Black male-female relationships.

In Hegelian terms, the two responses to the resurgence of the theme of sexual exploitation of the Black female in the Rhythm and Blues music of the 1970s can be characterized as thesis and antithesis. What may be an emergent synthesis is suggested in the song written and performed by Roberta Flack entitled "Why Don't You Move In with Me?"

There is an implicit value system embedded in the lyrics of "Why Don't You Move in With Me?" which emphasizes the need for mutual respect on the part of Black males and females that is not defined by traditional American norms in the face of socioeconomic pressures that constrain the structure of male-female relationships. Many would argue that the proliferation of this theme in contemporary Rhythm and Blues music would be a welcome development. Unfortunately, however, such a development does not seem likely given the contemporary impact of external forces on Black music. Instead, a more probable result is the continued growth of the sexual exploitation theme as a result of the impact of general societal values and technological developments. As April Reilly (1973: 137-138) notes, the use of electronic enhancement and derivation techniques has created a type of artificial Rhythm and Blues sound that is designed to appeal to the ear through the application of principles from psycho-acoustics and electronic music synthesis. The result is that modern music is increasingly "born" in the control room of a studio rather than representing the formalization of a folk articulation. In addition, as stated by noted musician Donald Byrd, the current structure of the music industry is such that "music is given its direction by non-creators as well as non-musicians," with the long-run effect that the artist's creativity is destroyed and his or her concern becomes "not straying from a code of acceptance" determined by "profit considerations" (Byrd 1978: 34).

The impact of modern technology and the structure of the music industry on Black Rhythm and Blues is producing an altered relationship between the music, writers, and performers and the Black community. In particular, it appears that there will be less chance in the future that Black Rhythm and Blues will be as good a barometer of shared perspectives in the community as had been the case in the past. With the exception of a few independent writer-producer-artists, e.g., Stevie Wonder, the control of such technologies is in the hands of large commercial concerns with little vested interest in the content of the studio output. This means that the potential is increasing for the "marketing" of values by such concerns through the medium of Rhythm and Blues. The potential implications of such a situation are mind-boggling. To the extent that people accept the proposition advanced by Ben Sidran that "music is not only a reflection of Black culture, but to some extent, the basis on which it is built," and further, that individuals appreciate the over-arching importance of the family in any culture, it is imperative that necessary steps be taken to ensure that the social commentary on Black male-female relationships contained in Black music again displays a direct correspondence to the feelings and aspirations of its constituency.[8]

NOTES

1. The proliferation of material examining the Black family is evidenced by the 386 entries included in Davis (1978).

2. Cited in Kofsky (1970: 102).

3. James B. Stewart, "Perspectives on the Changing Configuration of Black Families from Contemporary Soul Music: The Case of Millie Jackson," *Phylon*.

4. These interviews are contained as introductions to the songs included in the album, *The Motown Story*, Motown Records, 1970.

5. The fact that a disproportionate number of Black males served in the Armed Forces during this period has been noted in Moskos (1973: 94-106).

6. A seminal investigation of the scarcity of Black males is found in Jackson (1971: 30-41). See also Stewart and Scott (1978: 8-92).

7. Examples of studies which have investigated this phenomenon include Furstenberg (1970: 52-55); and Moore and Caldwell (1976).

8. Sidran (1971), cited in Byrd (1978). Byrd calls for a general movement to recapture the direction of Black music. Consistent with this call, this research constitutes a sub-component of a broader research project examining changes in the social-political thought embodied in Rhythm and Blues music and its derivatives.

REFERENCES

Byrd, Donald. 1978. "Music Without Aesthetics: How Some Non-Musical Forces and Institutions Influence Change in Black Music." *The Black Scholar*. July-August.

Cone, James. 1972. *The Spiritual and the Blues*. New York: Seabury Press.

Davis, Lenwood G. 1978. *The Black Family in the United States*. Westport, Conn.: Greenwood Press.

Furstenberg, Frank. 1970. "Premarital Pregnancy Among Black Teen-agers." *Trans-Action 7*.

Jackson, Jacqueline. 1971. "But Where Are the Men?" *The Black Scholar*. December.

Kamin, Jonathan. 1978. "Parallels in the Social Reaction to Jazz and Rock." *The Black Perspective in Music 3*.

Kofsky, Frank. 1970. *Black Nationalism and the Revolution in Music*. New York: Path Press, Inc.

Marcus, Greil. 1976. *Mystery Train: Images of America in Rock 'n' Roll Music*. New York: Dutton, E. P.

Moore, Kristin, and Steven B. Caldwell. 1976. "Out-of-Wedlock Child-bearing." *The Urban Institute*. September.

Moskos, Charles C. 1973. "The American Dilemma in Uniform: Race in the Armed Forces." The Annals of the American Academy of Political and Social Science 406.

Reilly, April. 1973. "The Impact of Technology on Rhythm 'n' Blues." *The Black Perspective in Music 1*.

Sidran, Ben. 1971. *Black Talk*. New York: Holt, Rinehart and Winston.

Southern, Eileen. 1971. *The Music of Black Americans*. New York: W. W. Norton and Co.

Springer, Robert. 1976. "The Regulatory Function of the Blues." *The Black Perspective in Music 4*.

Stewart, James B., and Joseph W. Scott. 1978. "The Institutional Decimation of Black American Males." *The Western Journal of Black Studies 2*.

The Heavy Blues of Sterling Brown: A Study of Craft and Tradition

Sterling Brown's poetry may profitably be studied, and his achievement precisely assessed, by implicating his work in the stylistics of the Afro-American culture in which it is saturated. There are, of course, aspects of the poetry which can properly be studied within other parameters—the formal Anglo-American tradition found in "Vestiges," for example, or the tradition of Frost and Masters, Sandburg and Robinson. But it is within the dimensions of Afro-American expressive culture that one may perceive most clearly the originality and subtlety of Brown's work.

Of the varied forms of Black expressive culture, music is indisputably the most dramatic, moving, and pervasive; and of the many forms which the music takes, the most typical, the most potently charged is the blues. At one end of the spectrum the blues are sensual ditties of lost love and hard times. At the other end they resonate on the same frequency with the spirituals, but in a somewhat different space, where the burden of salvation is equally weighty but the hope comes chiefly from self. The blues, then, are a music and a poetry of confrontation—with the self, with the family and loved ones, with the oppressive forces of society, with nature, and, on the heaviest level, with fate and the universe itself. And in the confrontation a man finds out who he is, a woman discovers

Reprinted from *Black American Literature Forum* 14 (Spring 1980), 32-44 (© The School of Education, Indiana State University).

her strengths, and if she is a Ma Rainey, she shares it with the community and in the process becomes immortal.[1]

The hallmark of Sterling Brown's poetry is its exploration of the
bitter dimension of the blues, which he links with a view of human-
kind that he shares with writers like Sandburg, Frost, and Edwin
Arlington Robinson. Their influence helps to catalyze the poet's
work without diluting it, and he extends the literary range of the
blues without losing their authenticity. When he employs other
folk forms such as the ballad, the "folk epic," the "lie," and the
song-sermon, he does so with complete confidence, not only in his
skill but in his models, both literary and folk. The literary models
merely confirm what he already knows from the folk: that these
forms embody a way of life that is valid and valuable.

Although most of the poems in *Southern Road* are not blues as
such, they are suffused with the blues tradition.[2] Indeed, one can
make the case that the entire volume is an extended treatment of the
blues mood and spirit, that each of the sections of the book presents
facets of the Black experience which evoke the world view and feel
of the blues. Even the last section of the book, "Vestiges," so named
because it contains poems written in the poet's earlier manner, in
the formal measures of the English poets, is caught up in this spirit
by virtue of its placement and its elegiac tone. Earlier in the book,
however, there are a number of poems which suggest a significant
range of the blues spectrum, although they are not written in blues
form.

"Kentucky Blues" is an example. It is blues-like chiefly in its
aphoristic imagery and its vernacular verve, as in the following
stanza:

> Women as purty
> As Kingdom Come,
> Ain't got no woman
> 'Cause I'm black and dumb.

In a poem like "Riverbank Blues" the emphasis is on the blues
mood rather than form. The mood is established in the first stanza:

> A man git his feet set in a sticky mudbank,
> A man git dis yellow water in his blood,
> No need for hopin', no need for doin',
> Muddy streams keep him fixed for good.

And the entire mood of seductive indolence is created through a description of the riverbank. There is an undertone of threat and danger which one associates with blues about the forces of nature:

> Towns are sinkin' deeper, deeper in de riverbank,
> Takin' on de ways of deir sulky Ole Man—
> Takin' on his creepy ways, takin' on his evil ways,
> "Bes' git way, a long way . . . whiles you can."

Two things stand out about this poem which justify its title: the mood created by the description, and the reaction of the persona. Blues, I observed earlier, are a music and a poetry of confrontation, and here the challenge to the persona is despair, which the poet presents in the personified river, where the persona

> Went down to the river, sot me down an' listened,
> Heard de water talkin' quiet lak an' slow:
> "Ain' no need fo' hurry, take yo' time, take yo' time . . ."
> Heard it sayin'—"Baby, hyeahs de way life go . . ."

The entire poem is related to traditional situations and imagery in blues poetry, as in the following:

> I'm goin' to the river
> I'm gonna buy me a rockin' chair
> If the blues overtake me,
> I'm gonna rock away from here.

But the crucial thing is the reaction—the heroic underpinning of the blues which so appeals to Brown and which merges in his poetry with the theme of the common man in the tradition of Whitman and Twain. As the man watches the slowly rolling river, something beside him

> . . . rared up an'say,
> "Better be movin' . . . better be travellin' . . .
> Riverbank'll git you ef you stay . . ."

"Riverbank Blues" serves to remind us that the blues are not only a music, but also a complex of emotions and a certain way of looking at life; thus the poet here is justified in titling the poem as he does. There, of course, was ample precedent in the music profes-

sion itself. One might observe that Langston Hughes also followed
this practice, his poem "The Weary Blues" being just one salient
example.

Hughes was able to evoke the blues feeling in sharp vignettes that
sometimes consist of no more than two or four lines. Brown too has
this ability to capture the pithy precision of folk speech and poetry.
In "Rent Day Blues" which first appeared in *Folk Say, IV* (Botkin
1932: 252ff) Brown's special brand of humor appears in a variation
on the blues form—a sort of blues ballad. The poet omits the
second line from the typical three-line blues stanza in "Rent Day
Blues," marking two lines, which he then breaks up into four.
Langston Hughes, by comparison, often wrote the stanza as six
lines. The short lines move swiftly, tersely, with snap. The opening
stanza retains the effect of a couplet in the statement about the rent:

> I says to my baby,
> "Baby, but de rent is due;
> "Can't noways figger
> What we ever gonna do."

The woman answers:

> My baby says, "Honey,
> Dontcha worry 'bout de rent;
> Looky here, daddy,
> At de money what de good Lord sent."

The pivoting of the voice on the word "baby" in the first stanza and
the enjambment of the last two lines help establish the sense of a
couplet, mentioned above. With the second stanza, however, with
the words "Honey" and "daddy," the rhythms of Black speech
demand a prolongation, an emphasis, which establishes the qua-
train for the ear as well as the eye. The resulting ballad movement
of the poem thus carries something of the flavor of a compressed
blues stanza. Amplified by the typical blues situation, this handling
of the poem's rhythm and movement is a further indication of
Brown's skill.

"Long Track Blues," which also first appeared in *Folk Say, IV*
(Botkin 1932: 251ff), is closer to the tradition of blues composition,
in terms of its dramatic situation and mood. Note, however, that

this poem too omits the second line for conciseness, although the poet sometimes supplies it when reading in public:

> Went down to the yards
> To see the signal lights come on;
> Looked down the track
> Where my lovin' babe done gone.
>
> Red light in my block,
> Green light down the line;
> Lawdy, let yo' green light
> Shine down on that babe o'mine.

For specificity of detail and evocative power this is one of Sterling Brown's finest poems. Its ease is deceptive. In order to appreciate fully his achievement here, one must acquaint oneself with the body of blues and other songs which deal with railroads and trains, with leavings and heartbreaks, particularly with the cluster of songs in which the lover rebukes the train for taking his babe away, as in "Mean Old Frisco," perhaps the most famous:

> O that mean Ol' Frisco
> And that low-down Santa Fe—
> Say, that mean Ol' Frisco
> And that low-down Santa Fe
> Come and stole my baby 'way—
> Better blow her back to me
>
> Lord, I wonder do she ever think of me
> Lord, I wonder do she ever think of me
> Lord, I wonder, I wonder, do my baby think of me.

And Sterling Brown consciously deepened the meanings and multiplied the implications of a Black American folk base, to paraphrase James Weldon Johnson, by his skillful selection and synthesis of the imagery which often appeared in songs of quite different types. Thus the signal lights in Brown's poem call up not only the "train with the red and green lights behind" but also a related image found in many blues: "If I could shine like the headlight on some train." Grading into this image, one finds the "gospel train" and the "little black train of death." Other related images of light and trains are found in hymns, gospels, and spirituals. These associations are not at all gratuitous, as we shall see later in the discussion of "Memphis Blues."

Let us return now to *Southern Road* and look briefly at "Tin Roof Blues," which is written in classical blues form. It is a marvelous distillation of both blues method and blues substance. Echoes from traditional blues appear in the very first line:

I'm goin' where de Southern crosses top de C. & O.

One, of course, hears the undertone:

I'm goin' where the Southern cross the Yellow Dog.

And one probably hears it in Bessie Smith's voice. The third line, too, is a distillation of hundreds of blues songs, and it is especially poignant since it stands as the second clause:

I'm goin' down de country cause I cain't stay here no mo'.

This theme of leaving so typical of the blues appears in lines like:

I'm going to Chicago, sorry but I can't take you.

Or:

I'm going, I'm going, pin up black crepe on your door.

And:

I'm going down this road feelin' bad, baby.

And:

I'm going where the weather suits my clothes.

And what is the wanderer in "Tin Roof Blues" looking for? He's looking for a place where people are friendly, honest, and down-to-earth, where they take control of their own lives as best they can, where they don't wait for fate to give them a lucky hit on the numbers.

The theme of wandering is a powerful one in folk literature and occupies a prominent place in the blues and the ballads and tales which nurtured the art of Sterling Brown. There is a well-known historical matrix of this wanderlust and leaving, which includes the migration of Blacks after the Civil War—the northward and westward migrations which peaked during the two world wars, and the movement from rural to urban areas even within the South itself. This is, to be sure, not strictly a Black phenomenon, but the effect which it had upon Black life was profound. The examples cited above are fairly self-sufficient on a literal level. On a deeper level, the theme of wandering or leaving is concomitant with the notion of the blues as a poetry/music of confrontation. The confrontation is frequently with a loved one, though often it is with one's enemies or with specific unhappy conditions in society, or with oneself. And the resolution comes through sexual triumph, or through violence, an assertion of one's manhood/womanhood, or through a bitter acceptance of the harshness, even the absurdity of life, expressed with cunning humor and with wit, or irony. The final confrontation, of course, is with death, and here the motif of the wanderlust takes on a special irony. The folk expression for it is, "You can run, but you can't hide." And the blues poet knows this. It is an ultimate knowing, but one which requires a lifetime of repetition. A man may run away after committing a murder, for example, but he can't run away from himself. ("Cain't nobody hide from God.") He may try to run away from confrontation with self, but eventually life forces him to make decisions which reveal who he is. Characteristic of Sterling Brown's figures is the heroism which the confrontation reveals, even in the case of Joe Meek. In "Georgia Grimes," one could hardly call the character heroic, but he has his pride, and our grudging respect. He has just killed his woman. With his red suitcase in his hand he "sloshes onward through the rain . . . " He "remembers hot words, lies,/The knife, and a pool of blood . . . " And he remembers her sightless eyes, and he knows that fear will follow him for the rest of his life. As he stumbles through "the soggy clay," muttering to himself, "No livin' woman got de right/To do no man dat way," we realize a bitter, brutal dimension of the folk, and the blues, experience.

The three poems on Big Boy Davis which open *Southern Road* —"Long Gone," "When De Saints Go Ma'ching Home," and

"Odyssey of Big Boy"—explore three stages, as it were, of the
wanderlust theme. All of these poems are blues-like in tone and language, though not in overall structure. "Long Gone" depicts a
typical footloose man who leaves his woman despite his mixed
feelings. In "When De Saints Go Ma'ching Home," the poet's first
published poem, Big Boy, the wandering songster, plays music
which progresses from "the bawdy songs and blues," "the weary
plaints," to his mother's favorite song, with which he ended all of
the concerts for his middle-class friends. As persona, Big Boy, in
effect, asserts through the shape of his concert the unity and meaningfulness of his life. Technically, the "concert" section of the poem
is a microcosm of the musical tradition; and, further refined, the
second section, with its series of portraits evoked by the music, is
an emblem of folk society framed by the consciousness and craft of
the poet.

Big Boy Davis's concert also illustrates the mingling of the religious and the secular in Black music and Black life,[3] and although
that fact is now well-known, one must still realize that the means
for achieving that mingling or fusion are rather more complicated
than substituting "Baby" for "Jesus" in a song based on gospel tunes
or chord progressions. Brown learned this quite early in his career,
and expressed it with subtlety and power not only in "Odyssey of
Big Boy" but in poems like "Ma Rainey" and "Memphis Blues." The
wanderlust motif or feeling is an important ingredient in the Blues
Universe and in the notion of Soul as the embodiment or essence of
Black lifestyle.

In "Odyssey of Big Boy," one of Brown's finest and most characteristic poems, there is a classic statement of wanderlust as Soul.
Big Boy envisions the final confrontation after years of wandering.
He outlines his history in comico-heroic terms. He has been mule
skinner, steel driver, tobacco harvester, coal miner, farmhand,
roustabout, short-order cook, and dishwasher. And he has had his
good times with the women, running the gamut from a "Creole
gal" to a "stovepipe blond." He continues:

> Done took my livin' as it came,
> Done grabbed my joy, done risked my life;
> Train done caught me on de trestle,
> Man done caught me wid his wife,
> His doggone purty wife. . . .

So when his "jag is done," there is no room for complaining. He has lived his life and taken the risks, and the confrontation has produced a clear self-knowledge and a view of the moral order of the world, where he, indeed, is bone and flesh of John Henry and the archetypical Brother, the embodiment of Soul.

Although the outstanding feature of Sterling Brown's blues is their somber outlook, the poet's treatment of the blues material ranges from emphasis on mood and character, to a focus on the sociological, to an accent on the philosophical. Sometimes, as in "Odyssey of Big Boy," all three elements are present in the same poem. In "New St. Louis Blues," however, the sociological emphasis is almost clinical. The poem is a kind of blues suite, consisting of three separate but related poems entitled, "Market Street Woman," "Tornado Blues," and "Low Down." All three are written in the three-line blues stanza, but there is a scientific detachment from the subjects which recalls the proletarian literature of the 1930s. One can't easily imagine these poems as songs, as in the case of "Tin Roof Blues," for example, or "Long Track Blues," which Brown recorded with piano accompaniment for Folkways Records.[4] In other words, "Market Street Woman" and "Low Down" are case studies of social oppression.

Even in "Tornado Blues" protest against oppression is the central theme, for although the "Black wind" from "de Kansas plains" has caused the initial destruction, the suffering which preceded it and which surely follows is man-made, the result of an oppressive social and economic system. It was mostly "de Jews an' us" that the tornado ruined. "Many po' boys' castle done settled to a heap o' dus'." The "Newcomers"—Destruction, Fear, Death, and Sorrow— "dodged most of the mansions, and knocked down de po' folks' do'. . . ." And this is what they found:

> Foun' de moggidge unpaid, foun' de insurance long past due,
> Moggidge unpaid, de insurance very long past due,
> And de homes we wukked so hard for goes back to de Fay and Jew.

Technically, the achievement of "New St. Louis Blues" lies in the adaptation of the strict blues form to precise socio-political statement, and the organization of the three separate but complementary poems into a tonal whole. But the achievement goes beyond isolated technicalities or social protest. Certainly, protest is an important part of the blues tradition, but it is an implicit protest, as Albert Murray observes. The crucial thing is that Brown goes beyond the social protest writers of his time and finds in the blues a philosophical position which is compatible with his own. It is this position, this attitude, this tone which most clearly sets him apart from others who employ the folk idiom. This "grim" perspective, to use the poet's own word, has some of its roots, at least, in the blues. There is, to be sure, a dimension of the blues which is unmistakably tragic, even fatalistic, in which human activity is pitted against the overwhelming forces of nature, depicted at times as impersonal, objective, or indifferent, at other times as the embodiment of a malevolent teleology. It appeared in the "blues suite," for example, in lines like these from "Tornado Blues":

> De Black wind evil, done done its dirty work an' gone,
> Black wind evil, done done its dirty work an' gone,
> Lawd help de folks what de wind ain't had no mercy on.

In the down-home blues tradition, Furry Lewis of Memphis sings:

> Wind storm come, an' it blowed my house away.
> Wind storm come, and it blowed my house away.
> I'm a good old boy, but I ain't got nowhere to stay.

And Mississippian Son House sings of a devastating drought in "Dry Spell Blues":

> The dry spell blues have fallen, drove me from door to door.
> Dry spell blues have fallen, drove me from door to door.
> The dry spell blues have put everybody on the killing floor. . . .
> Oh Lord, have mercy if you please.
> Oh Lord, have mercy if you please.
> Let your rain come down, and give our poor hearts ease.

The language in the song moves from the literal to the symbolic as the singer establishes a landscape worthy of Eliot's *The Waste Land*, as it moves from references to parched cotton and corn, the price of meat against that of cotton, to a description of the world as a powder-house where all the money men sit in their coil. With that range of language in mind, then, how lyrically right becomes the line "Let your rain come down, and give our poor hearts ease." Even the cliche of the second clause is restored to its pristine sincerity.

In a symbolic landscape, the precocious Robert Johnson sang of a veritable blues storm, through which he stumbled much like Sterling Brown's Georgie Grimes. Johnson's imagery, however, is at once biblical and hallucinatory, in the manner of the old sermons:

> I got to keep movinn', I got to keep movinnn'
> Blues fallin' down like hail, blues fallin' down like hail,
> Mmmmmmmmmmmmmmmmm-mmmm-mmm, blues fallin' down
> like hail, blues fallin' down like hail, blues fallin' down
> like hail.
> And the days keep on worryin' me, for a hell-hound on my trail,
> Hell-hound on my trail, hell-hound on my trail.

But Johnson and other blues people lived and sang in the real world, not in a symbolic landscape, and that world was harsh and oppressive, and dangerous. There were floods and droughts and tornadoes, and a merciless social order, built on the Black man's subjugation. Even in times of natural disaster Black folks seemed singled out for special punishment. Such a time was the great flood of 1927 which left an indelible impression on blues literature. Paul Oliver (1965), the blues historian, has a highly compressed account which warrants quotation:

No one had anticipated the full horror of the 1927 floods. Houses were washed away with their terrified occupants still clinging to the roof-tops; the carcasses of cattle and mules floated in the swirling, deep brown water; isolated figures whom none could rescue were last seen crying for help as they hung in the gaunt branches of shattered trees. Dressers and table-tops, clothes and toys were caught in the driftwood and floating timbers, to twist madly in a sudden whirlpool, and then sweep out of sight in the surging, eddying, boiling waters which extended as far as eyes could see.

From the town of Cairo, one could accurately judge the extent of the flooding at the towns farther down river. A rise of fifty feet above minimal level indicated that a severe flood was imminent. Oliver continues, "In 1927 the water had risen to 56.4 feet—nearly two feet above the previous highest reading." And at Vicksburg, the level had risen some sixty-five feet and with such a tremendous volume of water that the devastation was on an immense scale. Breaches—or "crevasses"—in the levees were recorded in fifty places and twenty-eight thousand square miles of land were under water. Whole townships were engulfed and the frightened people—largely Negroes—made for the hills at Helena and Vicksburg.

Some 600,000 people "were rendered completely destitute," and Blacks were at the mercy of white landlords who exploited a corruptly administered relief program. Total damage to the region was assessed at more than 350 million dollars (Oliver 1963: 263, 266, 267).

Many songs were written about the 1927 flood, but surely the best known was "Backwater Blues," which received majestic treatment by both Ma Rainey and Bessie Smith and moving treatment by others.

Sterling Brown had seen Ma Rainey in his youth, and her voice and her dignity had made a tremendous impression on him. Although he hadn't heard her sing "Backwater Blues," he had met someone who had, and he fused that account with his own impressions, his own knowledge of the people and the region and the music into one of the finest evocations of Black life that anybody has ever written, his poem "Ma Rainey." Sterling Stuckey calls it "perhaps *the* Blues poem,"[5] but to be precise, it is not a blues poem at all, in terms of structure, the way that "Tin Roof Blues" is, for example. It is, instead, a consummate dramatization of the spirit and power of the blues and their historic role as ritual in Black life.

The poem is divided into four stanzas which function in effect as movements in a musical sense. In the first, the tone is light and festive, capturing the excitement of the singer's personal fame:

> When Ma Rainey
> Comes to town,
> Folks from anyplace
> Miles aroun'
> From Cape Girardeau,
> Poplar Bluff
> Flocks in to hear
> Ma do her stuff. . . .

It's a holiday, when "Ma hits/Anywheres around'." Quickly the poet has established not only Ma's fame but the geography of the backwaters as well—Cape Girardeau, Poplar Bluff, all the way "fo' miles on down/To New Orleans delta/An' Mobile Town." In the second stanza the pace changes as the line lengthens and the focus is closer, tighter. People come "from de little river settlements," from "blackbottom cornrows and from lumber camps." The lens zooms in, as people "stumble in de hall, jes' a-laughin' an' a-cracklin', /Cheerin' lak roarin' water, lak wind in river swamps." The high feelings and the good times and the joking keep going in the "crowded aisles." But others wait for a deeper reason. Then Ma makes her entrance, flashing her famous smile, and "Long Boy ripples minors on de black an' yellow keys." And the poet in stark dramatic terms speaks with the voice of the people. It is the communal voice, the response of the ancient ritual pattern, the answer to Ma Rainey's call to "deir aches an' miseries":

> O Ma Rainey,
> Sing yo' song;
> Now you's back
> Whah you belong,
> Git way inside us,
> Keep us strong. . . .
> O Ma Rainey,
> Li'l an' low;
> Sing us 'bout de hard luck
> Roun' our do';
> Sing us 'bout de lonesome road
> We mus' go. . . .

The expression "Sing yo' song" is still current in the Black community. People say it spontaneously when they are moved by someone who appeals to their deepest concerns, whether a gospel singer or Aretha Franklin singing about hard times in love. And they complement her by saying, Sing *your* song, because the song is theirs too. She gives them back themselves and they return the love and the truth: "Now you's back" with us, "Whah you belong"—and now with *this* kind of singing, you're affirming our truth. And the language resonates on the mythic level, for the

singer is priestess and, before that, the surrogate of the god. This
was her role, in that time before time. But here it is compressed,
transubstantiated into song, personal commentary transmuted into
communal statement. And they know, they understand the ultimate tragic truth of human experience, and they accept it and
thereby transcend it. Hard luck is irrational, but there it is. Call it
fate, call it mischance, it is still there. And it will remain. So sing yo'
song: "Sing us 'bout de lonesome road/We mus' go. . . ."

One would think perhaps that the possibilities of the poem had
been exhausted at this point, but the poet moves into a different
perspective and amplifies his effect by letting the *blues* speak for
themselves. In stanza four, then, he returns to the narrative mode
of stanza two. Here the point of view changes to that of a single
persona:

> I talked to a fellow, an' the fellow say,
> "She jes' catch hold of us, somekindaway.
> She sang Backwater Blues one day:
>
> > *'It rained fo' days an' de skies was dark as night,*
> > *Trouble taken place in de lowlands at night.*
> >
> > *'Thundered an' lightened an' the storm begin to roll*
> > *Thousan's of people ain't got no place to go.*
> >
> > *'Den I went an' stood upon some high ol' lonesome hill,*
> > *An' looked down on the place where I used to live.'*
>
> An' den de folks, dey natchally bowed dey heads an' cried,
> Bowed dey heavy heads, shet dey moufs up tight an' cried,
> An' Ma lef' de stage, an' followed some de folks outside."
>
> Dere wasn't much more de fellow say:
> She jes' gits hold of us dataway.

The communion is complete. Even song now is unnecessary, and
Ma Rainey, the priestess, is spent—the spirit has left her, the spirit
is loosed and surrounds and hallows them all. It is like the end of a
sermon, or a baptism.

Technically, there's one final touch as the persona picks up the
language of the "fellow," which had been enclosed in quotes, as an
account, and repeats it, compressing and melding the account, the
reminiscence, the historical flood, and the present into an acknowl-

edgment of his oneness with the people and the experience. "Dere wasn't much more de fellow say/She jes' gits hold of us dataway." Not "somekindaway" but the way you have just experienced it— "dataway."

Just as Sterling Brown celebrates his people's health and sanity and their heroic confrontation with adversity, he attacks anything which oppresses or corrupts them. The vehemence of his attack is proportionate to his outrage and his sense of the people's loss. In "Children's Children" he directs a stream of elegant sarcasm at an unfaithful generation bent on abandoning its heritage. But in "Cabaret," one of his most important poems, the target is larger—it is nothing less than the prostituting of Black life by the larger society and the capitalistic system. Here he dramatizes not only the struggle of man against nature, but the conflicts between Black and white, the powerful and the powerless, the overlords and the underlings, and the complicity of Black people in their own degradation. The enveloping event of the poem again is the great flooding of the Mississippi in 1927, but whereas "Ma Rainey" demonstrates the heroic resiliency and philosophic maturity of the people through an authentic blues ritual, "Cabaret" becomes a complex vehicle for devastating satire on all that is false and parasitical in the American way of life. It is thus a poem on the anti-blues spirit, the dialectical opposite of "Ma Rainey." Just as "Backwater Blues" provides the emotional mainspring for "Ma Rainey," the banal Tin Pan Alley song "Muddy Water Blues" provides the basis of the satire in "Cabaret." The words of the song, drifting in and out of the narrative flow, help to shape it by providing a chronological base for the action, which is amplified in the event of the poem proper, a floor show at the Black and Tan Club of Chicago, in 1927, as we learn from the poem's subtitle. The two events which govern the poem may be viewed as two concentric circles, the larger one symbolizing the outside world with the conflicts between man and nature, overlords and underlings, powerful and powerless, white and Black—the sociopolitical conditions of the Mississippi Delta, and the country itself. The smaller circle, symbolizing the event of the Club, is a microcosm of the world outside. But here there is a suspension of real time, historical time, so to speak, and substituted for it is the time of the floor show, a hollow ersatz art. The poem itself is a verbal construct which mediates between the two "events."

Figure 9.1
Modality—Levels of Feeling—in "Cabaret"

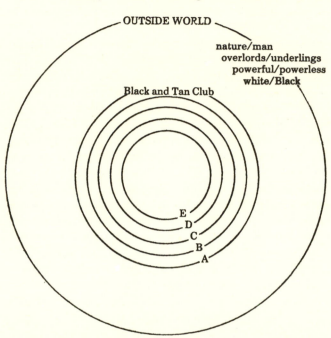

The reader is guided through a set of interlocking levels of perception and commentary, which may themselves be viewed as sub-
events of the action in the Club. The historical event of the flood is
refracted through various modalities, which we perceive as levels
of feeling or meaning, as voices, or angles of perception and commentary. The first level, "A," is the narrative. The poem opens here
with a scene of the rich "overlords" and their "glittering darlings"
(ll. 1-10). It occurs also at ll. 14-16, 20-24, 26-31, 33-34, 44, 58-63,
and 76-81; for a total of 35 lines. The other voices/levels are as
follows:

"B"—Sardonic #1. Here are reactions to the behavior of the participants in the Club event—the band, the chorus, the waiters, and
the overlords. It occurs at ll. 11-13, 25, and 45-49; for a total of 9
lines.

"C"—Music/Chorus. Lyrics of "Muddy Water Blues" sung by the chorus of "Creole" beauties provide a chronological base for the action. Along with voice/level A this level provides the main structural lines of the poem. It occurs at ll. 17-19, 32, 35-36, 50-52, 57, 68-69, 74-75, and 82-83; for a total of 12 lines.

"D"—Sardonic #2. This voice/level provides reaction to the Club event by the juxtaposition of images of toil, suffering destruction, and death resulting from the Mississippi floods. The sociological tone shades into the naturalistic and the fatalistic. It occurs at ll. 37-42, 53-56, 64-67, 70-73, and 84-86; for a total of 23 lines.

"E"—Music/Instrumental. This voice/level is represented through onomatopoeia as the music is left to speak for itself in a manner comparable to the quotation of "Backwater Blues" in "Ma Rainey." It occurs at ll. 43 and 87, at the midpoint and the end of the poem.

Let us return to the poem itself. It opens with the rich "overlords" and their "glittering darlings":

> Rich, flashy, puffy-faced,
> Hebrew and Anglo-Saxon
> The overlords sprawl here with their glittering darlings.
> The smoke curls thick, in the dimmed light
> Surreptitiously, deaf-mute waiters
> Flatter the grandees,
> Going easily over the rich carpets,
> Wary lest they kick over the bottles
> Under the tables.

Then "the jazzband unleashes its frenzy." Up to this point the action of the poem is presented on level A, narrative; but suddenly we encounter a sardonic voice, printed in italics, which comments on the band, trained "doggies" performing for the overlords. We are on level B:

> *Now, now,*
> *To it, Roger; that's a nice doggie,*
> *Show your tricks to the gentlemen.*

When we are returned to the narrative level, A, the band is depicted in pathological images:

> The trombone belches, and the saxophone
> Wails curdlingly, the cymbals clash,
> The drummer twitches in an epileptic fit

At level C (ll. 17-19), we hear the voice of the chorus singing the obscene banalities of the Tin Pan Alley song about the flood. We remember, of course, "Backwater Blues" and Ma Rainey singing *her* song. But the chorus sings:

> Muddy water
> Round my feet
> Muddy water

Back on the narrative level, A (ll. 20-24), we are informed that "the chorus sways in," and in an aside, we are told that they are not really "Creole Beauties from New Orleans," as billed, but come from almost everywhere else—Atlanta, Louisville, Washington, Yonkers. And on level B (l. 25), the Sardonic Voice #1 exclaims with mock preciousness:

> *O, le bal des belles quarterounes!*

The narrative voice creates a picture of mock romantic sensuality as it describes the "shapely bodies" of the chorus in their pirates' costumes, and it reflects with sarcasm upon the maudlin images of river life conjured up by the dancing, the music, and "the bottles under the tables" (ll. 26-31). And it reminds us of Lafitte, the real pirate (ll. 33-34), and his modern counterparts, the "overlords" themselves. There is a rich interplay of voices, tones, and perspectives at this point in the poem, as the voice of the chorus (C) surfaces—"Muddy water, river sweet" (l. 32)—and the narrative voice (A) refers us to Lafitte's "doughty diggers of gold" (ll. 33-34). The words of the chorus become unbearably unreal as they sing of the "peace and happiness" of the Delta (C, ll. 35-36) in 1927. Sardonic Voice #2 (level D) crashes in, distinguished by parentheses, its grim tone, and its naturalistic depiction of the sociology of the flood. First, there is the virtual slavery of the Black convicts who have been pressed to work on the levees (ll. 37-42):

(In Arkansas,
Poor half-naked fools, tagged with identification numbers,
Worn out upon the levees,
Are carted back to the serfdom
They had never left before
And may never leave again)

Amplifying these lines, in the music of the period, one finds Leadbelly singing "Red Cross Store Blues" and Big Bill Broonzy who
sang:

You'll never get to do me like you did my buddy Shine;
You'll never get to do me like you did my buddy Shine
You worked him so hard on the levee till he went stone blind.

On the deepest level/voice, E, the drummer makes a break which
the poet captures in terms that anticipate Langston Hughes's ren-
dering of Be-Bop sounds in his *Montage of a Dream Deferred*. In
fact, the term Be-Bop itself as a name for the music probably had its
origin in onomatopoeia, and just as "Bop" singing tended toward
the use of wordless "lyrics," the heart of Brown's poem demonstrates the tendency of Black musicians to employ the instrument as
an extension of the voice. In certain situations, in the scat singing of
Dizzy Gillespie, for example, the result is a teasing expression of the
antirational, dadaistic impulse. And so the drummer plays (l. 43):

Bee—dap—ee—DOOP, dee—ba—dee—BOOP

As "the girls wiggle and twist" to the music (A, l. 44), Sardonic
Voice #1 (B) offers them at auction (ll. 45-49). They, like the musicians, are ordered to go through their paces for the "gentlemen":

A prime filly, seh.
What am I offered, gentlemen, gentlemen. . . .

The song continues its phony sentiment (C, ll. 50-52), interrupted
by Sardonic Voice #2 (D), which now asks without bitterness (ll.
53-56, "What is there left the miserable folk?" In reply, the voice of
the chorus chimes in (C, l. 57), "Still it's my home, sweet home," as

the poet emphasizes the falseness with the "moans and deep cries for home" coming from the "lovely throats" of these displaced "Creoles." And the alcohol heightens the illusion they create (A, ll. 58-63).

In the real world of the Mississippi Delta (D, ll. 64-67), "*The black folk huddle, mute, uncomprehending*" the ways of " '*the good Lord.*' " They have no "shelter/Down in the Delta," as the song goes (C, ll. 68-69). On the level of Sardonic Voice #2 (D, ll. 70-73), the heavy-bellied buzzards fly low over the Yazoo, "Glutted, but with their scrawny necks stretching,/Peering still." This counterpoint of images is striking, this interweaving of voices and levels, the commercial song moving in and out of the real world of the Delta, the make-believe of the cabaret, all of it held in dynamic suspension in the world of the poem. As the song, as the event for the interior scene comes to a close, the band goes mad (A, ll. 76-81; C, ll. 82-83; D, ll. 84-86; E, l. 87):

> The band goes mad, the drummer throws his sticks
> At the moon, a papier-mâché moon,
> The chorus leaps into weird posturings,
> The firm flesh had arms plucking at grapes to stain
> Their coralled mouths; seductive bodies weaving
> Bending, writhing, turning
>
> My heart cries out for
> M U D D Y   W A T E R
>
> (*Down in the valleys*
> *The stench of the drying mud*
> *Is a bitter reminder of death.*)
>
> Dee da dee D A A A A H

The final notes of the trumpet, if one must seek a literary comparison, are the equivalent of Hemingway's "Nada" in "A Clean, Well-Lighted Place," in which the writer parodies the Lord's Prayer with the Spanish word for "nothing." And again one must note the anticipation of Be-Bop and the dadaist element in it especially in the singing. However, in characteristic style, Brown has arrived at this position through essentially realistic means. On the sociological level, the political level, and the moral level, there is a powerful indictment of modern slavery, in the exploitation and prostitution of the musicians and their music. They are, in effect, no better than the poor victims of the flood, or the convicts; and if they were aware of their condition, they too could ask " 'how come the good Lord/Could treat them this a way.' " These are the heaviest blues of all, and the poet has presented them to us through an elegant indirection.[6]

To appreciate Brown's craftsmanship it would be useful to study the relationship between the various voices/levels of the poem both as they fit together in a thematic scheme, as in figure 9.1, and as they produce a pattern left by the poem itself as its action moves through the "time" of the poem, as in figure 9.2. Here the "time" is indicated by the lines of the poem, perpendicular to which appear the levels/voices which I have just enumerated (see figure 9.2).

Figure 9.2
The Movement of the Poem's Action According to Levels in "Cabaret"

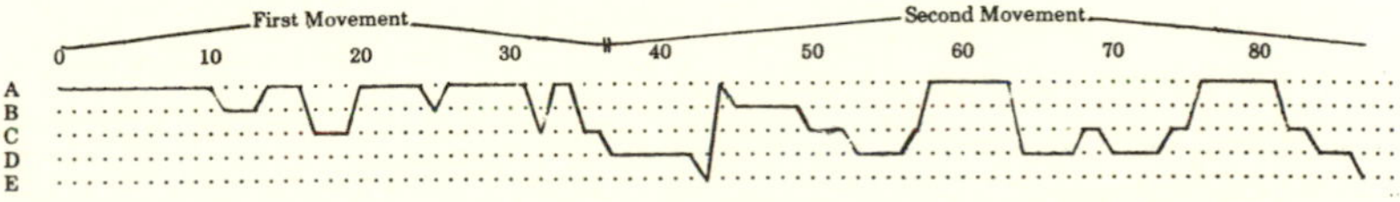

We now have a kind of grid on which we can trace the movement, the action, and, indeed, the geometry of the poem, its essence summed up in an action that flows like an arpeggio of downward turning blues. At a glance we see the movement to the various levels, the duration of the stay, and the intervals between jumps, which vary from the dramatic movement from E to A (ll. 43-44), after the descending pattern begun at l. 34, to jumps of a single level, as from A to B in ll. 44-45. If we check the text at the movement from E to A, we discover that here at the midpoint of the poem the drummer has just played a break which makes a frivolous and ironic comment on the preceding level, D, which had just introduced the real world into the poem. In its frivolous ambiguity, the break is a dramatic introduction to the second movement of the poem at the same time that it propels the movement along as "the girls wiggle and twist." We may note also that, at the last time at this level of the poem (E, l. 87), the trumpet unmistakably echoes the words "MUDDY WATER" from level C, l. 83, commenting in its dadaistic way on the nothingness of life. One notes too, by way of structure, that the first instrumental appearance seems to be the drums; the second, the trumpet. Finally, level E represents an ono-matopoetic extension and intensification of level C, thus faithfully following the tradition in Black music of employing the voice as an instrument.

If the poet presents the blues through indirection in "Cabaret," in "Memphis Blues" he presents them through the matrix of the oral tradition which helped to shape their growth. The poem partly draws upon the traditional notion of "preaching the blues" found in both music and oral literature, but significantly it is not a parody of the sermon but a brilliant exploration of the song-sermon form in which the blues are historically and formally grounded. Its A-B-A form is a common song pattern and is shared by jazz and the sonata form. It is also the pattern which typical sermons take—text, devel-opment and application, repetition.[7] In the poem the enveloping sections are historical parallels to the present:

> Was another Memphis
> Mongst de olden days,
> Done been destroyed
> In many ways. . . .
> Dis here Memphis
> It may go. . . .

The persona cites the dangers:

> Floods may drown it;
> Tornado blow;
> Mississippi wash it
> Down to sea—
> Like de other Memphis in
> History.

That is the warning of apocalypse, the sign of the Judgment. The poem is a blues sermon on the Last Judgment. The language evokes the hymns of Blind Willie Johnson, the Texas preacher who sang and played in blues style and tonality:

> See the sign of the Judgment
> Yes, yes!

> See the sign of the Judgment
> Oh, yes, my Lord,
> Time is drawing nigh!

And the stage is set.

The long middle section of the poem consists of six stanzas, each posing the ultimate question in the life of a Christian: Where will you be on the day when God sends down Judgment? It is the Dies Irae—Day of Anger, Day of Judgment, and a central theme of Western literature and art. One recalls the medieval plays *Everyman* and *The Castle of Perseverance*, and the other moralities which address the theme in a form comprehensible to the common man in fourteenth century England. One remembers, too, Marlowe's Dr. Faustus imploring the heavenly spheres to cease and bring time to a halt. And who can forget the peal of the *Dies Irae* as it strikes fear and repentance into the heart of Goethe's Gretchen?

Most of the old-time preachers were probably ignorant of Goethe and the Faust legend, but they knew the Bible fairly well, especially the Book of Revelations, and the most gifted of them knew enough history to draw lessons from it and to incorporate them into their sermons. Their knowledge was matched if not surpassed by superb rhetorical skills. The love of language was rooted in their culture. They sang as their parents had sung: "My Lord, what a mournin'/When the stars begin to fall." They sang: "Run, sinner, run and find yourself a hiding place." They admonished their congregations to work on the "building" for the Lord. They warned the gambler, the dancer, the drunkard, the "cussin' man," and the whoremonger to work on the building too, for the day was coming when "God's gonna separate the wheat from the tares." They questioned the sinner in his headlong flight: "O whar you runnin', sinner?" They asked him: "Sinner, what you goin' to do/When de devil git you?" And there would be nowhere for the sinner to go, for "there's no hiding place down here" (Odum and Johnson 1925, rpt. 1964: 72, 77).

Brown builds the middle section of his poem on the pattern of these songs of the Last Judgment, a pattern which is also used in the sermon. That pattern is reinforced by a smaller rhetorical pattern of concentrated and compressed Black cultural experience, a *mascon*, and in choosing it the poet goes to the ambivalent heart of the Black man's Christian heritage. He is both Christian and Black. He is a child of God, yet not a man. There are contradictions, and conflicts, but one kind of resolution is found in the blues. However, the blues lie outside the church, are the devil's music. Still the blues came out of the church, as the singers themselves say. Thus there is no contradiction in the development of the poem. The first person to be addressed in the "Judgment Day pattern" is the Preacher Man—

> Watcha gonna do when Memphis on fire,
>   Memphis on fire, Mistah Preachin' Man?

And the Preachin' Man replies:

> Gonna pray to Jesus and nebber tire,
>   Gonna pray to Jesus, loud as I can,
>   Gonna pray to my Jesus, oh, my Lawd!

This is correct Christian behavior and the language and sentiments echo the Judgment Day spirituals cited above. Had the poet continued in this vein, the poem might have ended with a tonality and structure akin to the sermon-poems of James Weldon Johnson. But the poem is to be an experiment in blues tonality, as the title suggests, and we are not disappointed. Something remarkable and subtle begins to happen with the introduction of this answering refrain. For one thing, the poet has established perhaps the most characteristic pattern of Black oral/musical tradition, the call-and-response, and both parts of the pattern take delightful variations of rhythm, tone, and diction as the poem proceeds. Each variation in the "call" is like a chord change, which is developed by the "response."

Although tonally and thematically the first response recalls the spirituals, the rhythm is jazzy as in gospel music. In addition, a closer examination will reveal that the call-and-response pattern is enhanced by the familiar mascon qualities of the call and the anaphora of the response. The pattern also contains an artfully concealed extension of the blues form in which the two lines of the call constitute, in effect, the first two lines of a blues stanza, while the response is a rhetorical elaboration of the third line. However, instead of the quick turn or the punch line of the blues stanza, the response stretches out into a kind of jazz melody.

Although each "change" is distinctive, we remain in the same key, as it were, as the calls are made in sequence to the Preachin' Man, the Lovin' Man, the Music Man, the Workin' Man, the Drinkin' Man, and the Gamblin' Man. Each responds in his own way, in his own rhythm and accent, but all end up with the refrain "oh, my Lawd!" first spoken by the Preachin' Man. This expression not only links the personae together, it allows for ironic variation of tone from the religious somberness of the opening section. In effect, the "Lawd" of the spirituals is subtly transformed by the "Lawd" of the blues.

The call also is a kind of blues riff which is found not only in blues songs but in other areas of the oral tradition. Thus Big Bill Broonzy sings a song called "Honey O Babe" in which these lines appear:

Whatcha gonna do when the pond goes dry, honey, honey?
Whatcha gonna do when the pond goes dry, babe, babe?
Whatcha gonna do when the pond goes dry?

And the response is:

Sit up on the bank and watch the poor things die,
Honey, O babe o'mine.

Novelist John O. Killens recalls a chant which children of his generation sang in Valdosta, Georgia. The first line is the call; the second, the response:

Watcha gonna do when the world's on fire?
Run like hell and holler, "Fire!"

And Blind Lemon Jefferson sang, when John Killens was a little boy:

Watcha gonna do when they send your man to war?
Watcha gonna do—they send your man to war?

It is important, then, to realize that the call is a fundamental feature of blues style, and this particular call is one of the most deeply engrained in the oral tradition. This realization helps us to understand the structure of "Memphis Blues" and the reason that the title is justified. Each individual call, we may note further, is a kind of compressed blues experience, for the blues are a poetry of challenge and confrontation, and this fact is reflected in the poem's thematic concerns and its structure—its stanzas, its imagery, its rhythm, its diction, its overall shape.

In Memphis, Furry Lewis sings:

> Whatcha gonna do, your troubles get like mine?
> Whatcha gonna do, your troubles get like mine?

The wordless response comes ringing in from the guitar, but one ever-present possibility occurs in the response of another song:

> Get a handful of sugar and a mouthful of turpentine.

Again, diagrams help one to appreciate the poet's skill in the construction of "Memphis Blues."[8] Each of the six stanzas of the middle section possesses the following structure. First is the *call*, which is a kind of "riff" that may be diagramed as follows:

Figure 9.3
Structure Diagram of the "Call"

Mascon	Challenge
Challenge (repeat)	Persona

Next is the *response*, which may be diagramed thus:

Figure 9.4
Diagram of the "Response"

Anaphora ⟵	⟶ Statement
Anaphora ⟵	⟶ Intensification
Anaphora ⟵	⟶ Elaboration & Refrain

As figure 9.3 dramatically demonstrates, the call is rather rigid. with a kind of singsong rhythm, characteristic of certain ritual language and of children's song. That quality is heightened by the repetition of the challenge. Variation is achieved and the poem is activated by changing the specific challenge in each call and, of course, by addressing a different persona. So we may list these elements in order: (1) "Memphis on fire," Preachin' Man; (2) "tall flames"—a variation—Lovin' Man; (3) "Memphis falls down," Music Man; (4) "de hurricane," Workin' Man; (5) "Memphis near gone," Drinkin' Man; and (6) "de flood roll fas'," Gamblin' Man. We may note that the poet achieves coherence in the call by specific mention of Memphis in calls 1, 3, and 5, and by citing the destructive forces of nature in 2, 4, and 6.

It is the response, however, in which we best see the skillful work in the poem. The anaphora builds up a driving, jazzy pattern which the second part of the line develops into a series of brilliant explorations of the melodic variety of Afro-American speech. In the first, the preacher's voice reaches a tender intensity when he prays to "my Jesus," with the initial fillip of "oh, my Lawd!" In the second, the Lovin' Man in a sensual stammer of alliteration is "gonna love my brownskin better'n before," and the emphasis is not on his being a "do right man," but on the miracle of "my brown baby," which parallels the language of the preacher. One of the most felicitous of the responses is the third, in which the poet sets up a rocking rhythm that suggests the piano's bass line, then suddenly shifts into a lovely scattering of treble notes. Here is the entire stanza:

Watcha gonna do when Memphis fall down,
Memphis falls down, Mistah Music Man?
Gonna plunk on dat box as long as it soun',
Gonna pluck dat box fo' to beat de ban',
Gonna tickle dem ivories, oh, my Lawd!

When questioned about the hurricane, the Workin' Man in the fourth stanza makes a heroic personal response which is crucial to an appreciation of the tone and significance of the entire poem. He will not give up, and he will not be content with praying. He'll put the buildings back again, to stand, and he takes pride in his energy, his will, and above all in his style: "Gonna push a wicked wheelbarrow, oh, my Lawd!" Even the Drinkin' Man will go down in

style with his "pint bottle of Mountain Corn," and the stopper in
his hand. Finally, we come to the Gamblin' Man:

> Watcha gonna do when de flood roll fas',
> Flood roll fas', Mistah Gamblin' Man?
> Gonna pick up my dice fo' one las' pass—
> Gonna fade my way to de lucky lan',
> Gonna throw my las' seven—oh, my Lawd!

At this point we realize that the language of the poem in these six
blues vignettes reflects Black life's emphasis upon style. That emphasis is at times overlooked and frequently misunderstood although it has attracted considerable attention from the media as
well as the scholarly community. In effect, the style or the styling is
an assertion of meaningfulness, not of frivolity or illusion, although there are, of course, assertions which may be so classified.
An examination of the last response, then, is in order. The
Gamblin' Man is not going to panic and fall down on his knees and
beg God for mercy. That would be the coward's way. It would also
be very "unhip." Death is final, but he meets it with a gambler's
nerve, which is a kind of courage. He's not going to the Promised
Land, but to the "lucky lan'," which he has created out of his own
life, his own experience and values. He does not live in illusion and
he takes responsibility for his life. The same thing applies to the
Drinkin' Man, probably the most unsavory character of the
group. Even he is going out in style: "Gonna get a *mean* jag on, oh,
my Lawd!" These are not poor, benighted, superstitious foundlings
in the hands of Fate, as Jean Wagner, for example, interprets
Sterling Brown's characters (Wagner 1973: 483-490), but ordinary
blues people heroic in their own way. As for the Drinkin' Man, we
understand him better when we recall Bill Broonzy's words: "I'm
gonna keep on a drinkin'/Till good liquor carry me down." Note
that it's *good* liquor and "Mountain Corn," made by experts for
virtuoso drinkers. And lurking behind the response are the immortal lines: "I got the world in a jug, the stopper's in my hand." So
sang Bessie Smith.

   These last stanzas of the group prepare us for the return to the
somber theme of mutability in the final section of the poem:

Memphis go
By Flood or Flame;
Nigger won't worry
All de same—
Memphis go
Memphis come back
Ain't no skin
Off de nigger's back.
All dese cities
Ashes, rust. . . .
De win' sing sperrichals
Through deir dus'.

What warrants attention here is the loaded ambiguity of the last two lines, which one can read as an equation of the spirituals with the moaning of the wind, or as an existential projection of human value upon "objective" impersonal nature. And the songs are spirituals, not the blues, nor yet the songs of Tin Pan Alley, and the people have made them out of the substance of their lives, bleak though they might have been. An affirmation is made out of their courage, their strength, and their resilience, but equally out of their faith in themselves and their style. So when one reexamines the poem with the haunting lyricism of its enveloping sections and the artful mastery and development of folk resources in the middle, one wonders why it has not received its critical due. And one has to conclude that some of the fault, at least, can be attributed to a patronizing attitude toward the folk themselves, whom the poem celebrates.

In this brief assessment of the "blues" poetry of Sterling Brown, I have tried to demonstrate that a closer examination of the work reveals that he is, indeed, a skillful and careful craftsman, but a full appreciation of his achievement is dependent on a knowledge of and a feeling for the dynamics of the folk culture, some aspects of which have only begun to receive serious and systematic attention during the past fifteen years. Failure to appreciate these dynamics leads on one hand to the casual snobbery of a usually judicious critic like Nathan I. Huggins, who writes after a brief look at "Memphis Blues":

Such poems of Langston Hughes's and Sterling Brown's defy criticism because they lack pretension. They do not ask for academic acclaim; thus they are exempt from its contempt. In truth, Hughes was not writing to be approved as a literary poet (Brown sometimes did).

He continues, asserting that Hughes "expected his poems to be taken on the simple and unpretentious level on which they were written." By adopting folk forms, Huggins states, Hughes, and presumably Brown, obtained a freedom which while important in itself "deprived him of the control and mastery that might make each (or indeed any) of his poems really singular. Langston Hughes avoided the Scylla of formalism only to founder in the Charybdis of folk art" (Huggins 1971: 226-227).

On the other hand, failure to respect the dynamics of the folk base also leads to distortions, and misinterpretation of the thematic aspects of Brown's art. In this regard, Jean Wagner—despite Robert Bone's citation of his "capacity for empathy" and his ability to "surmount linguistic and cultural barriers" (Wagner 1973: xiii) —manages to cramp the blues nuances of Brown's poetry into a rather mechanical universe of foolish faith and stoic endurance.[9] That Brown's view of life as expressed in the poems is tragic there is no doubt, but that view is expressed in terms which grow naturally out of the blues perspective, and, at times, the blues form in its many permutations. Brown's achievement, like that of the blues themselves, is a special kind of synthesis. Brown is not a folk poet, but a poet in the folk manner, who cunningly conceals his craft in the stylistics of the tradition itself. He mastered not only the academic studies and sources of his people's lore but the principles undergirding the lore itself. Thus his remarkable ability to render the sounds of speech, its nuances of rhythm and texture and meaning, was nourished not so much by his thorough knowledge of the literature written in dialect as by his immersion in the actual flow of the oral tradition, in the country homes of his students, in the barbershops and cafes of the South—Lynchburg, Atlanta, New Orleans—in all the varied places where Black folks gathered and talked and told lies, screamed at children, and sang the blues, or moaned the spirituals. He understood the contradictions in the people and in himself, and he did not sentimentalize them. He treated them roughly in his analysis, as Wagner indicates, but no rougher really than they treated themselves, not only in the dozens

but in the whole range of the tradition, because survival and affirmation were their implicit objectives. If he is cynical at times and
despairing, so are they. But the cynicism of the blues is ultimately
cleansing. It sets limits and reinforces them—the blues allow for
hope, for endurance, and, above all, for the very control that
Huggins speaks of, but control of a deeper sort—moral control.
Big Bill Broonzy, for example, recalls working deep in a hole under
a city street. As he glanced up, he noticed another, earlier level
where workers used to stand. He laughed to himself at the irony.
Here he was a Black man "lookin' up at down." And he wrote a
song about it. Memphis singer Furry Lewis, still alive at this writing, once sang about his misfortune: "My shoes done got thin./I'm
back on my feet again." So much for progress. And even before the
Depression, long before then, someone sang, "I been down so long
it seems like up to me." And we link up the insights with Sterling
Brown's poetry, in which the heavy water blues absorb the
"chilling" social analysis and transmute the elegiac vestiges of his
youth into a unique testament of the human will to endure.

NOTES

1. On the blues as a poetry of confrontation see Henderson (1967, 1975);
Murray (1976: 250-252). Note, too, Murray's caption to the photos of
dancers at the Savoy Ballroom (p. 12), which reads, "Saturday Night *pas
de deux* uptown any night, confrontation . . . improvisation . . . affirmation . . . celebration."

2. All references refer to Brown (1932, rpt. 1974). Reproduced by permission of the author.

3. For further discussion, see Murray (1976: 23-42) especially for the
important distinction made between the "Saturday night function" and the
"Sunday morning service." See also Cone (1972: 108-137); Oliver (1965);
and Ferris (1970). Comment on the unity of Black music from the viewpoint of jazz musicians appears in the Summer, 1972, issue of *The Black
Scholar*. Donald Byrd, in his article, "The Meaning of Black Music," states,
"When I use the term jazz, I speak of all black music" (p. 30). Max Roach,
in "What 'Jazz' means to me," takes a different approach. "They are mis-
nomers: Jazz music, rhythm and blues, rock and roll, gospel, spirituals,
blues, folk music" (p. 6).

4. *Sixteen Poems of Sterling A. Brown Read by Sterling A. Brown*
produced and edited by Frederic Ramsey, Jr. (Folkways Records FL 9794).

5. Introduction to Brown (1932, rpt. 1974: XXVII).

6. On "elegant indirection," see Henderson (1973: 33-41). Cf. Murray (1976: 214): "The preeminent embodiment of the blues musician as artist was Duke Ellington, who, in the course of fulfilling the role of entertainer, not only came to address himself to the basic imperatives of music as a fine art but also achieved the most comprehensive synthesis, extension, and refinement to date of all the elements of blues musicianship."

7. The repetition may be obliquely expressed or expressed through non-verbal means. In either case the completion is recognized by the congregation. In an unpublished doctoral dissertation, Davis (1978) develops a model of the sermon from intensive fieldwork and a study of recordings. He provides a close critique of the scholarly literature, especially the work of Rosenberg (1970).

8. The diagrams, especially figure 9.3, are intended chiefly to show the location of structural elements, not this function.

9. See Wagner's entire discussion of Sterling Brown, especially his discussion of the poem "Southern Road" (p. 489), and the section entitled 'The inanity of Faith." Wagner misses the nuances of Brown's position and, apparently, much of his art.

REFERENCES

Botkin, B. A., ed. 1932. *Folk-Say IV: The Land Is Ours*. (Norman: University of Oklahoma Press).

Brown, Sterling A. 1932. *Southern Road*. Boston: Beacon Press.

Cone, James H. 1972. *The Spirituals and the Blues*. New York: The Seabury Press.

Davis, Gerald L. 1978. "The Performed African-American Sermon." Ph.D. dissertation, University of California, Berkeley.

Ferris, William. 1970. *Blues from the Delta*. London: Studio Vista, Ltd.

Henderson, S. E. 1967. "Blues for the Young Blackman." *Negro Digest*. August.

———. 1973. *Understanding the New Black Poetry: Black Speech and Black Music as Poetic References*. New York: William Morrow.

———. 1975. "Southern Road: A Blues Perspective." *New Directions* (Howard University). July.

Huggins, Nathan I. 1971. *Harlem Renaissance*. New York: Oxford University Press.

Lord, Albert B. 1965. *The Singer of Tales*. New York: Atheneum Publishers.

Murray, Albert. 1976. *Stomping the Blues*. New York: McGraw-Hill.

Odum, Howard W., and Guy B. Johnson. 1925, rpt. 1964. *The Negro and His Songs*. Hatboro: Folklore Associates, Inc.

Oliver, Paul. 1965. *Conversation with the Blues*. London: Cassell.

Rosenberg, Bruce A. 1970. *The Art of the American Folk Preacher*. New York: Oxford University Press.

Wagner, Jean. (Douglas, Kenneth, trans.) 1973. *Black Poets of the United States*. Urbana: University of Illinois Press.

10

LORETTA S. BURNS

The Structure of Blues Lyrics

There is some disagreement among scholars as to the relative importance of the lyrics of the blues. Harold Courlander (1963: 145) feels that the blues in their natural milieu are "not primarily conceived as 'music' but as a verbalization of deeply felt personal meanings. It is a convention that this verbalization is sung." Albert Murray (1976: 79) on the other hand, asserts that "the definitive element of a blues statement is not verbal," and maintains that the lyrics are always secondary to the music. It is probably more accurate to say that the blues as they are performed involve a symbiotic esthetic relationship between music and lyrics that is, at times, quite complex. In the discussion that follows it is assumed that, whatever the importance of the lyrics vis-à-vis the music in actual performances, the lyrics themselves have a vitality that is realized within a musical context but does not require one.

In a comparison of poetry and instrumental music, Barbara Smith explains the dual quality of language:

The principles of poetic and musical structure are comparable insofar as both forms of art produce experiences which occur over a period of time and are continuously modified by successive events. Because language, however, has semantic or symbolic as well as physical properties, poetic structure is considerably more complex. A sonata consists only of an organization of sounds, but a sonnet consists of an organization of symbols as well. The conclusion of a poem is, therefore, doubly determined. . . .

The consequences of the double nature of language become even more relevant to poetic structure and closure when we consider that a poem is an
utterance or . . . the imitation of an utterance. A sonnet is not merely a
syntactically correct organization of linguistic symbols, but it also represents a statement or speech of some kind: an argument, perhaps, or a decla-
ration, or lament. . . . The division of structural principles into two kinds,
formal and thematic, corresponds to a more general division which,
because it is inherent in the double nature of language, can be observed in
all the elements of a poem. *Formal elements* are defined as those which arise
from the physical nature of words, and would include such features as
rhyme, alliteration, and syllabic meter. The *thematic elements* of a poem
are those which arise from the symbolic or conventional nature of words,
and to which only someone familiar with the language could respond; they
would include everything from reference to syntax to tone. (Smith 1968: 46)

Without attempting to resolve the question as to whether the essential element of a blues statement is musical or verbal, I would like
to examine the linear structure of the blues lyric, viewing it as a
poetic text that incorporates the formal and thematic elements
Smith defines. In attempting to distinguish between different types
of blues songs, some scholars have found it useful to speak of a
country-city-urban continuum,[1] and the lyrics under consideration
here fall within the country-city expanse of the continuum.

In terms of formal structure, the most rigidly constructed lyrics
are, of course, made up of stanzas. The classic three-line stanza is
the most prevalent unit. It consists of an original statement, repetition of the original statement with optional variation, and a resolving line that rhymes with the first two lines. Each line consists of
two sections of similar duration, with a caesura in the middle.
There are, however, other forms that are just as rigidly structured
and the general structural devices I will discuss apply to any lyric
that consists of a succession of identical or similar stanzas or
patterns.

When confronted with such a lyric, it is difficult at first to perceive any formal devices marking the beginning, middle, or end.
Because the lyrics are most often sung, few strictly formal devices
are essential, and the musical context may, in large part, structure
the lyric. For example, a musical introduction and conclusion may
frame the lyric. The singer's voice, together with the musical
accompaniment, may also give structure to the song. For example,

the singer may indicate the end of the lyric by retarding the vocal and musical tempo of the last phrase or line. Nonetheless, verbal devices are used as formal structuring strategies.

A blues lyric that consists of formally identical or similar stanzas usually begins by introducing its formal conventions and patterns. In short, the lyric begins by beginning. We do not perceive these formal devices as patterns, however, until they are systematically repeated. For example, the three-line, rhymed stanza is not perceived as the stanzaic pattern of a lyric unless its structure is repeated in subsequent stanzas. Smith (1968: 13) explains:

poetic structure is, in a sense, an inference which we draw from the evidence of a series of events. As we read the poem, it is a hypothesis whose probability is tested as we move from line to line and adjusted in response to what we find there. And . . . the conclusion of a poem has special status in the process, for it is only at that point that the total pattern—the structural principles which we have been testing—is revealed.

Closure is especially important in the blues because the end of a lyric is often the only conspicuously marked segment. While a blues lyric is not typically narrative, it usually proceeds according to the emotional association between the structural units. In terms of thematic structure, the coherence and unity of a blues lyric does not usually depend on the sequence of its structural units. Therefore, the sense of order and completeness that we experience is, in part, dependent on the coalescence of the lyric's structural patterns within the last stanza.

In a blues lyric made up of stanzas, then, formal strophic units begin the song and are systematically repeated as the lyric continues. (Here it is useful to regard the stanza as a single structural unit forged from a complex of smaller elements.) Once this process has been set in motion, however, is there any formal signal to indicate its close? Smith (1968: 56) points out that "the systematic repetition of formal elements is fundamentally a force for continuation, and closure is, of course, always weakened by the expectation of continuation."

Although many of the ending devices of the blues lyric are thematic, there are some formal devices that signal or reinforce closure. One of the most effective, discussed by Smith throughout her study, is terminal modification. In the blues lyric, this involves a change in the structure of the final stanza so that it is not identical to the ones that precede it. The following lyric illustrates this principle:

Baby I can see just what's on your mind
Baby I can see just what's on your mind
You got a long black woman with her gold teeth in her face

I take a long look right smack down in your mind
I take a long look right smack down in your mind
And I don't see but one woman rambling up and down the line

Don't kid your mama [,] you ain't fooling nobody but yourself
Oh don't kid your mama [,] you ain't fooling nobody but yourself
And what I see on your mind you would not have no friend

I remember the day when I was living at Lula town
I remember the day when I was living at Lula town
My man did so many wrong things that I had to leave the town

I caught the riverside [,] my man caught the transfer boat
I caught the riverside [,] my man caught the transfer boat
And the last time I seed him he had a gal way up the road

Well I'm worried now and I won't be worried long
Well I'm worried now and I won't be worried long
Well I'm worried now and I won't be worried long. (Sackheim
   1969: 36)

Here the formal elements are established through their systematic repetition in stanzas one through five: the three-line unit—original statement; repetition of original statement with optional variation; and resolving line—is consistent throughout these stanzas, but not the element of rhyme. The variations include rhyme, near rhyme, exact duplication of sound, and absence of rhyme. Since there is no firm rhyme pattern, an ending rhyme cannot by itself act as the formal closure device. Rather, closure is signaled by modification of the established structural norm, that is, the final stanza has three identical lines. This persistent repetition adds a note of finality and completion.

Another type of terminal modification occurs in this next lyric:

Won't you be my chauffeur
Won't you be my chauffeur
   I want someone to drive me
   I want someone to drive me Downtown
Baby drives so easy I can't turn him down

But I don't want him
But I don't want him
   To be riding these girls
   To be riding these girls A-round
You know I'm gonna steal me a pistol [,] shoot my chauffeur down

Well I must buy him
Well I must buy him
   A brand new V-8
   A brand new V-8 Ford[2]
And he won't need no passengers [,] I will be his load
   (Yeah, take it away)

Going to let my chauffeur
Going to let my chauffeur
   Drive me around the
   Drive me around the World
Then he can be my little boy [,] Yes I'll treat him good. (Sackheim
     1969: 58)

The last stanza of the lyric signals closure through the terminal modification because rhyme is sometimes thought of as a natural ending device. Smith (1968: 49) points out, however, that "rhyme is neither the *sine qua non* of poetic closure nor a sufficient condition for its occurrence." Indeed, if rhyme alone were sufficient to indicate closure, the blues audience would expect closure at the end of each rhymed stanza. Instead, once the convention of rhymed stanzas has been established, we expect them to continue.

In certain instances, of course, rhyme may reinforce closure—for example, in an isolated stanza—but when rhyme functions as an element of systematic repetition, it represents a "force for continuation that must be overcome if closure is to occur" (Smith 1968: 48). In the above lyric, the absence of rhyme in the last stanza arrests the forces of continuation.

Other formal devices may also modify the terminal stanza. In a lyric entitled, "Traveling Riverside Blues," the singer, after delivering four, three-line stanzas with varying rhyme patterns, uses the familiar technique of improvisation to signal the end of his lyric:

> Now you can squeeze my lemon till the juice run down my
>   (till the juice run down my leg baby
>   you know what I'm talking about)
> You can squeeze my lemon till the juice run down my *bed*[3]
>   (That's what I'm talking about now)
> But I'm going back to Friar's Point *if I be* rocking *to* my head.
>   (Sackheim 1969: 220)

Some formal devices are, of course more subtle than others. In the following lyric, the closure is achieved, in part, with a variation in meter:

> I want all you women to listen to my tale of woe
> I want all you women to listen to my tale of woe
> I've got consumption of the heart [,] I feel myself sinking so
>
> Oh my heart is aching and the blues are all around my room
> Oh my heart is aching and the blues are all around my room
> Blues is like the devil [,] they'll have me hell-bound soon
>
> Blues, you made me roll and tumble [,] you made me weep and sigh
> Lordy lordy lordy blues you roll and tumble [,] you made me weep
>   and sigh
> Made me use cocaine and whiskey but you wouldn't let me die
>
> Blues: blues: blues: why did you bring trouble to me?
> Blues: blues: blues: why did you bring trouble to me?
> Oh death please sting me, and take me out of my misery.
>   (Sackheim 1969: 55)

The first and second lines of the last stanza are arresting because they begin with three primary stresses—a rather dramatic departure from the flowing rhythm of the preceding lines. There is somewhat similar stress pattern in the second line of the third stanza ("Lordy lordy lordy"), but here the result is not as striking because the hammering effect of the primary stresses is mitigated by the unstressed second syllables. The effect is also muted because this phrase occurs, not in the first line of the stanza, but as the variation in the second line. The primary stresses at the closure, however, have maximum effect because they begin the stanza.

Another formal closing device is a return to the norm following a deviation. In the blues this device is often used in conjunction with musical modification. All of the following lyrics contain deviations in their penultimate stanzas:

> I got stones in my passway and my road seem dark at night
> I got stones in my passway and my road seem dark at night
> I have pains in my heart [,] they have taken my appetite
>
> I have a bird to whistle and I have a bird to sing
> Have a bird to whistle and I have a bird to sing
> I got a woman that I'm loving, boy but she don't mean a thing . . .
>
> Now you trying to take my life
> And all my loving too
> You laid a passway for me
> Now what are you trying to do
> I'm crying please please let us be friends
> And when you hear me howling in my passway, rider please open
> your door and let me in
>
> I got three legs to truck on boys please don't block my road
> I got three legs to truck on boys please don't block my road
> I been feeling asham' 'bout my rider [,] babe I'm booked and I got
> to go. (Sackheim 1969: 219)

> So many wagons they have cut that good road down
> I said so many wagons have cut that good road down
> And the girl I love [,] her mama don't want me around
>
> Baby I can't drink whiskey but I'm a fool about my homemade wine
> Baby I can't drink whiskey but I'm a fool about my homemade wine
> Ain't no sense in leaving Dallas [,] they makes it there all the
> time . . .
>
> I got a girl for Monday Tuesday Wednesday Thursday Friday too
> I got a girl for Monday Tuesday Wednesday Thursday Friday too

I'm gonna sweeten up on a Saturday [,] what are the women
    through the week going to do

Don't look for me on Sunday [,] I want to take baby to Sunday
    school
Don't look for me on Sunday [,] I want to take baby to Sunday
    school
She's a fine looking fair brown but she ain't never learned Lemon's
    rule. (Sackheim 1969: 83)

Make me a pallet on your floor
Make me a pallet on your floor
    Just make me a, a pallet
    Baby, down upon your floor
    When your main girl come
    I swear, she will never know

Just make it, baby, make it very soft and low
If you will make it, baby, make it very soft and low
    If you feel like—lying down
    With me on the pallet on the floor
    When your main girl come
    I swear, she will never know

I'll get up in the morning, and I'll make you a red hot meal
I'll get up in the morning, and I'll make you a red hot meal
    Just to show you I—appreciated
    Baby, baby, what you done for me
    When you made me that pallet
    Down upon your floor

Won't you make it, baby, make it very soft and low
Make it, baby, make it near the kitchen door
    If she comes in the front door
    I swear, I swear she will never know
    That you made me that pallet
    Down upon your floor. (Sackheim 1969: 65)

In the first example, the penultimate stanza contains obvious deviations from the norm of the three-line, rhymed stanza. In the second
lyric, the pounding stress of the phrase, "Monday Tuesday Wed-
nesday Thursday Friday," provides rhythmic deviation. In the last

example, the variation is more subtle in that it involves the omission of a clause found in the other stanzas of the lyric: "I swear, she will never know." This line functions as a refrain in the earlier stanzas. Although the last stanza does not conclude with this statement as stanzas one and two do, the statement's concluding force is strengthened by the repetition of the phrase, "I swear."

Of the three examples, the deviation in the first has the greatest impact. Because the variation is so conspicuous, the return to the norm in the last paragraph has the strongest concluding effect.

Another terminal modification device is the repetition, sometimes with variation, of the first stanza at the conclusion of the lyric. Smith (1968: 66) comments on the effectiveness of this device:

To begin with, . . . it is effective because, as in music, it reproduces a familiar group of sounds. This is not in itself a sufficient condition for closure, but its force is strengthened by the fact that the first stanza constitutes an integral formal structure in its own right. Consequently, any part of it, when it reappears, will cause the reader to expect the rest to follow; and when it does follow, closure will be strengthened. . . . Second, the repetition of an entire stanza is not only a formal repetition but a thematic one as well: it is the reassertion of an utterance. . . . Finally, the terminal repetition of an initial stanza is effective in strengthening closure . . . in weakening the expectation of continuation.

The following stanzas are the first and last components of a lyric entitled, "Ain't No Tellin' ":

Don't you let my good girl catch you here
Don't you let my good girl catch you here
She might shoot you [,] may cut you and stob you too
Ain't no telling what she might do . . .

Don't you let my good girl catch you here
She might shoot you [,] may cut you and stob you too
Ain't no telling what she might do. (Sackheim 1969: 232)

Here, closure is strengthened, not only by the repetition of the first stanza, but also by a further terminal modification device: the last stanza is the only one in which the first line is not sung twice.

Sometimes, even when the wording of the first stanza is not repeated, the first and last stanzas provide a contrast to the middle stanzas:

Oh you used to told me you could drive me like a cow
Oh you used to told me you could drive me like a cow
Well now you can't drive me, 'cause you don't know how

From now on, mama, I tell you just like that
From now on, mama, I tell you just like that
If you hit my dog, sure gonna kick your cat

From now on, mama, I ain't gonna have no rule
From now on, mama, I ain't gonna have no rule
I'm gonna get hard-headed, and act just like a doggone mule

From now on, mama, you gonna do what I say
From now on, mama, you gonna do what I say
You must understand, you can't have your way

From now on, mama, this way you got of doing
From now on, mama, this way you got of doing
Sugar you better stop that, lord it's sure gonna be your ruin

From now on, mama, starting from this very day
From now on, mama, starting from this very day
I'm gonna get some one, who can drive my blues away

I want her to drive them off, so they won't come back no more
Want her to drive them off, so they won't come back no more
From now on, mama, I said I'm gonna let you go. (Sackheim
        1969: 297)

Here, the first and last stanzas provide an effective frame for the
middle stanzas because neither has the phrase, "From now on,
mama," in its first two lines. With the occurrence of this phrase in
the final line of the last stanza, however, the closure is strengthened.
Thematically, a concluding note is expressed with the phrase, "I'm
gonna let you go." Of all the changes the singer set forth in the
song, this is the most final. Lyrics like these in which formal devices
sharply delineate the beginning, middle, and end are relatively rare
but, as this song shows, the pattern does occur, especially in city
blues.

The formal devices discussed above, although effective in themselves to a degree, are most often combined with thematic structuring elements. Before discussing the thematic structure of the blues, I
would like to stress that the examples I have used so far to illustrate
formal structuring devices are from more or less rigidly structured

lyrics. Please bear in mind, however, that improvisation and certain other nonsystematic elements are often important components in the composition and performance of blues songs. Indeed, an important function of these elements is to break the monotony of systematic repetition and add freshness and vigor to the lyrics.

Paradoxically, both lyrics that consist of formally identical stanzas and those with minimal formal structure face the same structural problem: how to give shape to the text. In the less rigidly structured lyrics, the devices that determine structure are mostly thematic. In lyrics like the ones we just considered, formal and thematic devices function together as determining forces. The surface thematic structure of most blues lyrics is paratactic rather than narrative. In a sequential structure the sequence itself often determines the beginning, middle, and end. In a paratactic structure, however, other thematic devices are employed. For example, we noted earlier that the formal device of repeating the first stanza at the conclusion of a lyric is also a thematic device because it reaffirms an utterance, as the following lyric illustrates:

> Yes, I know I been talked about, people everybody knowed it in
>   town,
> I know I have been talked about, everybody knowed it in town,
> Said my home in Mississippi, but you know I'm Chicago boun'.
>
> Well, I'm goin' to see my baby, people she done moved all up there,
> Well, I'm goin' to see my baby, people she done moved all up there,
> I say I'm gonna work hard, I'm gonna try to get my fare.
>
> I'm gonna leave town, everybody know it all aroun',
> I'm gonna leave town, everybody know it all aroun',
> I say I just wanta fin' my woman, I'm gonna be Chicago boun'.
>
> *Spoken*: Yeah, I got to leave, my baby gone,
> What do I wanta hang aroun' here about?
> Now you know I been talked about, yeah, everybody know it in
>   town,
> No sooner do I get my fare, you know I sho' Chicago boun'.
>   (Oster 1969: 268)

The first and last stanzas serve as a formal and thematic frame for the middle stanzas, which focus on the reasons for the singer's departure—to find his lover. The lyric's conclusion is strengthened

by the interplay of the thematic device or the various formal structuring devices. While the final strophe repeats the basic thematic
elements of the first stanza, the principle of terminal modification is
also formally at work—that is, the first line of the stanza is not
repeated. Also, deviation precedes the last stanza so that this stanza
has a stabilizing effect. Thus, in this seemingly simple lyric, several
formal and thematic devices are at work to give the lyric structure.

In the lyric above, the first and last stanzas are thematically little
more than affirmations of the same idea. In the following lyric,
however, the last stanza goes beyond more mere repetition:

> I been drifting and rolling along the road
> Looking for my room and board
>
> Like a log I've been jammed on the bank
> So hungry I've grew lean and lank
>
> Get me a pick and shovel, dig down in the ground
> Gonna keep on digging till the blues come down
>
> I've got the blues for my sweet man in jail
> Now and the judge won't let me go his bail
>
> I've been rolling and drifting from shore to shore
> Gonna fix it so I won't have to drive no more. (Sackheim 1969: 33)

The theme of lonely, destitute wandering is introduced and
repeated throughout the lyric, but the last stanza does not merely
reaffirm this idea, it offers a thematic resolution: The woman
asserts that her drifting days will end.

It may be argued that the resolution is weak because it does not
seem to follow logically from anything that has gone before, but
surface logic is not the determining factor in the structure of the
blues. In any case, the fact remains that, logical or not, the
"resolving line" of the last stanza has a strong concluding effect.

In other lyrics, concrete expression of the theme and repetition of
that theme with variations make up the beginning and middle
stanzas, while the final stanza makes a general comment or
observation:

> I had the blues last night [,] I've got 'em again today
> My man told me he was going away . . .

Just let me tell you what your friends will do
Grin in your face and then they'll talk about you

Me and my girl friend went out for a little run
When she seen my man she told him what I had done . . .

Take me back baby [,] try me one more time
I'll do everything to satisfy your mind

Listen people, hear what I'm telling you
Don't let your left hand know what your right hand do. (Sackheim
    1969: 43)

The proverbial quality of that last stanza strengthens its terminal effect. Although the comment is a generalization, it is a thematically sound one because of what we have been told in an earlier stanza: The woman's friend betrayed her confidence. In a lyric already cited—the first line of which is "Baby I can see just what's on your mind"—the last stanza also makes a rather general statement, but in this instance the listener is subtly prepared for the statement since in the first three stanzas, the speaker addresses her lover directly and accuses him of disloyalty:

Baby I can see just what's on your mind
Baby I can see just what's on your mind
You got a long black woman with her gold teeth in her face. . . .

In the next two stanzas, she abandons this manner of address and speaks of him in the third person:

I remember the day when I was living at Lula town
I remember the day when I was living at Lula town
My man did so many wrong things that I had to leave the town. . . .

Referring to her lover in the third person creates a certain emotional distance, as does the reflective phrase, "I remember the day." This distance is increased by the general statement in the final stanza, which summarizes the singer's feelings and offers a resolution as well:

Well I'm worried now and I won't be worried long
Well I'm worried now and I won't be worried long
Well I'm worried now and I won't be worried long

As most of the above examples illustrate, though relatively few blues lyrics proceed in a narrative fashion from beginning to end, many of them do have strong narrative elements. However, these elements are insufficient in themselves to determine the lyric's structure. The following lyric is typical of many that contain bits of narrative:

> House catch on fire and ain't no water 'round
> If your house catch on fire, ain't no water 'round
> Throw your trunk out the window [,] building burn on down
>
> I went to the Gypsy to have my fortune told
> I went to the Gypsy to have my fortune told
> He said, Doggone, you, girlie [,] doggone your bad luck soul
>
> I turned around [,] went to the Gypsy next door
> I turned around [,] went to the Gypsy next door
> He said, you'll get a many anywhere you go
>
> Let me be your rag-doll until your chiny come
> Let me be your rag-doll till your chiny come
> If he beats me ragged he's got to rag it some.
> (Sackheim 1969: 49)

The first stanza gives some succinct advice on how to manage when things are less than perfect. This theme is developed further by the brief shift to narrative form in stanzas two and three where we are told that instead of accepting the first gypsy's dire assessment, the woman seeks a second opinion and is rewarded. The lyric ends with an amorous variation on the same basic theme: hang tough and do the best with what you've got. Stanzas one and four, then, are effective framing devices for the short narrative in the middle stanzas.

What is most essential in the structure of the blues lyric, however, is neither narrative sequence nor narrow thematic consistency, but rather, emotional association among the structural elements. Given the fact that this association is, at times, highly personal and that the structure of the blues is generally paratactic, the internal coherence of certain lyrics may seem very elusive. Indeed, sometimes the structural units seem to contradict one another. Quite often, however, blues songs are structured, in part, by seemingly arbitrary closing allusions to finality. Sometimes, of course, these allusions relate directly to the thematic content of the lyric, but often the relationship is obscure. For example, many lyrics end with an allusion to departure which is, in many instances, consistent with the overall thematic content of the lyric—wandering being one of the most common of blues themes. In these instances, the final reference to departure may be a variation on or reaffirmation of what has already been stated or implied. Or, the reference to leaving may be a plausible response to some other experience— for example, abuse by a lover. Sometimes, however, the connection between an allusion to departure and the rest of the lyric is not clear-cut, as the next lyric illustrates:

Now tell me where my easy rider gone
Tell me where my easy rider gone
I need one of these women always in the wrong

Well, easy rider, standing on the road
And it's easy rider standing on the road
I'm a poor blind man, ain't got no where to go

It's gonna be the time when a woman don't need no man
Well it's gonna be a time when a woman don't need no man
Then, baby, shut your mouth: it's gonna be raising sand

The train I ride don't burn no coal at all
Train I ride don't burn no coal at all
The coal house burner: everybody's snapping cannonballs

I went to the depot
I means I went to the depot and set my pistol down
The blues overtake me and tears come rolling down

The woman I love, she must be out of town
Woman I love, man she's out of town
She left me this morning with a face that's travel bound

I got a gal 'cross town, she crochets all the time
I got a gal 'cross town, crochets all the time
Baby, if you don't quit crocheting, you gonna lose your mind

Goodbye brown, what's the matter now
Goodbye brown, what's the matter now
You turn your back to quit me: woman, and you don't know how.
  (Sackheim 1969: 91)

It is obvious that these stanzas are not sequential in any conventional sense and the singer could conceivably go on indefinitely. The conclusion is signaled, however, by the phrase, "Goodbye brown." This statement is not unrelated to what has gone before, for there are references to travel and movement throughout the lyric, but it is difficult to determine the exact connection. Is the singer saying good-bye to the woman who has already departed? To the "gal 'cross town"? Is he actually leaving or is the phrase merely a figurative expression of his loneliness? Whatever the relationship, the allusion to departure has a concluding effect because it suggests that something has ended.

A similar effect is achieved through references to death and other final allusions, whether or not the references specifically relate to the preceding lines. When there is a direct relationship, however, closure, as well as the lyric's overall structural integrity, is strengthened.

Although I have focused on the surface, linear structure of the blues lyric, it is important to note that this is only one aspect of blues structure. A broader analysis of blues form reveals that linear structure, as well as the patterns of imagery and theme, is controlled by an underlying thematic structure.[4] In order to discover the essential meaning and function of the blues, it is important to understand this underlying framework.

NOTES

1. For a discussion of a country-city-urban continuum, see Keil (1966: 217-224).

2. Rhyme is systematically repeated in stanzas one, two, and three. Although the rhyme in the third stanza appears imprecise on the page, in actual performance, postvocalic r in the word Ford would probably be deleted.

3. Sackheim (1969) italicizes words and phrases of which he is uncertain and uses parentheses to indicate spoken words.

4. See Burns (1977).

REFERENCES

Burns, Loretta. 1977. "A Stylistic Analysis of Blues Lyrics." Ph.D. dissertation, University of Michigan.

Courlander, Harold. 1963. *Negro Folk Music, U.S.A.* New York: Columbia University Press.
Keil, Charles. 1966. *Urban Blues.* Chicago: University of Chicago Press.
Murray, Albert. 1976. *Stomping the Blues.* New York: McGraw-Hill.
Oster, Harry. 1969. *Living Country Blues.* Detroit: Folklore Associates.
Sackheim, Eric. 1969. *The Blues Line.* New York: Grossman Publishers.
Smith, Barbara Herrnstein. 1968. *Poetic Closure: A Study of How Poems End.* Chicago: University of Chicago Press.

The Music Program of the Works Progress Administration: A Documentation and Description of Its Activities with Special Reference to Afro-Americans

At a time when there is deep concern about national budget cuts across the board and high unemployment, one can gain strength and encouragement from investigating the struggles of our fore-fathers. Much can be learned from studying their successes and failures, their hardships and prosperity, the hopes and fears of a people experiencing hard times.

History often repeats itself.

The Works Progress Administration (WPA), later renamed the Works Project Administration, was an outgrowth of a critical time —the Great Depression. Established by President Roosevelt in 1935, this relief program provided employment for the jobless in the fields of art, music, theatre, and writing. Although not the first national relief program,[1] the WPA of 1935 was unique because for the first time, with the creation of a Federal Music Project, under WPA,[2] special provisions were made for bringing instrumentalists into efficient, performing organizations.

Even before the Depression, trained Black musicians found that their incomes were becoming increasingly precarious for several reasons. While, in 1900, there were over five thousand theaters in

Motivation to undertake this research project began with a concentrated summer program for college teachers in 1979, supported by a stipend from the National Endowment for the Humanities.

the country and the Black entertainer seemed omnipresent, thanks to the rise of the radio and sound-film industries by 1940, there were fewer than two hundred theaters. Blacks had owned or operated a large number of these theaters in major cities, such as Washington, D.C., Philadelphia, Atlanta, and New York. As long as theaters provided the major source of entertainment for the American people, agencies assured Black entertainers regular employment. The old minstrel tradition of singing spirituals in the theater had created employment for even more musicians. There was also the vaudeville circuit, as well as jobs for Black musicians as accompanists for theatre acts and silent movies. The sound movie industry and the appearance of sound technicians, however, put many musicians out of work. Musicians also felt the economic crunch, in music schools, which reduced their faculties. In addition, private music teachers found their classes dwindling.

When the Federal Music Project (FMP) was initiated under WPA hundreds of musicians were taken from the labor jobs to which they had been assigned—they made notoriously poor ditch-diggers and clerks—and placed in new units for which their training equipped them. While initially, the musicians were skeptical, they were won over by promises of quality control. Musicians responded promptly when they learned that untalented individuals would be transferred out quickly. They were also attracted by the fact that the project aimed to make music an integral part of their community, a permanent civic program.

The potential impact of the WPA project was great. For years, up until World War I, American music was almost completely dominated by foreigners. This was true despite the love for Stephen Foster, Edward MacDowell, and a few other American composers. In addition, until the turn of the century, people were too busy, often too emotionally occupied with material advancement, to concern themselves with great music. With the advent of the FMP came the first real commitment to professionalism in music and support for fine arts as an aesthetic experience. Music in America then became a communal art as more than twenty million Americans attended concerts given by FMP musicians.

The goal of this essay is to highlight the relationship between Black Americans and the WPA and to turn attention to the contributions of Black Americans to the WPA Music Project Program.[3] It remains for future researchers to determine the impact of this program on the Black community and its role in preserving Afro-American culture.

Research on the activities of the Federal Music Project (FMP) has been extremely limited for several reasons. First, the FMP came to a complete halt following America's entry into World War II. Its most innovative plans to publish musical works were abandoned, and the potential of the collections was never realized. Second, much of the unpublished musical material was sitting in a small, windowless room at the end of a labyrinth in the Library of Congress (officially called the "rare book room"). Third, there was no comprehensive inventory of the collection. Finally, the political and cultural climate of the postwar years has not been conducive to interest in the project's activities. Today, the information is more readily available to the public, now that the Library of Congress has acquired an additional facility.

Besides the holdings in the Library of Congress, which consist of forty-one exhibits, some of the most important information about the FMP, including thousands of narratives in the form of monthly reports from the various divisions within the FMP, is housed in the National Archives of the United States, also in Washington, D.C. These narratives describe numerous creative acts carried out by the musicians involved in the project. In addition to the narratives, there are press clippings, educational reports, reports on activities of the states, performance reports, employment reports, national and special reports, and miscellaneous reports.

Information on the WPA—though not extensive—appears in several sources. Eileen Southern in *Music of Black Americans: A History* (1971) gives a half-page discussion of Afro-American involvement in the FMP.[4] She notes that for the first time Blacks were able to participate fully in all of the complex musical activities of bands and orchestras, that Black singers were placed in choruses and opera groups and Black music teachers given classes of children and adults. The most published information on the WPA projects is found in *Federal Relief Administration and the Arts: The Origins and Administrative History of the Arts Projects of the Works Progress Administration*. In 1980 the Library of Congress published a sourcebook of WPA materials. *Pickaxe and Pencil* is also a compilation of references for the study of the WPA.[5]

DESCRIPTION OF THE FEDERAL MUSIC PROJECT

National in scope, the Federal Music Project had a multipurpose goal: to provide employment for needy professional musicians, to involve them in socially useful projects, to preserve their skills by maintaining high standards of musicianship, and to offer the less privileged citizens throughout the nation opportunities to enjoy music. There were four major sections: educational, choral, instrumental, and composer's forum. By 1939, the program involved forty-two states and the District of Columbia. At its peak employment period during the spring of 1936, 15,842 persons were participating, including instrumentalists, vocalists, composers, teachers, librarians, copyists, arrangers, tuners, and music binders. There were symphony and concert orchestras, bands, chamber music ensembles, dance theater and novelty orchestras, choruses, copyists, and vocal ensembles, a composer's project, teachers projects, grand opera, chamber operas, operetta projects, a soloists project, projects for copyists and librarians, and a folk song project charged with the preservation of early vernacular music.[6]

Conferences were established with local sponsors of FMP, including state universities; municipal, county, and township boards; chambers of commerce; boards of education and school superintendents; service clubs, veterans organizations, fraternal and social groups, and such far-reaching organizations as the National Council of Women.

Of the four projects under WPA (art, music, theatre, and writing) the music project employed the most people.[7] The FMP, through its concert bureau and radio broadcasts, was able to make a real contribution to musical enjoyment in the local communities. (See Appendix A, showing WPA employment in community service programs from March 1940 through March 1941.) In 1939, the FMP was transferred from federal to state control and renamed the WPA Music Program.

Afro-American Participation

While it is estimated that Afro-American involvement in the total WPA relief program was less than five percent, in the FMP Afro-American participation was considerably higher. From the

FMP's inception in 1935 to its dissolution in 1943, there was Afro-American participation at every level—that is, except at the national executive level. This writer found no evidence of the involvement of Afro-Americans as state supervisor; however, they were represented in all four sections—educational, choral, instrumental, and composer's forum. Of the 3,146 adults in the education program for the District of Columbia, for example, only 331 were white. Some people were enrolled in more than one type of class and therefore were counted twice. In any case, however, Afro-Americans participated on a large scale in the overall WPA Music Program, particularly in the District of Columbia and Alabama (see Appendix B).

Let us now examine each section of Afro-American involvement within it, as revealed in the narratives of conductors, directors, teachers, and musicians, who were required to make monthly reports to the state directors and supervisors.

EDUCATIONAL

When in 1939 the FMP was transferred to state control and gained a new administrator in Earl Moore, he ushered in a strong concern for and commitment to education and community service. Previously under the direction of Nikolai Sokoloff, there was greater emphasis on performance and the creation of large symphonies. Moore was eager also to provide opportunities for Afro-Americans to participate in musical performances.

Small units, such as eighteen- and twenty-piece bands, which were not large and diversified enough to warrant notable public performances, devoted part of their time to teaching and sponsored band clinics. Many of these small groups were directed by Afro-Americans (see Appendix C). Throughout the country, there were hundreds of community orchestras, composed mainly of nonprofessional musicians. These orchestras, although lacking enough qualified musicians for a complete section, had good individual performers. For example, they may have had one fine flutist in a limited woodwind section. At the same time, there were WPA Music Program orchestras of eighteen, twenty-five or thirty good musicians in need of a good flutist. The key to productivity was the combination of these units and the absorption of individual musicians into the community orchestras that desperately needed their help. Sometimes, musicians were joined on a regularly scheduled basis; other times, combinations were temporary or periodic.

Musical instruction classes were held in New York, Pennsylvania, Ohio, Virginia, Illinois, North Carolina, South Carolina, Florida, Mississippi, Louisiana, and California. The monthly educational report from Virginia reveals:

Three members of the Colored Orchestra in Richmond teach 250 colored men, women and children in piano and choral groups after their rehearsals are over, and some very fine spiritual singers are being developed.[8]

In the Texas Educational Report,[9] it is reported:

Classes in piano, violin, vocal and guitar taught by members of the orchestra—*El Paso.*
Following lessons given:

Colored people (piano-choral)	226
Mexican people (piano-choral)	260
Violin lessons	12
Guitar	8
American children	90

The Florida Educational Report of December 30, 1936, shows major Afro-American participation. The North Carolina summary report,[10] submitted by sponsor supervisors to state supervisors, indicates that Nell Hunter, a Black teacher and choral director, and others made astounding contributions in fostering music appreciation, especially in rural depressed areas where many Afro-Americans could not afford to pay for tickets to a concert. Furthermore, the report notes, Afro-Americans exhibited a keen appreciation and sincere love for concert music. E. Stapleton, state supervisor of North Carolina writes:

More requests for new teaching units come in than can be filled. Another instrument has been added to subjects taught since the underprivileged Negro children asked for pipe organ lessons. Arrangements were made with a church in Wilmington for use of the instruments.[11]

In an examination of educational reports, several interesting notions come to the forefront. First, in Richmond, we see that Afro-Americans made a double impact. Vocal and instrumental groups performed concerts as a part of the Concert Bureau's music appreciation program. In addition, the musicians exended their services beyond the call of duty by offering an overtime program. By today's standards, their overtime activities would be equivalent to a full-time performance schedule. The Richmond Report also indicates that the music education classes of WPA were conducted primarily in recreational centers, community centers, and the like, revealing that these programs supplemented the music programs of the public schools.

CHORAL AND INSTRUMENTAL

Afro-American musicians found performance outlets in various settings. Through the FMP, they appeared, for example, in opera productions. The FMP performances of Verdi's *Il Trovatore* in New York and Auber's comic opera, *Fra Diavole*, in Los Angeles had all Afro-American casts. In California, Verdi's *Aida* was performed with an entirely Black choral unit. In North Carolina, music productions successfully joined Black and white musicians. Nell Hunter made an outstanding contribution. From the narrative reports that Hunter submitted weekly, we learn of Hunter's creative projects and humanitarian spirit.

As Hunter states: "I have been gathering Negro folk music in the various sections of the state and have compiled and organized it into a pageant which I am preparing to present in Durham within the next eight weeks."[12]

Hunter continues:

It is worthy of note that there is a complete lack of friction in the groups wherever I work. All seem to catch the spirit of harmony that, to my mind, is the primary mission of music. It is my hope that this same spirit of harmony will carry through all their acivities and will help each one to make the proper adjustments to daily living.[13] (See Appendix D.)

Nell Hunter was very highly respected, not only by musicians and members of the community but also in the higher echelon of the WPA bureaucracy. E. Stapleton reports on her accomplishments:

An outstanding piece of work was done by Nell Hunter, State Choral Director, with a chorus of one hundred Negroes from Durham and Winston-Salem in a program of spirituals for an audience of ten thousand in Chapel Hill. This program was sponsored by the Carolina Political Union of the University of North Carolina, where the President of the United States was guest of honor and spoke to this large audience.[14]

It must be remembered that without the WPA Music Program, Afro-Americans would not have been afforded the opportunity to participate in the concert world.

From 1935 to 1939, there were seventeen bands or orchestras and nine choral groups of Black musicians in the FMP. During the life-time of the WPA Music Program—1939 to 1943—there were many more. Concert bands and dance orchestras, composed entirely of Black musicians, were in evidence in California—the Los Angeles Colored Chorus, the Los Angeles Concert Band, and the Oakland Choral Group. In Illinois, there were the Chicago Dixie Orchestra, the Chicago Jubilee Singers, the Chicago Columbia Band, and the Herrin Jubilee Singers. Kansas had the Kansas City Negro Concert Band and Louisiana, the New Orleans Negro Military Band. Massachusetts had the Boston Southland Singers, the Springfield Colored Novelty Orchestra, and the Cambridge American Folk Singers. In Michigan there was the Detroit Dance Band; in Minnesota, the Twin Cities Jubilee Singers; in Missouri, the Kansas City Colored Orchestra and the St. Louis Colored Orchestra; in Nebraska, the Omaha Negro Unit; in New York City, the Negro Melody Singers, the Negro Art Singers Dance Band, and the Instrumental Trio. Ohio had the Cleveland Choral Group and the Toledo Dance Orchestra, while in Pennsylvania there were the Philadelphia-Lincoln Dance Band and the Pittsburgh Colored Dance Band. Virginia had the Richmond Colored Concert Orchestra and Wisconsin, the Milwaukee Dance Orchestra. Whereas the white orchestras and concert bands performed extensively and exclusively in the cities and suburbs, the Afro-Americans covered more territory and gave still more concerts.

COMPOSER'S FORUM

Afro-American composers worked with contemporary American composers. Through FMP, Black composers were able to get their compositions published and performed. William Grant Still, often called "dean of Afro-American composers," lecturer, and educator, was one of the participants in the composer's forum.

Blacks were integrally involved in the "Electric Radio Broadcast."[15] This program included two hundred and thirty master electrical transcriptions, produced by WPA and broadcast coast to coast from April 1936 to November 1939. Thirty-one of these broadcasts included music composed, performed, and/or conducted by Afro-Americans. On these programs FMP concerts were aired; later, during the lifetime of WPA, these broadcasts were used not only to promote music appreciation but also to further the purposes of national defense.

Many Black composers' works were given exposure through these broadcasts—for example, William Grant Still's "Lenox Avenue Suite" was played by the Los Angeles Federal Symphony and conducted by Still (see Appendix E).

Other composers featured were Clarence Cameron White, who was a violinist, composer, arranger, and music educator, as well as an organizer in the community music programs of the WPA; Julian Work, brother of John Wesley Work III; John Work III, also an arranger, music educator, and author who was best known for research in the field of Black folk songs; Harry T. Burleigh, singer, composer, and arranger, who composed more than ninety songs and received numerous honorary doctorate degrees; Nathaniel Dett, an arranger, pianist, conductor, and music educator who wrote and arranged works based on the Negro folk song and was best known for piano and choral works; Carl Diton, also a pianist, composer, and teacher, who was the first Afro-American concert pianist to tour the United States; W. C. Handy, an arranger, bandmaster, cornetist, and publisher, who is often called the "Father of the Blues"; and Eva Jessye, an arranger and conductor who organized and conducted the first all-Black choir to tour the United States.

All of the above composers achieved national recognition and were aided in building their initial reputations by participating in the WPA Music Program.

SPECIAL ACTIVITIES

There were three special activities conducted by the FMP and later by the WPA Music Program: Recreational Services, National Defense, and Music Therapy. In addition to these, the FMP and WPA Music Program developed a Braille music segment under the music therapy activity program.

Afro-Americans made tremendous contributions in these areas. In National Defense, for example, they played a key role. By January 1941, twenty-one state music projects were doing their part for the military. The army had no musical bands in the early days of mobilization nor enough special service officers, so the state music projects were called on to provide leaders for musical activities in the camps. Chorus leaders and instructors for musical instruments were in great demand. Army recreation was not sufficiently well organized to provide healthful recreation activities for all the men, and the commanding officers were desperate for help. Consequently, the state music projects heavily increased their services to the military. The Report on National Defense Activities for the month of June 1941 reflects the accelerated schedule of assistance to the military: forty-two state music projects were involved; in some states, all civilian services had ceased.

Blacks played a very important role in keeping the spirit and morale of the men in the Armed Forces high, as the National Defense Narrative report from the state director in Northern California reveals:

The first program presented at Moffett Field, February 26, featuring the Northern California WPA Symphony Orchestra of 100 pieces, and the WPA Negro chorus of 37 voices, was wildly applauded by the men and most favorably commented on by critics in their columns the following day. Choruses generally, it seems, are popular with the boys, and the Negro Chorus especially so. Indicative of the enthusiasm aroused was the fact that when the time for intermission arrived the officers begged that no intermission be observed—the men didn't want the music to stop. When the carefully planned concert reached its climax with a presentation of the exciting "Ballad for Americans" the soldiers stood in their places and cheered.[16]

In Georgia, a narrative report submitted in May 1941 relates:

A group of colored spiritual singers is busy entertaining both white and colored soldiers and is being received with enthusiasm. The colored teacher in Americus has developed a fine group of singers who present spirituals and other choral music in the colored CCC camps. The Atlanta Philharmonic, for which the Atlanta Civic (WPA) Orchestra supplies the professional nucleus, gives special programs for young men having military training in the region of Atlanta.[17]

The day Pearl Harbor was bombed, December 7, 1941, marked the end of the WPA Music Program as such. From that date on, no activity was continued that did not directly serve the armed forces or the sale of war bonds and stamps. While several symphony orchestras continued to give concerts in large military areas and to give performances sponsored by the U.S. Treasury Department, most of the smaller units were converted into dance bands for the army camps and naval bases. The music education activities disappeared almost overnight.

Surely, the entire story of Afro-American involvement in the FMP and the WPA Music Program cannot be told in this brief essay. It will require volumes of research data and many investigators to unravel the life history of this important relief program.

Nevertheless, I have attempted to expose this storehouse of an all but forgotten resource. There is little question that the FMP and the WPA Music Program made important contributions to the cultural life of the United States during their eight years of existence. By the same token, it is clear that Afro-Americans were most important participants and their participation had a profound effect on Black America.

It has been suggested by Richard Long of Atlanta University that more Afro-Americans attended more musical concerts during the lifetimes of the FMP and WPA than at any other time in American history. (Many Afro-Americans made tremendous sacrifices in order to purchase their own musical instruments.)

Some of the narratives cited here support Long's conjecture. There is a need for more research to find out why Blacks were more involved with musical concerts in previous decades. Perhaps research will uncover reasons other than the appearance of television.

Researchers are needed to document the relationship between Black Americans and the WPA. State records must be examined, various programs evaluated, and people interviewed for firsthand information.

Although the logistics, operation, and implementation of the WPA could not be considered in this essay, another area for future research is the disparity in salaries between Afro-Americans and whites within the WPA. John Hope Franklin (1969: 538) reports

There was a greater inclination toward fairness to Negroes in providing employment. Under the WPA there was such a variation in policy from place to place as to make impossible any general statement with regard to the treatment of Negroes. The wage differentials in some communities were great, and the administrators made no apologies for them.

Nevertheless, more than a million Afro-Americans owed their living to the WPA in 1939; this relief program was surpassed only by agricultural and domestic service as a source of income for the Black population.

By June 1936, approximately twenty million people had heard "in the flesh" performances by the units of the FMP. In addition to the concerts, operas, choral and band programs, and chamber and quartet recitals, there were hundreds of radio broadcasts that reached an audience so vast that it escapes computation. With the golden anniversary of the FMP's inception approaching, it is hoped that documentation of Afro-American involvement in the WPA Music Program will be undertaken as a tribute to Afro-American achievements in perpetuating and preserving a national treasure.

APPENDIX A

EMPLOYMENT ON WPA COMMUNITY SERVICE PROGRAMS,[1]

BY PROGRAM AND TYPE OF PROJECT, UNITED STATES

TERRITORIES, MARCH 27, 1940, FEBRUARY 28,

1941, AND MARCH 28, 1941

| Program and type | March 27, 1940 | |
| | Number of | |
of project	Persons	Percent
All projects generated		
by WPA...............	2,212,233	---
Division of Community		
Service Programs--total..	542,108	100.0
Public activities		
programs--total........	127,286	23.5
Education.............	31,185	5.8
Recreation............	38,559	7.1
Library...............	29,723	5.5
Museum................	7,715	1.4
Art...................	6,011	1.1
Music.................	10,312	1.9
Writing...............	3,781	0.7
Research and records programs--		
total...................	85,943	15.8
Research and surveys...	39,738	7.3
Public records........	37,449	6.9
Historical records		
survey.............	8,756	1.6

Program and type of project	March 27, 1940 Number of Persons	Percent
Welfare programs--total.....	310,574	57.3
Public health and hospital work.......	13,083	2.4
Sewing.................	183,001	33.7
Production projects (ex. sewing).........	17,768	3.3
Housekeeping aides.....	36,940	6.8
Household workers' training...........	960	6.2
School lunches........	36,297	6.7
Distribution of surplus commodities.........	22,525	4.2
Other programs.............	18,305	3.4

[1]Does not include employment on WPA projects operated
by other Federal agencies and financed by allocation
of WPA funds. Revised through April 21, 1941.

W.P.A. Statistical Summary Report, 1941.

APPENDIX A

EMPLOYMENT ON WPA COMMUNITY SERVICE PROGRAMS,[1]

BY PROGRAM AND TYPE OF PROJECT, UNITED STATES

TERRITORIES, MARCH 27, 1940, FEBRUARY 28,

1941, AND MARCH 28, 1941

| Program and type | February 26, 1941 | |
of project	Number of Persons	Percent
All projects generated		
by WPA...............	1,820,453	---
Division of Community		
Service Programs--total..	491,448	100.0
Public activities		
programs--total........	119,473	21.3
Education.............	29,078	5.9
Recreation............	36,581	7.5
Library...............	27,506	5.6
Museum................	6,073	1.2
Art...................	6,023	1.2
Music.................	10,499	2.1
Writing...............	3,713	0.8
Research and records programs--		
total..................	69,615	14.2
Research and surveys...	29,799	6.1
Public records........	31,486	6.4
Historical records		
survey.............	8,330	1.7

Program and type of project	February 26, 1941 Number of Persons	Percent
Welfare programs--total.....	290,712	59.1
Public health and hospital work.......	14,527	2.9
Sewing................	128,893	26.2
Production projects (ex. sewing).........	16,110	3.3
Housekeeping aides......	38,538	7.8
Household workers' training.............	884	0.2
School lunches.........	64,426	13.1
Distribution of surplus commodities..........	27,334	5.6
Other programs..............	11,618	2.4

[1]Does not include employment on WPA projects operated
by other Federal agencies and financed by allocation
of WPA funds. Revised through April 21, 1941.

W.P.A. Statistical Summary Report, 1941.

APPENDIX A

EMPLOYMENT ON WPA COMMUNITY SERVICE PROGRAMS,[1]

BY PROGRAM AND TYPE OF PROJECT, UNITED STATES

TERRITORIES, MARCH 27, 1940, FEBRUARY 28,

1941, AND MARCH 28, 1941

Program and type of project	Number of Persons	March 26, 1941 Percent
All projects generated by WPA................	1,663,856	---
Division of Community Service Programs--total..	491,448	100.0
Public activities programs--total........	111,635	24.5
Education..............	27,219	6.0
Recreation.............	34,759	7.6
Library...............	25,193	5.5
Museum................	5,520	1.2
Art...................	6,128	1.3
Music.................	9,670	2.1
Writing...............	3,547	0.8
Research and records programs-- total...................	64,762	14.2
Research and surveys...	27,812	6.1
Public records.........	29,249	6.4
Historical records survey.............	7,701	1.7

Program and type of project	March 26, 1941	
	Number of Persons	Percent
Welfare programs--total.....	268,155	50.0
Public health and hospital work.......	11,137	3.1
Sewing.................	111,563	25.2
Production projects (ex. sewing)..........	13,377	3.1
Housekeeping aides......	36,078	7.9
Household workers' training.............	785	0.2
School lunches..........	64,298	14.1
Distribution of surplus commodities..........	24,317	5.4
Other programs..............	10,396	2.3

[1]Does not include employment on WPA projects operated by other Federal agencies and financed by allocation of WPA funds. Revised through April 21, 1941.

W.P.A. Statistical Summary Report, 1941.

APPENDIX B

ENROLLMENT[1] IN ADULT CLASSES OF THE WPA

EDUCATION PROGRAM, BY TYPE OF CLASS AND

STATE, JANUARY 1941

	WPA Region and State	
	District of Columbia	Alabama
Enrollment		
All classes[2]		
Total	3,146	30,984
White	331	16,232
Negro	2,815	14,734
Other	---	28
Literacy classes	631	4,731
Naturalization classes	---	81
Vocational		
training classes		
Total	725	89
Radio engineering	---	---
Aeronautics	---	---
Commercial training	438	236
Other	287	661
Homemaking and parent-		
education classes	166	3,622
Other classes	1,624	23,253

[1]Data represent the number of persons enrolled in each type of class who attended at least 1/2 of the scheduled class meetings during January 1941.

[2]Data do not represent the number of different persons enrolled, since some persons are enrolled in more than 1 type of class, and therefore counted more than once in this tabulation. Revised through Apr. 28, 1941. W.P.A. Statistical Summary Report, Jan. 1941, excerpts.

APPENDIX C

NEW JERSEY

Location	Unit	Employment
Asbury Park	Concert Orchestra	15
	Dance orchestra	5
Atlantic City	Concert Orchestra	21
	Concert Band	32
	Dance Orchestra	9
	Negro concert and dance orchestra	17
Beachwood	Concert Orchestra	7
Camden	Concert Orchestra	26
	Dance Orchestra (D.)	10
	Dance Orchestra (N.)	9
Elizabeth	Concert Orchestra	18
	Dance Orchestra	4
Hackensack	Concert Orchestra	34
	Dance Orchestra	10
Hudson County	Concert Orchestra	31
	Concert Band	31
	Dance Orchestra	16
Morristown	Concert Orchestra	20
Newark	Symphony Orchestra	56
	Concert Band	36
	Dance Orchestra	23
	Negro Dance Orchestra	6
	Opera Unit	34
	Library, copying, etc.	3

Location	Unit	Employment
Paterson	Concert Orchestra	36
	Dance Orchestra	15
Perth Amboy	Concert Orchestra	15
	Dance Orchestra	6
Trenton	Concert Band	23
	Dance Orchestra	9
Statewide	Other	46
	TOTAL	634

The Boards of Education in New Jersey make continuing demands upon the Music Project playing units for school concerts. Three concerts are requested in many high schools where formerly one only was given. Recently the opera chorus was scheduled for five 25-minute performances in one day. The dance bands and orchestras provide entertainment for community centers and institutions. The Essex County Opera Company has given numerous performances of opera. The Newark Symphony Orchestra is engaged in a series of sponsored concerts in the Mosque Theatre. It is expected that this private sponsorship will soon be replaced by direct sponsorship by Mayor Ellenstein. W.P.A. Statistical Summary Report, June 1940.

APPENDIX C

NEW JERSEY

Location	Unit	Performance
Asbury Park	Concert Orchestra	20
	Dance orchestra	11
Atlantic City	Concert Orchestra	71
	Concert Band	38
	Dance Orchestra	40
	Negro concert and dance orchestra	32
Beachwood	Concert Orchestra	25
Camden	Concert Orchestra	14
	Dance Orchestra (D.)	4
	Dance Orchestra (N.)	10
Elizabeth	Concert Orchestra	12
	Dance Orchestra	16
Hackensack	Concert Orchestra	23
	Dance Orchestra	17
Hudson County	Concert Orchestra	30
	Concert Band	15
	Dance Orchestra	40
Morristown	Concert Orchestra	18
Newark	Symphony Orchestra	2
	Concert Band	23
	Dance Orchestra	17
	Negro Dance Orchestra	8
	Opera Unit	
	Library, copying, etc.	

Location	Unit	Performance
Paterson	Concert Orchestra	37
	Dance Orchestra	39
Perth Amboy	Concert Orchestra	14
	Dance Orchestra	23
Trenton	Concert Band	42
	Dance Orchestra	33
Statewide	Other	___
	TOTAL	702

The Boards of Education in New Jersey make continuing demands upon the Music Project playing units for school concerts. Three concerts are requested in many high schools where formerly one only was given. Recently the opera chorus was scheduled for five 25-minute performances in one day. The dance bands and orchestras provide entertainment for community centers and institutions. The Essex County Opera Company has given numerous performances of opera. The Newark Symphony Orchestra is engaged in a series of sponsored concerts in the Mosque Theatre. It is expected that this private sponsorship will soon be replaced by direct sponsorship by Mayor Ellenstein. W.P.A. Statistical Summary Report, June 1940.

APPENDIX C

NEW JERSEY

Location	Unit	Attendance
Asbury Park	Concert Orchestra	9,945
	Dance orchestra	4,390
Atlantic City	Concert Orchestra	24,650
	Concert Band	29,100
	Dance Orchestra	17,000
	Negro concert and dance orchestra	11,050
Beachwood	Concert Orchestra	5,070
Camden	Concert Orchestra	8,400
	Dance Orchestra (D.)	750
	Dance Orchestra (N.)	3,900
Elizabeth	Concert Orchestra	6,995
	Dance Orchestra	3,920
Hackensack	Concert Orchestra	9,210
	Dance Orchestra	6,185
Hudson County	Concert Orchestra	29,000
	Concert Band	13,900
	Dance Orchestra	42,700
Morristown	Concert Orchestra	6,250
Newark	Symphony Orchestra	2,589
	Concert Band	12,950
	Dance Orchestra	5,350
	Negro Dance Orchestra	2,100
	Opera Unit	
	Library, copying, etc.	

Location	Unit	Attendance
Paterson	Concert Orchestra	14,900
	Dance Orchestra	15,300
Perth Amboy	Concert Orchestra	2,505
	Dance Orchestra	2,750
Trenton	Concert Band	22,242
	Dance Orchestra	43,750
Statewide	Other	_____
	TOTAL	366,646

The Boards of Education in New Jersey make continuing
demands upon the Music Project playing units for
school concerts. Three concerts are requested in many
high schools where formerly one only was given.
Recently the opera chorus was scheduled for five
25-minute performances in one day. The dance bands
and orchestras provide entertainment for community
centers and institutions. The Essex County Opera
Company has given numerous performances of opera.
The Newark Symphony Orchestra is engaged in a series
of sponsored concerts in the Mosque Theatre. It is
expected that this private sponsorship will soon be
replaced by direct sponsorship by Mayor Ellenstein.
W.P.A. Statistical Summary Report, June 1940.

APPENDIX D

NARRATIVE REPORT FOR JANUARY

With the closing program in Wilmington on January 16th,
the Choral Project of the Federal Music Project has
about completed its program of "North Carolina
Singing".

Early in the fall I worked in Asheville and then
went directly to New Bern, the western and eastern
extremities of the state. I found a marked contrast
in activities, habits and reactions of the people,
all of which is reflected in their singing. In the
western and Piedmont sections there is a snappiness
and briskness not found in the easy-going, slow-moving
easterners.

I found fewer good voices in Wilmington and a
less highly developed sense of rhythm. However,
what was lacking in musical sense was made up for in
zeal and enthusiasm.

In most places, the large community chorus has
been made up of all ages, but not so in Wilmington.
The younger singers refused to sing with the older
and less talented ones. As a consequence, I had
several groups of younger singers which I prepared
for a separate program. They sang on Sunday
afternoon, December 12th, at the Central Baptist
Church and broadcast the following Sunday afternoon.

The final program was on January 16th by a
chorus of seventy-eight (78) voices. This chorus
was made up largely of elderly people who had had no
previous training. They gave the most satisfactory
program I have ever had, not because of the caliber
of the voices, but their reaction and response to
direction. I am urged to return and repeat this
program at an early date. As in other places, this
group has been formally organized and they promised
to keep going under the leadership of a local director.

January 31, 1938   _____(Signed)
                                    Nell Hunter

WPA Narrative Report, January, 1938

APPENDIX E

PROGRAM NO. 59

MANHATTAN CONCERT BAND

ANTHONY GIAMMATTEO

CONDUCTOR

Overture to "Pique Dame".......... Franz von Sunpe

Malaguena from "Boabdil".......... Moritz Moszkowski

PROGRAM NO. 60

NEW YORK FEDERAL SYMPHONY ORCHESTRA

CHALMERS CLIFTON

CONDUCTOR

Andante Movement from Symphony

    No. 4 in A Major .... Mendelssohn

Dance of the Flutes from "The

    Nutcracker Suite"............... Tschaikowsky

Tsar's Journey from "Musical

    Pictures"...................... Rimsky-Korsakoff

PROGRAM NO. 61

MANHATTAN CONCERT BAND

ANTHONY GIAMMATTEO

CONDUCTOR

Waldemere........................... F.H. Losey

Overture to "The Sicilian Vespers".... Guiseppe Verdi

PROGRAM NO. 62

LOS ANGELES FEDERAL SYMPHONY

WM. GRANT STILL, CONDUCTOR

VERNA ARVEY, GUEST PIANO SOLOIST

Excerpts from "Lenox Avenue Suite"... Wm. Grant Still

Street Scene

A Flirtation

A Fight

The Intervention of the Law

Dancing Boys

The Dancing Drunkard

The Philosopher

W.P.A. Elective Radio Broadcasts Transcripts, 1939

NOTES

1. The list of Federal Involvement in Relief and Work Relief Programs—1935-1943—were many.

2. Federal One was the name given to the professional arts projects of the WPA. There were four such projects—music, art, theater, and writers.

3. The Federal Music Project was discontinued in 1939 and the WPA continued the music project of Federal One under the WPA Music Program.

4. See Southern (1971: 446).

5. See McDonald (1969) for the origins and administrative history of the Arts Projects of the Works Project Administration. Bloxom, Marguerite D. *Pickaxe and Pencil*, Bibliography section, General Reading Rooms Division, Library of Congress, Washington, D.C., 1983.

6. *United States WPA Exhibit No. I.* "A Preliminary Report of the Work on the Federal Music Congress, Washington, D.C."

7. For employment on WPA Community Service Programs by program and type of project see *Statistical Summary Report*, 1941. Exhibit No. 3. WPA Collection, Library of Congress.

8. *United States WPA Narrative Education Report*, Virginia, December 30, 1936. National Archives of the United States, Washington, D.C.

9. *United States WPA Narrative Educational Report*, Texas, December 30, 1936. National Archives of the United States, Washington, D.C.

10. *United States WPA Narrative Report*, North Carolina, November 1940.

11. Ibid.

12. *United States WPA Narrative Report*, North Carolina, May 1938.

13. Ibid.

14. *United States WPA Narrative Report*, North Carolina, March 31, 1938.

15. *United States WPA Electric Radio Transcriptions*, 1939.

16. *United States WPA Narrative Report*, Northern California, March 1941.

17. *United States WPA Narrative Report*, Georgia, May 1941.

REFERENCES

References given are relevant to this subject and provide a general background.

Adams, Grace. 1939. *Workers on Relief*. New Haven: Yale University Press.

Banks, Ann. 1980. *First Person American*. New York: Knopf Publishers.

Botkin, Benjamin A. 1945. *Lay My Burden Down: A Folk History of Slavery*. Chicago: University of Chicago Press.

Franklin, John Hope. 1969. *From Slavery to Freedom: A History of Negro Americans*. New York: Vintage Books.

Jones, Alfred H. 1971. "The Search for a Usable American Past in the New Deal Era." *American Quarterly* 23, No. 4 (December).

Mathews, Janet D. 1967. *The Federal Theatre, 1935-1939: Plays, Relief, and Politics*. Princeton: Princeton University Press.

MacMahon, Arthur, Millett, and Ogden. 1941. "The Administration of Federal Work Relief." Chicago, Committee on Public Administration of the Social Science Research Council by Public Administration Service.

McDonald, William F. 1969. *Federal Relief Administration and the Arts: The Origins and Administrative History of the Arts Projects of the Works Progress Administration*. Ohio: Ohio State University Press.

Southern, Eileen. 1971. *Music of Black Americans: A History*. New York: W. W. Norton and Co.

Stewart, Maxwell S. 1940. *The Question of Relief*. Public Affairs Pamphlets. Prepared by staff of Committee on Social Security of the Social Science Research Council.

Terkel, Studs. 1970. *Hard Times: An Oral History of the Great Depression*. New York: Pantheon Books.

Terrill, Tom, and Jerrold Hirsch. 1978. *Such as Us: Southern Voices of the Thirties*. Chapel Hill: University of North Carolina Press.

U.S. Senate. 1938. Hearings before Special Committee to Investigate Unemployment and Relief. 75th Congress, 3rd session. S. Res. 36—a Resolution Creating a Special Committee to Investigate Unemployment and Relief, Vol., 1, Jan. 4-22.

U.S. Works Projects Administration. 1935-1943. U.S. Records of Works Projects Administration, Federal Music Project and W.P.A. Music Program. National Archives, Washington, D.C.

———. 1935-1943. U.S. Works Projects Administration Collection, Exhibits Collection. Library of Congress, Washington, D.C.

———. 1936. Works Progress Administration. Government Aid During the Depression to Professional Technical and Other Service Workers.

———. 1939. "W.P.A. and Folklore Research: Bread and Song." *Southern Folkore Quarterly*, Vol. 3, No. 1 (March).

———. 1943. United States Federal Works Agency, W.P.A. Final Statistical Report of the Federal Emergency Relief Administration.

White, Evelyn D. 1975. *Selected Bibliography of Published Choral Music by Black Composers*. Washington, D.C.: Howard University.

Index

The Contributors

HORACE CLARENCE BOYER is Associate Professor of Music Theory and Afro-American music in the department of Music and Dance at the University of Massachusetts at Amherst. He has contributed articles to such Journals as *Music Educators Journal, Black Perspective in Music, First World,* and *Black World.* He is presently preparing a book on pioneers in gospel music.

MELLONEE V. BURNIM is Assistant Professor in the Department of Afro-American studies and Director of the Afro-American choral ensemble at Indiana University. She has conducted extensive fieldwork in gospel music in black communities throughout the United States. Her research has focused on developing a theoretical framework for understanding and analyzing Afro-American gospel music.

LORETTA S. BURNS, Associate Professor of English at Tuskegee Institute, has held appointments at Fisk University and the University of Florida. Her research has centered around sociolinguistics and Afro-American folklore.

LORRAINE M. FAXIO, Assistant Professor of Music in the Department of Music at Howard University, has received research grants including awards from the National Endowment for the Humanities. Presently, her research activities involve the Works Progress Administration music project and the contributions of Black Americans to the WPA.

STEPHEN E. HENDERSON is Director of the Institute for the Arts and Humanities at Howard University, Washington, D.C., and a faculty member of the Afro-American Studies Department. He is co-author with Mercer Cook of the *Militant Black Writer* and the editor of *Understanding the New Black Poetry*. His work centers on the relationship of the folk base to contemporary Black literary expression.

IRENE V. JACKSON is former Program Director of the Center for Ethnic Music at Howard University and an Assistant Professor in the Music Department. Her research and several articles have focused on Afro-American religious music and the role of the Black woman in music. Her book, *Afro-American Religious Music* (1979) is a publication of Greenwood Press. She is editor of *Lift Every Voice and Sing: A Collection of Spirituals and Other Songs* (New York: Church Hymnal Corporation 1982).

PORTIA K. MAULTSBY is presently a postdoctoral fellow, American Culture Program, Smithsonian Institution. She is an Associate Professor in the Department of Afro-American Studies and the Ethnomusicology Program at Indiana University-Bloomington. Her current research has centered on the influence of social environments and cultural perceptions/attitudes on the evolution of contemporary Afro-American music.

DORIS EVANS McGINTY is Professor of Musicology and Chairman of the Department of Music at Howard University. She has written articles and reviews for scholarly journals such as the *Journal of Human Relations, The Black Perspective in Music,* and *Fontes Artis Musicae* and is a contributing editor to the *Black Perspective in Music*. Her studies of music in the Black community of Washington, D.C., include a forthcoming book, an account of the history of music at Howard University.

GEORGE L. STARKS, JR., an ethnomusicologist, is Associate Professor of Music at Drexel University. His research and publications have been concerned with new world musics of African origin. He has conducted field research in the South Carolina Sea Islands, the Bahamas, and the West Indies. As an alto saxophonist, he was listed in the talent deserving of wider recognition category of the 1972 *Down Beat* International jazz critics poll.

JAMES B. STEWART is Director of the Black Studies Program and Assistant Professor of Economics at the Pennsylvania State University. He held similar positions at the University of Notre Dame. He is co-author of the volume *Regulation, Values and the Public Interest* and has had articles published in several journals including the *Review of Black Political*

Economy, the *Western Journal of Black Studies,* the *Journal of Black Studies, Umoja,* and *Phylon.*

OLLY WILSON is a composer and Professor of Music at The University of California, Berkeley. His compositions, performed by major orchestras, have received numerous awards and commissions. His research area has been the relationship between African and Afro-American music and he has published on this subject.